The
Buddy Holly
Story

The Buddy Holly Story

John Goldrosen

New York   London   Tokyo

International Standard Book Number: 0-8256-3936-0
Library of Congress Catalog Card Number: 79-84323

In Great Britain: Book Sales Ltd., 78 Newman Street,
London W1P 3 LA.

In Canada: Gage Trade Publishing, P.O. Box 5000, 164
Commander Blvd., Agincourt, Ontario M1S 3C7.

In Japan: Music Sales Corporation, 4-26-22 Jingumae,
Shibuya-ku, Tokyo 150.

Book design: Suzanne Newman/Crackerjack Studio
Cover painting: Robert Burger

To Marian,
for whom it was written

Contents

Foreword

February 3, 1979 looms just ahead as I write this, taunting me with its inevitable question. Has "the music" really been dead for so long now, as the poet first dreamed out loud back in 1971? Has it actually been 20 years since rock 'n' roll so badly misplayed its hole card, somehow sending us all crashing into the Iowa snow?

The answer, of course, is obvious: while the music of Buddy Holly may have been abruptly cut off at the source, it surely did not die. Instead, it flowed naturally along, pushing, shaping, drawing into the current everything that it touched, eventually becoming part of the larger body of music downstream. "Buddy Holly was one of the giants of early rock," said the late Lillian Roxon nearly a decade ago, "a figure so important in the history of popular music that it is impossible to hear a song on the charts that does not owe something to the bespectacled boy from Lubbock, Texas."

However valid that assessment may have been in 1969, it is even more so today—not only does the Holly fiber run through a great deal of what we hear, but through much of what we see as well. As rock becomes increasingly more visual yet beholden to its roots, trendsetters such as Elvis Costello emerge with the total Holly look and attitude, right down to the frantic red Stratocaster at the fore. A leather-jacketed Springsteen proclaims: "I play Holly every night before I go on—it keeps me honest," while the granddaddy of contemporary visual pop-rock, Elton John, reveals: "I began wearing glasses when I was thirteen to copy Buddy Holly. After eighteen months, I found I couldn't see without them. If any young fans are thinking of copying *me*, I'd advise them to forget it!"

Buddy Holly's posthumous ascendancy has been remarkable and totally without parallel. It began, predictably, with the likes of Bobby Vee and Tommy Roe, the well-intentioned if less than adequate Holly imitators seeking to fill the vacuum. But, as it has been with so many other areas of music, it took the curiosity and sensitivity of the fledgling British rock bands to initiate a widespread awareness of the music's real value. It took the Stones (first American hit: "Not Fade Away"), the Beatles (who borrowed their very name and instrumental lineup from the Crickets), Peter & Gordon (whose Peter Asher continues to perpetuate the Holly legacy via his renowned

Ronstadt productions), and the Hullaballoos to open the floodgates, helping to expose the uncompromising Hollyesque west-Texas rock 'n' roll of the Bobby Fuller Four, and to inspire all which has followed.

Most fortunately, the events of the early 1960's also stimulated the curiosity of young John Goldrosen, who had been totally unacquainted with Holly and the Crickets when he was blown away by the first hearing of a record called "Oh Boy!" So moved was he by the music that he endeavored to hit the road, to find out firsthand where these sounds came from and where they went. And so, much like John Wayne in *The Searchers* (the legendary John Ford film which gave rise to "That'll Be The Day"), Goldrosen began his relentless pursuit, logging more than 20,000 miles in the process of creating this extraordinary volume. Loving in his approach, the author moves us, teaches us, entertains us, and above all manages to produce a definitive work which will strip the vast legion of "music experts" of all its defenses.

John Goldrosen's *The Buddy Holly Story* is a monument to the Man and his Music, and to a long underappreciated and misunderstood area of popular music history.

RALPH M. NEWMAN
publisher, *Time Barrier Express*
and co-author of *Rock On Vol. 2*
(The Modern Years)
January, 1979

Introduction

It's easiest to think of Buddy Holly as the archetypal pop star, whose light melodies and star-crossed life set the pattern for those teen idols who have followed him. Holly had a couple of hot years at the top, after untutored beginnings. His looks were utterly unlikely. He found a moonstruck romance in an alien, glittering city. And in the end, he met a macabre, sensational death.

That's the picture Hollywood offers us, but for once—thanks to this volume—it is not the one we are stuck with. The bare facts of Holly's life are actually more dramatic, almost unbelievably so—the source of genuine legend. His story does not belong to a pop star, who is by definition fixed and limited by his times and their circumstances and thereafter available only to nostalgists. Cultists like to say that "Buddy Holly Lives." While I doubt that's true (at least, not this side of an afterlife), there is no question that Buddy Holly's music lives, and not only because his songs continue to top the charts.

What I'm trying to suggest is that Holly is a great American popular artist. Taking the title of his first hit song, "That'll Be the Day," from John Ford's *The Searchers,* which may be the greatest American film of the Fifties, seems to me no more than the intuitive homage a young master pays an older one.

Like Ford, Holly is often underestimated. The sentimental veneer of both men's work, their casual familiarity with period and genre conventions belies their underlying emotional resiliency, their passion for beauty, their consummate control of superficially mundane elements. So just as *The Searchers* has come to mean as much to children of the Sixties as those of the Fifties, Holly's songs have continued to be enormously meaningful to people who couldn't possibly have known them firsthand. And that is one test of their intrinsic worth.

The Hollywood myth about Holly is correct in one crucial respect, however. He was a prophetic figure. The story of rock 'n' roll is, in some sense, the tale of outsiders gaining control of an entertainment mechanism in order to extract from it personal significance (which is the only way to achieve mass significance). Holly was the first to involve himself in all phases of his work—performing, writing, production, guitar-playing, arrangements. While he certainly did not achieve as much in this respect as contemporary performers often find themselves granted as a matter of course, that is only an additional measure of his accomplishments. What Buddy Holly might have done in ensuing years, when artistic freedom in popular music became a given, is virtually unimaginable.

Holly left an enormous legacy, both in quantity (there is that nine-volume German set of his recordings) and in quality. And in some ways, it is his simplest material which seems freshest. The winsome grandeur of his understated reading of "Love Is Strange," for instance, or the guitar break in the slower version of "Slippin' and Slidin' " which is virtually the theme of Peter Townshend's *Tommy* in miniature. Or to be more exact, some of his own songs which were not big American hits: the opening yowl of "Rave On," which forever stands as a monument to rock's ability to communicate in a language all its own, or the simple poetry of "Well All Right" or "I'm Changing All Those Changes," which are truly artful renderings of American vernacular. It may be too early to guarantee that Holly will eventually be regarded as one of the great American artists of his era, but like love that's real, those moments will not fade away.

DAVE MARSH

Author's Introduction: In Search of the Singer

> *For Lycidas is dead, dead ere his prime,*
> *Young Lycidas, and hath not left his peer:*
> *Who would not sing for Lycidas? He knew*
> *Himself to sing, and build the lofty rhyme.*
> —John Milton, *Lycidas*

I never saw Buddy Holly perform, and I can't remember hearing his songs before his death in 1959. (I was eight years old at the time, but that's not much of an excuse—one friend of mine was seven when he bought a copy of "Peggy Sue.") But I do remember just where I was a couple of years later when I first heard one of Holly's songs—the tune was "Oh Boy!"—and how the name and the song stayed in my mind, then futilely occupied with studying the 1962 Red Sox for signs of life. A couple of more years and I was an affluent teenager, able to buy whole albums of Holly's songs. Like so many other fans, I found that the age of the records was unimportant. All I knew was that the songs spoke to *me*, right then. All my feelings and experiences, good and bad, were expressed within the variety of Holly's style and matter. I did not have to wait for a rock 'n' roll revival craze before deciding that contemporary rock music offered nothing so exciting, moving, and meaningful as what Buddy Holly had composed and recorded years before.

When we fans wanted to go beyond the records—when we wanted to learn more about the background of Holly and his contemporaries—we found that the record was blank. Early rock 'n' roll was treated as frivolous music at the time it was popular and for over a decade thereafter, and so there was little firsthand information about those early artists available in this country. Nobody had reviewed Buddy Holly's concerts for *The New York Times;* Leonard Bernstein had not given Holly the New York Philharmonic seal of approval; and there had been no young journalists waiting to interview him to take down his thoughts about his own music. Nobody had filmed him, on stage or off. What little did appear in print was often contradictory or biased, and never seemed to answer the questions most important to the fans.

There was nothing for a fan to do but save up some dough, set aside a year or two, and go out and find the answers. This book is the product, then, of a twenty-thousand-mile cross-country drive in search of the people and the places that were part of Buddy Holly's life. The image of Holly which emerged was an intriguing and complicated one, not very easily put into words. Holly presented different sides of himself to different people, and never revealed himself totally to anyone. Only after talking with those who knew him can the pieces be fitted together, and the conflicting accounts and legends weighed. As it turned out, the Buddy Holly story is indeed one which deserves to be told.

Without the assistance of those who were so generous with their time and recollections, I would have found it next to impossible to write a biography of Holly. I am especially grateful to Holly's parents, Ella and Lawrence Holley; his widow, Mrs. Maria E. Diaz; and the original Crickets, Jerry Allison, Joe Mauldin, and Niki Sullivan. They spent many hours discussing the details of Buddy's life and gave me access to tapes, clippings, and photographs in their possession—without demanding any control whatsoever over the final content of the book.

All of the following also offered their own memories of Buddy Holly and the rock 'n' roll era, or helped put me in contact with Holly's acquaintances. Resolving any conflicts among the various accounts was my own responsibility, and as with any such work, the author must be held accountable for any errors in fact or judgment.

Those whose help should be acknowledged include: Sonny Curtis, "Pappy" Dave Stone, Dick Jacobs, Bob Montgomery, Ben Hall, Norman Petty, "Hipockets" Duncan, Larry Holley, Scotty Moore, Tommy Allsup, Mrs. Jo Walker of the Country Music Association, Ralph Peer II, Larry Welborn, Don Guess, George Atwood, Daniel Dougherty, Bob Linville, Bill Hall, Carroll Anderson, Bud Andrews, Jerry Coleman, Murray Deutch, Bob Thiele, Owen Bradley, and Luke McDaniel.

This present book is a revised edition of the book first published by The Popular Press. In enlarging and revising this book, I have drawn on additional interviews which I have conducted since the first publication; I have also been aided by several Holly fans and collectors, both in the United States and in Britain. Foremost among these is Bill Griggs of Wethersfield, Connecticut, president of the Buddy Holly Memorial Society. Bill has lent special assistance to this edition by supplying photographs and discographical information (especially on cover records and tribute songs). In addition, Bill has allowed me to use material first published in *Reminiscing*, the Memorial Society's quarterly newsletter, which has been a trove of information and a means of communication for Holly fans since the Society's inception in 1976. Other fans who deserve special mention are Joan Turner, Steve Bonner, Wayne Jones, John Beecher, and Malcolm Jones.

Finally, my thanks are due to my family and my friends, for their support and encouragement.

JOHN GOLDROSEN

The
Buddy Holly
Story

Buddy Holly, 1958 (From the Buddy Holly Memorial Society Collection)

1. Home Town: Lubbock, Texas

Two full decades have now passed since Buddy Holly's life and career ended with such suddenness one wintry night in Iowa. No present-day teenager today was even alive when Buddy Holly died; only older rock 'n' roll fans can remember seeing or hearing him in person or on television. His memory lives on in his recordings, in the music that was the devotion of his short life. When someone asks "Who was Buddy Holly?" the music furnishes the most immediate answer. And yet, it is not enough—the music only raises more questions. Where did Buddy Holly and his music come from? Why does his music have the sound it does? How much was his own creation, and how much drawn from his musical environment? If the melodies and lyrics suggest something to you or make you feel a certain way, how can you be sure that that is how he meant it to be? What sort of person was he, and what drove him to become a musical performer? What were his successes and failures in life, and what were his goals for the years that never came?

When I first decided to seek answers to these questions, the answers were not to be found in any ready source—at least, there was hardly anything in print based on reliable, first-hand knowledge. In search of the answers—in search of the singer—it was necessary to put aside what I had read and heard before, and instead to seek out those who had known Buddy Holly and worked with him. And the search brought me to the city which was his birthplace and lifelong home.

When Buddy Holly was born in 1936, Lubbock, Texas had just twenty-five thousand inhabitants—only one-seventh of its present population—and had existed as a permanent settlement for only forty-five years. Its economy was based on a college—Texas Tech, a state school which the young community had won for itself in 1923—and on cotton, which had come to be widely planted in the region during the same decade. There was little large-scale industry; the college provided jobs in the construction trades and student business for small retailers, while the farms produced a demand for agricultural supplies and implements. Even when the small town grew into a good-sized city, it still looked to the college and the farms for its prosperity, and kept the appearance and attitudes of a rural community.

Lubbock lies three hundred miles west of Dallas on a broad plateau that offered an unbroken sea of grass to the view of the first settlers. They did not arrive until the 1890's; the growth of the region since then has been so rapid that ambitious goals and optimism about reaching them come naturally to the inhabitants. The census figures alone tell a story. As late as 1920, Lubbock had just four thousand residents; a decade later, there were twenty thousand people there; by 1950, the population had reached seventy thousand; and today, the city has over one hundred and seventy thousand people. It's only natural, too, that the town should present a strong sense of individual and community pride. From the moment the town was founded in 1891, its citizens have always believed that Lubbock was destined to become the central city of west Texas—and whether or not destiny had anything to do with it, their faith was justified. At the start, this was just another of the tiny frontier towns dotting the area; now it is the largest city for three hundred miles around and has earned the title "Hub City of the South Plains." Explaining how this happened isn't easy, but the community believes, with some justification, that the growth was due to the town's efforts on its own behalf. Town leaders rarely fought each other—town politics are simply dull—but instead concentrated on winning the town's battles for railroads and colleges; when the battles were won, Lubbock's primacy was practically assured. This competitive spirit still dominates the town's outlook on life and success—whether in business, sports, or culture.

Despite this expansive optimism—or is it because of it?—Lubbock remains conservative in thought and morals. "This isn't just the Bible Belt," jokes one resident, "it's the *buckle* of the Bible Belt." The three leading religious denominations are Baptist, Church of Christ, and Methodist; the congregations at their main Lubbock churches rank among the largest anywhere for those sects. The total number of all religious groups must run into the hundreds, explaining why Lubbock has as one nickname "The City of Churches." The town has no wild frontier past to look back on; organized religion asserted itself early, and the town grew partly on its reputation as a good place to bring up a family. Prohibition was only repealed in April 1972. Until then, no package stores were allowed within the city limits and no liquor could be sold by the drink except at "private" clubs. As in other Southern towns with similar regulations, the result was a string of clubs, honky-tonks, and liquor stores lying just beyond the town line along the highways leading out of the city.

Lubbock is linked to the older South too in its history of racial discrimination. "Lubbock is farther south than Georgia," said one citizen laconically, in explaining the state of race relations in the town. Blacks and Chicanos each make up about ten per cent of the population, with Chicanos, who have only appeared in sizable numbers since the fifties, on the increase. Until recent years, school segregation was fairly complete. Even now, the residential patterns are obvious: whites move out into the new subdivisions on the west and south sides, while the older, less desirable neighborhoods in the north and east quarters are left to the blacks and Chicanos. Actually, there is probably less contact between the races—and certainly more ignorance about the existence of a racial problem—than there is in the older parts of the South. When Buddy Holly was growing up in Lubbock, he had only limited contact with local blacks and their music, in contrast to the experience of Elvis Presley, Jerry Lee Lewis, or Carl Perkins.

Because Lubbock's rapid growth occurred after 1920, when Congress limited immigration, there are few foreign-born or first-generation American citizens among the town's Anglo population. The diversity of ethnic groups to be found in older Eastern cities is missing here; most of Lubbock's settlers came from the WASP-ish older sections of Texas.

All the same, there are still social divisions within the white population, and a person's cultural tastes can depend on his social status. Lubbock supports theater groups and a symphony, and plays host to theatrical road companies, ballets, chamber groups, and pop and rock music shows—all of which receive attention and support from the city newspaper, the *Avalanche-Journal*. But when a country music show comes to town featuring a Conway Twitty or a Buck Owens, the newspaper ignores the concert. At least until recent years, country music has been thought of in Lubbock as music for poor people; as a result, the "better" element in town—and anyone who wants to be considered in that class—has avoided any association with country music. (The reaction is a common one wherever country music is popular—even in Nashville.) Anyone caught listening to it feels compelled to make excuses— "I just had the radio on, I wasn't really *listening* to it."

However invisible it may be to the public journal, country music does still flourish in Lubbock, as it did when Buddy Holly was growing up there. Since the thirties, live country music "jamborees" have been a Saturday night feature in the cities and small towns of west Texas. Often sponsored by radio stations, these musical get-togethers offer local artists opportunities to perform, compete, and share styles and techniques with each other. Most of the numerous clubs and honky-tonks in the area feature country music, whether performed live by bands or played on jukeboxes.

In the Southwest, country music has always been dance music, not just music to sit and listen to. It was here that, in the thirties and forties, country bands began to use steel and electric guitars, tenor banjos, string basses, and occasionally drums, to provide more rhythm and a louder sound. It was here, too, that "honky-tonk" vocalists and the famous "western swing" bands of Bob Wills and Hank Thompson first became popular. All this went largely unnoticed in the North, and was not entirely welcomed by the older parts of the South, where more traditional instrumental and vocal performers had been popular before—it was only grudgingly that the Grand Ole Opry allowed Bob Wills to use drums when he appeared on the Opry in 1945; it was some time after the start of the rock 'n' roll era before the Opry routinely allowed drums on its stage. But in the Southwest, the assumption that country music was dance music, and the concept of country vocalists as lead singers for small rhythm groups, were familiar to country music fans of all ages well in advance of the rock 'n' roll movement.

These assumptions partly explain why the west Texas area produced more than its share of rockabilly artists, songwriters, sidemen, and producers. The gap between country vocalists and combos of the forties and early fifties and rockabilly performers who appeared just afterwards was not all that great; at the least, a young performer trained in these country music styles could move into rock 'n' roll. The same held true for performers raised on rhythm & blues traditions, but not for those raised in a pop music environment. Moreover, no matter what established country music stars thought of the young rockabilly intruders into the recording world and of their effect on country music, rockabilly performers were in fact accepted as country singers in the Southwest—and given the support and encouragement of local country music fans and musicians there. In such a town as Lubbock, the major opposition to the new music actually came from the elements in the population which had never cared for country music either.

Obviously, the brand of music popular in west Texas encouraged young country performers trying to make a career out of their music; but so too did the prevailing attitude toward music in general—and who should play it. Americans, a nation of spectators in sports, are often the same in the arts. We listen to music on recordings or in concerts, and maybe play an instrument privately without getting too far with it—we draw too sharp a line between "professionals" and "amateurs." In most places, music has ceased to be a family activity. In the Lubbock area, however, interest in music is more personal, and performers of all ages take more pride in their talents and set high goals for themselves. Each high school has a band, orchestra, and chorus, and the junior high schools face a large demand for classes offering instruction in all band instruments. It's not easy to be specific in explaining all this. When asked why so many musicians have come out of the area, the musicians themselves find the question difficult to answer. One replied, "Well, there isn't anything else out there to do *but* pick." Isolation and boredom may have something to do with it; but after all, Lubbock has movies, radio stations, and television, just like any other American city of similar size. The answer lies in the way the whole community approaches music. Among a part of the population, popular music is encouraged as much as "serious" music, and even in preference to it. Among country musicians especially, music is a strong force in family life. Furthermore, the performers share the area's sense of pride and desire for improvement. Explains one musician who was a contemporary of Holly's:

"Lubbock has always had this attitude, that you move ahead by being just a little better than someone else. It was the same for the musicians—there was this sense of pride in improving, in being good. There was competition, and people you could learn from; and once you started, you felt like you had to reach up to the level already established."

As a result of its geographical isolation, Lubbock attracts a number of concerts and shows out of proportion to its size. In more crowded areas of the nation, any city of Lubbock's size is usually so close to a much larger metropolis that local cultural life is stifled by the competition of the big city.

But because it is three hundred miles from any larger town, Lubbock remains an independent market—and its residents, lacking steady access to such entertainment, turn out well for visiting one-night shows. The city boasts convention and auditorium facilities superior to those of cities several times its size. An aspiring musician thus has not just the opportunity to play regularly at local functions, but also the chance to hear and see his models in person.

For all their pride in the town's growth and importance, Lubbock residents cling to the city's small-town past and all the good and bad which that implies. Lubbock has grown too fast to realize how large it is. Besides, its citizens are largely immigrants from small towns and farming communities who have not left all their habits behind; friends and strangers still say hello to each other when they pass on the street. The city itself has nothing rural to it. The population is strangely crowded together; house lots are small, and with the flat land almost entirely usable for buildings, adjacent houses are often just a few feet apart. There are no real suburbs, since the city limits contain almost all of the residential sections.

Beyond the city itself are only open fields of cotton and feed lots for cattle raising. The flat terrain stretches endlessly under a warm, blue sky to sharp, distant horizons, visible clearly in the dry air. It is a land that rarely leaves a neutral impression; to some, it is unbearably boring, while others find it exhilarating—"There's just something about it," is all they can say. And if it strikes you that way, then you can understand the confidence and urgent ambition that so many of the inhabitants possess. The land offers no boundaries to the sight; it promises opportunity, and provides the urge to be on the move, outwards and upwards. The countryside bare of trees and mountains offers no cover and hides no secrets; and so too the people are outspoken, unafraid to bare themselves to outsiders, and as eager to learn the stories of newcomers and strangers—for few families have lived here more than a generation or two, and so all are still newcomers of a sort. It is a country where the frontier has been settled only yesterday, where an elderly schoolteacher remembers the hitching post outside her school and the sons of cowboys who rode to class each morning. The frontier is now a memory, but not a distant one, and the old American faith that hard work and determination bring success has not yet been tarnished by doubt.

It was in this town and among such people that Buddy Holly grew up and formed his hopes. When the building of Texas Tech in 1923 and the spread of cotton farming to the west Texas plains created an economic boom in Lubbock, thousands left the poorer towns and villages of east and central Texas and sought work in the young city. Among the newcomers were Lawrence and Ella (Drake) Holley.[1] Mr. Holley had been raised on a farm near Honey Grove, a small town close to Paris in northeastern Texas. As a

---

[1]The difference in spelling between the last name of Buddy Holly and that of his parents arose when the family name was misspelled on Holly's first recording contract in 1956. Holly did not bother to have the error corrected; perhaps he preferred the simpler spelling anyway, since his family name was likely to be frequently misspelled in the same accidental manner if he chose to keep the original spelling. For the sake of consistency, throughout this book Buddy's last name has been spelled "Holly" and that of his parents "Holley."

young man, he moved west to Vernon and became a short-order cook. It was in Vernon that he met Ella; the two were married in 1924. The promise of employment in Lubbock, the opportunity to be part of a new and growing town, and the prior move of Mrs. Holley's own family to Lubbock all led the Holleys to go there themselves the year after they were married.

Even in the years of the Depression, there was work for Mr. Holley, but the family never had much more than just enough to make ends meet. "I guess we were poor—but of course, we didn't *know* that we were poor," Mrs. Holley recalls now. And although she will not talk of it herself, Buddy's friends are quick to point out that the Holleys, in spite of their low income, always managed to come up with the money for what they thought was important for their children—including musical instruments and lessons.

During the first few years after his arrival in Lubbock, Mr. Holley worked as a cook and a carpenter; through most of the thirties and forties he was employed as a tailor and salesman in a clothing store. The Holleys lived in rented houses, moving almost yearly. Their first child, Larry, was born in 1925; a second son, Travis, followed in 1927; and their one daughter, Patricia, was born in 1929. The family was living in a one-story house at 1911 Sixth Street when their last child was born on September 7, 1936. He was named Charles Hardin Holley, after his two grandfathers, Charles Drake and John Hardin Holley. Though his birth certificate carried his official given name, Mr. and Mrs. Holley decided right then that "it was too long a name for such a little boy." They decided to call him Buddy, a popular nickname for the youngest in a family, and it was by that name that he was known throughout his life.

Holly's birthplace at 1911 6th Street in Lubbock, 1972 (John Goldrosen)

2. Growing Up in Lubbock

There were no musical virtuosos among Buddy Holly's kin; but as a young child, he was surrounded by a family in which—as in many other families in that part of the country—practically everyone played some instrument or sang, on an amateur basis. At family get-togethers, he would have heard his mother singing duets with her twin sister, sometimes joined by Buddy's sister Pat. He would also have listened to his oldest brother Larry, who played the violin and the guitar, and to his other brother Travis, who played the guitar, accordion, and piano. (Buddy's father was the only family member who didn't join in the music—"*Someone* had to listen," he jokes now.)

Even so, Buddy did not show a strong personal interest in music until he reached his teens. The one exception to this was his first appearance on stage—at the age of five. His brothers were preparing to enter a talent show at the nearby town of County Line, with Larry playing violin and guitar, and both joining on the vocal. Mrs. Holley suggested that they take Buddy along and let him sing a number, too. "You know how they felt about *that*," she recalls. "Said they didn't see why their kid brother had to tag along, and so on. But after arguing about it a while, they gave in." Mr. Holley had given Buddy a small toy violin—and greased the strings so that Buddy could play with his toy without bothering others. At the talent show, Larry and Travis played their own number; and then Buddy carried his violin onto the stage and, accompanied by his brothers, sang a song his mother had taught him called "Down the River of Memories." His brothers failed to win anything for their duet; but to their surprise and chagrin, Buddy won a five-dollar prize for his performance.

As was said, though, that was an exception, and it was several years before Buddy, spurred a bit by his parents, showed any desire to sing or play an instrument. A fanciful account of the origins of Buddy's music was later offered in record company publicity write-ups, and set down in the liner notes to his first solo album:

> *Buddy's interest in music began at the age of eight, at which time he enthusiastically took up the violin. Unfortunately, his enthusiasm was not shared by those who heard his rather squeaky efforts. Soon, after he had driven everyone within earshot wild, he switched to the*

Holly as a young child (Lawrence and Ella Holley)

*guitar—an instrument which proved to be a natural for him. At
fifteen, Buddy began singing and accompanying himself on the
guitar.*

Actually, Buddy did not play the violin or any other instrument until he was
about eleven years old. At that time, his mother suggested that he take up the
piano. She explains, "Larry and Travis already played a couple of
instruments, and I thought it was about time Buddy learned to play
something too." Mrs. Holley doesn't remember Buddy having much feeling
about it one way or the other—"He was kind of quiet then—mostly kept his
thoughts to himself. We asked him to try this, and so he agreed."

Buddy took lessons from a teacher connected with the Lubbock school
system. Though his family did not notice any marked interest on his part, he
must have applied himself quietly to the subject, or else have just had a
natural aptitude for it; for after just a few months, his teacher reported to the
Holleys that Buddy was one of her best pupils—he learned quickly, and could
play some pieces by ear. After only nine months of piano, though, Buddy told
his parents that he wanted to stop taking lessons; as was his manner, he did
not bother to explain why. Actually, he continued to play piano on his own
through his life, though he never felt he played well enough to do so publicly.
Even during the time he was taking lessons, his interest ran to popular
rhythms—his brothers tell of him playing boogie-woogie figures after his
nine months of lessons. Years later, when he was a national star, he would sit
with his family and hometown friends during his visits home and accompany
himself while singing his new songs, or when playing some of his own
favorite recordings by such artists as pianist Fats Domino.

When Buddy dropped piano, it went without saying that he was going to
take up something in its place. He told his parents that he wanted to learn
how to play the guitar. They arranged for him to take lessons on steel guitar;
but after about twenty lessons, Buddy got more specific about what sort of
guitar he wanted to play: "The kind Travis has"—the standard acoustic
guitar. His obliging parents got him one. Buddy learned a few chords from
Travis and then learned on his own. Apparently, it didn't take too long for
him to become reasonably proficient; before the year was out, he was playing
his guitar on the bus to school and entertaining his friends with country
tunes, his favorite being Hank Williams's "Lovesick Blues."

Buddy was in the sixth grade then; in the fall of 1949, he entered
Hutchinson Junior High and met another young guitarist, Bob Montgomery, who was also entering the seventh grade. The two became close friends
and musical companions, practicing and performing together and sharing
their musical tastes. which came to be quite varied.

The foremost country singer and songwriter of the time, Hank Williams,
was probably the most profound early influence on Holly. Williams achieved
prominence when he joined the Louisiana Hayride, a live weekly country
music show which was broadcast over KWKH, a fifty-thousand-watt
Shreveport, Louisiana station easily audible at night in Lubbock. Williams
moved to the Grand Ole Opry on WSM in Nashville in 1949 and had his first

Holly at the age of thirteen (Lawrence and Ella Holley)

major record hits the same year; he remained the most significant performer in country music until his sudden death at the age of twenty-nine on January 1, 1953.

Williams's impact on such adolescent country music fans as Holly was much greater than that of other country singers whose styles and messages were more directly oriented to adult audiences. The songs of Hank Williams carried an intense personal touch; they revealed his life through his music. Other country singers were "sincere" in their singing—they could assume a role convincingly—but Williams wasn't even assuming a role, he was living it. There was a sense of romantic legend to his hard and sad life—a life which, while contributing so much to his music, also seemed to lead inexorably and inevitably to his early death. Even at the peak of his career, he was still a mysterious loner, a bit of a rebel against the conventions of his field. All this made him a figure of interest to some adolescents, as other country stars were much less frequently. His reaching tenor vocal style, haunting melodies, and plaintive lyrics, as well as simply the example of his individualistic career, all left their mark on young country performers.

When it came to performing as a team, Holly and Montgomery were more directly influenced by other country instrumental and vocal styles— especially bluegrass. Bill Monroe had established this traditional string band style in its modern form just before World War II, but it was in the late forties that bluegrass gained its greatest popularity among country music fans. Though most bluegrass musicians hailed from the eastern South, the style was not alien to areas like Texas where fiddle music was popular. In any case, Holly and Montgomery could listen to records played on the local country music radio shows or to Bill Monroe and the Bluegrass Boys and such Monroe "alumni" as Lester Flatt and Earl Scruggs when they appeared on the Grand Ole Opry. The high tenor harmonies common in bluegrass vocals were attractive to the two young musicians—whose voices had not yet changed—and so too were the brilliant and exciting instrumental patterns created by the bluegrass bands. (Holly in fact learned to play banjo and mandolin, though probably not to any high level of skill once he concentrated his attention on the guitar.) Holly and Montgomery were also fans of country duet teams whose close harmonies resembled those of the bluegrass singers, though their instrumental patterns were simpler; the Louvin Brothers and Johnnie and Jack were two of their favorite duos. This was the style Holly and Montgomery imitated most closely on the demonstration recordings made during their high school years which later appeared on an album, *Holly in the Hills*.

By the early fifties, Holly and Montgomery were expanding their interests to music outside the country vein. The clear channel stations in Nashville, Shreveport, and Dallas (KRLD) were bringing them live country music on the Grand Ole Opry, the Louisiana Hayride, and the Big D Jamboree respectively; but the pair were also using the radio to listen to black music as well. At the time, rhythm & blues and blues were not being played on any local Lubbock station; and, as has been mentioned, there was very little contact between whites and blacks in the town. All the same, there was, even then, an audience for such music among whites in the Lubbock area. Holly, Montgomery, and those with similar tastes found a more distant source for the sounds they could not hear in Lubbock: "Stan's Record Review," a radio show sponsored by Shreveport record shop owner Stan Lewis and hosted by a disc jockey named Frank "Gatemouth" Page, which was broadcast nightly at 10:30 on KWKH. Holly listened closely to the vocal and instrumental styles he heard on the radio (he and Montgomery being too poor to buy many records) and adapted them to his own playing years before the beginning of the rock 'n' roll era or the advent of Elvis Presley.

The rhythm & blues groups like the Clovers, the Dominoes, and Hank Ballard and the Midnighters were the ones which attracted increasing attention from whites in the early fifties; but interestingly enough, Holly and Montgomery were more interested in what was referred to as the "root blues" performed by such figures as Lightnin' Hopkins, Muddy Waters, Little Walter, and Howlin' Wolf. At first, the two held a purist attitude towards the rhythm & blues groups, even though they still enjoyed the music. Montgomery explains, "Blues to us was Muddy Waters, Little Walter, and Lightnin' Hopkins, and we didn't really think of the Drifters or the Clovers as being *blues* singers—because they *weren't*. They were pop artists, as far as we were concerned."

Not many of Holly's white contemporaries, in Lubbock or elsewhere, shared his interest in black blues styles—but among this minority were many of those who later became rock 'n' roll musicians. The game of picking this or that recording as the first rock 'n' roll hit has created the impression that the contact between white and black performers which produced rock 'n' roll did not take place until 1954 or so, when rhythm & blues records began to attract a wider white audience. In fact, musical tastes had stopped running strictly along racial lines well before 1954, particularly in the South: the existence of segregation did not mean that blacks and whites were ignorant of each other's musical idioms. The white musicians who were to enter the rock 'n' roll field constituted a sort of *avant-garde* among their contemporaries, taking a serious interest in black music five or ten years in advance of the actual popularization of rock 'n' roll. Scotty Moore, Elvis Presley's lead guitarist for many years, was as familiar with such black artists as Roy Hamilton, Howlin' Wolf, Junior Parker, and Lowell Fulson as he was with country music. "I'd always enjoyed R & B," he says. "It was just something we grew up with in Tennessee." The reason why he had a country band before teaming up with Presley was simply that a white band could get more jobs playing country music than it could playing rhythm & blues.

Ironically, Buddy and Bob, who were so ahead of the crowd in their taste for black music, were considered old-fashioned by Lubbock teenagers for their interest in bluegrass and country & western. Bob Montgomery remembers that "at that time, kids who listened to country & western much wouldn't admit it to the other kids, because it was 'hip' to like other things." A Lubbock disc jockey who was himself a teenager then puts it more bluntly:

Holly at the age of fifteen (Lawrence and Ella Holley)

"The kids would listen to *anything* else rather than listen to country & western. But before rock 'n' roll, they really didn't listen to anything at all."

As far as most of the teenagers in town were concerned, country music had little to do with them. They had reason to think so. Although postwar country songs frequently offered more graphic, realistic lyrics than pop music of the time, country music was still directed entirely at an adult audience. Country singers sang of marriage, adultery, religious salvation, the beer and blood of honky-tonk life, and other subjects without direct significance to most teenagers. The performers, too, were adults. Before the rock 'n' roll years, most country singers reached their thirties before they managed to work their way out of the provinces and gain national recognition. The same stars dominated the field from the end of World War II into the early fifties—new, younger stars were rare, Hank Williams being a prime exception. The middle-aged singers, producers, and songwriters became entrenched, aided perhaps by the disrupting effect World War II and the Korean War had on the development of younger performers. Those who were in control were satisfied with the size and the make-up of their audience, and called that time "The Golden Era of Country Music." But they failed to see the danger signals—they ignored the loss of the potential younger listeners. And they did not consider what would happen to their own field if younger stars ever broke through the traditional barriers.

Not that Holly and Montgomery had to hide their interests from their friends to avoid becoming social outcasts. Even though young people thought so little of country music then, Buddy and Bob could still entertain their peers without embarrassment. Whatever his brand of music, a musician enjoyed a high status in that society. "If you were a musician," explains one who was, "you were something special." And if you played an instrument in such a town, you grabbed every chance you got to perform for others. Holly and Montgomery started with school functions—assemblies, parents' night open houses, and the like. Stage fright was not a problem for them—they already played well enough to please, and their brash personalities were not cowed by the audience they might be facing. One time, the two were invited to appear on a parents' night program at their junior high school. No one thought to ask them what they intended to sing, and it was left up to them to introduce their song. When their turn came, they strode to the microphone and announced that they wished to dedicate their number to their teachers. The tune was a country novelty song made popular by the Carlisle Brothers (and revived in 1971 by Buck Owens)—"Too Old to Cut the Mustard":

> ...used to fight the girls off with a stick,
> But now they say, "He makes me sick!"
> Too old, too old,
> He's too old to cut the mustard anymore....[1]

"We were as surprised as the teachers were," says Mrs. Holley. "Oh, we

---

were so embarrassed—we felt like sinking right into the ground. Looking back on it now, it's pretty funny, really. But we thought they would get kicked out of school or something. Nothing happened, though. But that's what they were like, you know.''

Into their high school years, the pair continued to seize any opportunity to play in public. Live music was an important part of local business promotions and offered Buddy and Bob a chance to perform and be seen. When a new food market was about to open, or a car dealer made plans to expand his used car lot, or a department store scheduled a sale, a celebration was planned to attract public attention. The word passed among the local musicians, and the eager ones sought a place on the program—and a chance to be mentioned in the newspaper ad as the "live entertainment." Buddy and Bob played when they could, sometimes for nothing, sometimes for as much as five or ten dollars. As Montgomery puts it, "We played anywhere we could get to a microphone."

In the fall of 1953, when Montgomery and Holly were high school juniors, they got their first chance to perform on the radio. Before that time, the existing Lubbock stations had offered "block programming"—half an hour of this, an hour of that—most of which was supplied by the national radio networks. Then, in 1953, "Pappy" Dave Stone, a disc jockey on station KSEL, obtained the license for a new daytime station in Lubbock. Stone decided to devote the new station's entire airtime to country & western music. He was joined in this venture by two other KSEL announcers with a taste for country music, "Hipockets" Duncan and Ben Hall. The new station, KDAV, began operation in September 1953; to the best of anyone's knowledge, it was the first full-time country music station in the United States.

While on KSEL, Stone and Duncan had hosted the Saturday night "KSEL Jamboree," which had featured a bill of live local talent sometimes headed by a visiting name act or two. The Jamboree had at times attracted live audiences numbering in the thousands. The two men decided to bring the concept with them to KDAV. Since that station was limited to daylight operation, they scheduled the live show for Sunday afternoons and called it the "Sunday Party." The show went on the air within a few weeks after the station began broadcasting.

KDAV had announced that anyone who wished to perform could come down to the station that Sunday. Buddy and Bob showed up, of course, along with other acts of varied ages. Besides his interest in the radio station, Hipockets Duncan was also involved in booking and promoting talent, and so was alert to any new possibilities that he came across. Holly's very first appearance on the Sunday Party caught Duncan's attention.

"I could see right away that Buddy had it," Duncan says, "a lot of grit, a lot of determination—he just had more drive than the other youngsters there. He had a lot of talent, that's true. But then, everybody has a talent of some sort or another. What Buddy had was the determination to develop that talent."

Duncan encouraged Holly, Montgomery, and a younger bass player named Larry Welborn to form a trio, and the group was given a regular half-

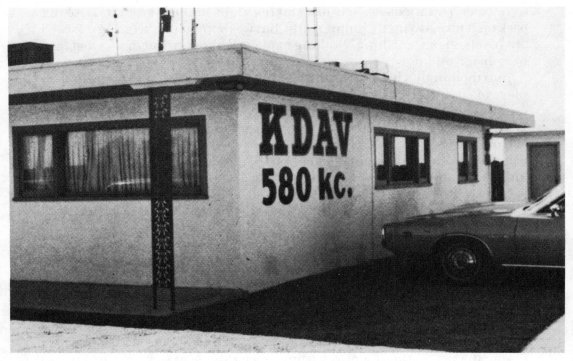

KDAV studios, Lubbock, Texas, 1972 (John Goldrosen)

hour slot on the Sunday Party, at 2:30 P.M.—like the Grand Ole Opry, the Sunday Party was divided into thirty-minute segments hosted by a regular act. The trio's segment was named "The Buddy and Bob Show," and it was by that title that the group came to be called. Sometimes they were referred to as Buddy, Bob, and Larry, but Buddy and Bob fit the name pattern of the time set by such country acts as Flatt and Scruggs, Johnnie and Jack, and Jim and Jesse.

Most of the time, they sang country duets in the harmony styles of Johnnie and Jack or the Louvin Brothers; on solo passages, Bob usually sang while Buddy played a guitar break. Occasionally, though, the trio played blues or rhythm & blues tunes, usually with Buddy performing the lead vocal. In 1954, one of Holly's favorites was the suggestive "Work With Me, Annie," a tune which was a great rhythm & blues hit for Hank Ballard and the Midnighters, but which was banned from most white pop stations because of its descriptive lyrics. Apparently, no pop station in Lubbock would play the recording, either; but Holly sang the song more than once on KDAV, which was proud of its status as Lubbock's first all-country station. The pattern does have a certain logic to it. Though country songs were rarely as explicit in dealing with sex as was "Work With Me, Annie," the earthiness of their lyrics might likewise have surprised pop listeners used to the bland sentimentality of Tin Pan Alley offerings. And conversely, at least some country fans, especially young adults, were interested in rhythm & blues but disliked

"Hipockets" Duncan, May 1978 (Bill Griggs)

standard white pop music. Buddy's brother Larry was that way himself. "When I was in the army," he recalls, "during World War II and right afterwards, they'd play a lot of pop music—slow ballads and syrupy-sweet songs with slick vocalists like Sinatra and Vaughn Monroe. Boy, I couldn't stand that stuff. Because I liked music with a beat—like country music and black music."

The "Buddy and Bob Show" gave the team more exposure, and they continued to grab whatever jobs came along. Hipockets Duncan noticed that people were often ready to take advantage of young musicians who were so willing to perform. "There was one fellow in Lubbock," Duncan remembers, "who would throw a party and 'invite' the boys, and tell them, 'Say, bring your instruments along and join in.' Sure enough, those kids were so eager to play, they'd wind up playing all night, and that guy would have entertainment for his party without paying anything for it." To prevent such cheating, the boys agreed to let Duncan serve as their manager. The contract was signed with the understanding that when the boys became successful enough to travel outside the west Texas area, Duncan would end his role.

Both sides to the agreement were equally sure that such a provision was necessary: the word "if" wasn't part of their vocabulary. The boys fully expected to make a career out of music and to become stars on stage and on record. When asked the question "At what age did you and Buddy decide that you wanted to be professional musicians?" Montgomery laughed and replied, "Oh, we always planned that, both of us. We never really considered anything else."

Even so, during his high school years, Buddy did prepare for a nonmusical career, just in case. He took courses in printing and drafting and worked part-time during his junior and senior years at Panhandle Steel Products as part of the high school's vocational education work-study program. His parents admit that he may have enrolled in the program partly because it offered the chance to spend less time in classrooms. By everyone's admission, Buddy was

Lubbock High School, 1955 (Lubbock Chamber of Commerce)

just an average student; he was never in any academic difficulty, but he was hardly outstanding, either. He doesn't seem to have left any more of an impression on his teachers than they left on him. One teacher still at Lubbock High says, "I taught him once. But to be honest, it was only after the news was in the paper about his death that I remembered that he had been in my class. He was a quiet kid—wasn't any great student, but didn't cause any trouble either, you understand. So I really don't remember anything about him."

"To Buddy, school was like prison," says Mrs. Holley. "But that was the way most of the kids felt then. They still do, don't they? I never saw him study at home. Every fall I'd say to him, 'Now Buddy, this year it's going to be harder, you know—you're going to have to start bringing your books home sometimes.' And he'd make some kind of promise to do that. But he never did; and he got by all right in school, so I guess he never had to."

The description of his school activities in the high school yearbook shows that they were related to his job or to the arts. He belonged to the Vocational Industrial Club of Industrial Cooperative Training, Chapter 95, and was its vice-president his senior year. (Montgomery also belonged to the club, and held an office the same year—the pair was intact in nonmusical activities too, it seemed.) Holly sang for two years in the high school's mixed *a cappella* choirs—the sophomore Choralaires, and the junior-senior Westernaires. (Holly didn't participate in the group his senior year, probably because of his job.) He belonged also to clubs for students interested in art and in classical and semi-classical music; of course, as any high school graduate knows, membership in such clubs doesn't necessarily mean productive participation. The only academic achievement by Holly that might be mentioned is a pin he won from a Fort Worth newspaper in a journalism contest. The Holleys know almost nothing about it. Buddy came home one day, handed his mother the pin and told her to put it away somewhere, and didn't tell his parents anything else about it. They never thought to ask, and they still don't have the faintest idea what he did to win the prize.

Together, Buddy, Bob, and Larry did win one school prize for their music. Lubbock High School students and teams are called the Westerners; once a year, up through the fifties, the school held a "Westerner Round-Up Day," with appropriate dress and music. During Buddy's junior year, the trio entered the song contest at the Round-Up, performed a tune Montgomery had written called "Flower of My Heart," and won the contest (and individual prizes of Westerner belts). It was small glory, but still, it meant something.

Music was foremost among Buddy's activities, but he exhibited related talents and interests, too. The dexterity and coordination he showed in playing musical instruments were exercised as well in handicrafts, notably leather work. He would make pocketbooks, wallets, and other articles as gifts for his friends and family. In late 1956, when Buddy was still a struggling artist, leading country star Marty Robbins saw Buddy's leather work and asked him to make some wallets—for distribution to Robbins's fans! Buddy at first agreed, but later decided that he was too busy for the job, no matter

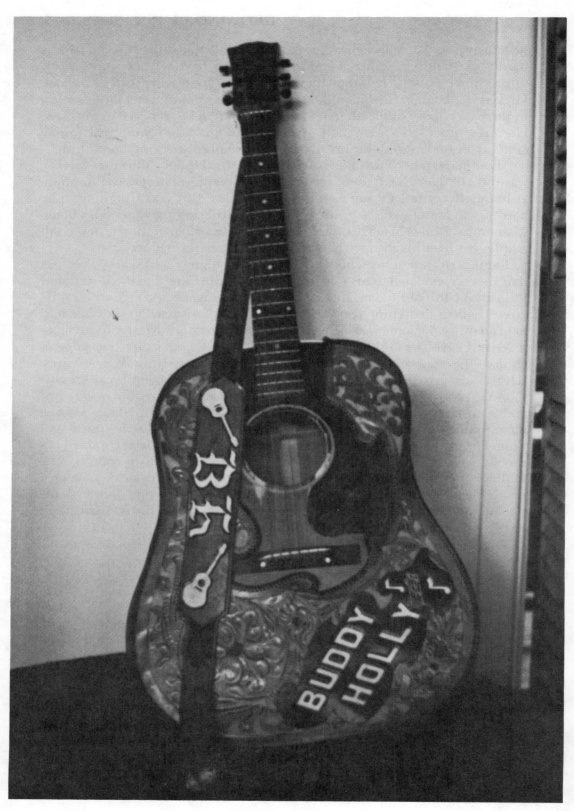

Holly's Gibson guitar, with the handmade leather cover
(John Goldrosen)

what price he was offered. His most ambitious project was a leather cover which he made for his Gibson acoustic guitar not long after his first record release in 1956. Buddy had seen the cover Elvis Presley had on *his* guitar and decided that he had to have one for his own. (Of course, Elvis could *buy* his.) After cutting, shaping, and tooling the leather, Holly traced designs on it, and colored the leather in blue and black. At opposite ends, he inscribed the titles of the cuts on his first record ("Blue Days, Black Nights" and "Love Me") and the name of his state, putting his own name on the body of the guitar. He showed his interest in design and arrangement in other ways, too, making a few paintings, and spending hours making architectural plans for hypothetical houses.

In the summer, his father would call on his manual abilities for more mundane tasks, such as helping in the residential construction business Mr. Holley and his two older sons had recently formed. "He could lay tile real well," Mr. Holley recalls with pride. "He was fast and neat—good with his hands." When Mr. Holley didn't have work for Buddy and his musical friends, Buddy's uncle, a bricklayer, could put the boys to work mixing mud and carrying bricks—no soft job, to be sure, in the west Texas summer sun.

Though Texas is even more devoted to sports than to country music, Buddy was not particularly sportsminded himself. He lacked the build for football, although he did play that and baseball informally with his friends. He sometimes went on fishing trips in the hills of New Mexico with his older brothers, and hunted rabbits in the fields around Lubbock during the early morning hours before school.

Music dominated all. Besides the performances of the Buddy, Bob, and Larry team, there were jam sessions with other local youths or occasional dates playing with the area's larger country bands, including one led by KDAV announcer Ben Hall. Bob Montgomery remained Buddy's closest companion. Often they would be at one or the other's house, listening to the radio or practicing by themselves. But both were filled with nervous energy, an urge to be going somewhere, to be doing something. More of their time would be spent "cruising," driving an old car around town and to the drive-in restaurants where Lubbock teenagers hung out, searching for action or activity in a town that offered very little to them. In the early fifties, television was a novelty and a popular rage (perhaps one reason why teenagers didn't listen much to the radio); but it was a sign of Buddy's restlessness and impatience that he almost never watched TV and couldn't see why anyone would spend time sitting quietly, entranced by a tiny screen. "I'll go into somebody's house," he told his parents once, "and they'll be sitting watching TV—they don't look up or anything. And if they're eating, they practically put the food in their ears. I just can't understand it." The only time the Holleys can remember their son staying home to watch TV was once in 1956—when Elvis Presley made his first appearance on *The Ed Sullivan Show*.

Buddy's impatience marked his method of practicing his music. He almost never practiced songs steadily and thoroughly, at least not when he was playing alone. Sometimes when he was home, he would mention a song or an instrumental and wonder out loud if he could play it. After playing a few bars and running through some chord progressions, he would stop and say with satisfaction, "Yup—I can play it"—and go on to something else. And of course, he *could* play it.

"The shy Texan" was the catch phrase applied to Buddy Holly years later, but those who knew him well have other memories. He was indeed often shy with strangers, even when he had gained national stardom. Maybe, though, there was more of caution than of shyness in his manner. His close boyhood friends remember instead that Buddy was brash, determined, aggressive, and a bit high-tempered. There was nothing shy or reserved about the way he drove a car—he piled up a good number of tickets, mostly for speeding, and lost his license for a time as a result. And when he had to deal with other people, he was often overbearing. He wanted everything done just right—and he was sure that he knew the right way of doing it. "He used to have his friends over to our house to play and practice," says his mother, "and one time he was really fussing and arguing with them about how something should be done. When the session was over and they all left, I said to him, 'Now Buddy, they're just kids—you can't yell at people like that, you've got to get along with them.' And he said, 'Mother, they just don't care—they don't take it seriously enough. But it's gotta be right, and so I have to get after them to play it like it should be played.'"

Larry Holley remembers that it took Buddy a while to grow up. "He was the youngest in the family, of course, and by the time he was a teenager he was the only one at home. He was pretty spoiled, to tell the truth. For a while he was awfully sassy to his parents. So one day—he was maybe seventeen or eighteen at the time—I just took him aside and told him, 'Now look, they're my parents too, and I'm not going to have you talking to them like that. I want that to stop, right now.' And after that, he really changed. Oh, he was just as determined in what he did and what he thought. He always did things like he wasn't going to have much time to do them. But he acted more respectful to his parents, and held his temper better, and was a little more considerate to other people."

Buddy was always close to his parents and to the other children in the family. Not every young musician at the time had parents who encouraged his music and even shared his tastes. "We never minded having him practicing at our house with his friends," says Mrs. Holley. "He was trying to be a success, so of course we were all for him. Anyway, I liked the sort of music he was listening to. Especially those black gospel singers—some of those songs were so pretty. He liked Ray Charles a lot. He had one record by Ray Charles, 'My Bonnie'—I still have it at home—and he'd play that and sing it, and I'd join in and sing along with the girls' chorus part on it. You see, some of those parents were really down on their kids, and made fun of their music—but the music Buddy was playing wasn't so very different from what we were used to, as far as we were concerned."

It was a very religious family, and one in which the "Protestant ethic" of

Larry Holley, May 1978 (John Goldrosen)

morality and success through hard work was stressed. The Holleys were
fundamentalist Baptists. According to their faith, one is not born into the
church; instead, each person must arrive at his or her own personal
acceptance of Christ as Saviour. His parents say that Buddy was fourteen
when he "came to know the Lord" and was baptised. Buddy's father and older
brothers served as officers of the Tabernacle Baptist Church in Lubbock; their
church, not just their faith, was an important part of their lives. Services at
the church avoid both the emotionalism of the pentecostal sects and the
formal ceremony of more organized faiths. The church music consists of
simple tunes—songs, really, not hymns—meant to be sung always by the
entire congregation without the leadership or domination of a choir.
Sometimes the songs are written in parts, and the congregation follows the
familiar phrases with everybody singing what suits them. When you attend
such a service and sing the songs, you are reminded of the background vocal
patterns which Holly introduced on his Crickets records, and you gain a good
idea of where the style originated.

His fellow musicians confirm Buddy's faith. Crickets drummer Jerry
Allison says, "Oh yeah, Buddy was very religious. I mean, when we were
playing together, he didn't go to church every Sunday or preach to everybody;
but I knew that he felt very deeply about his convictions." "We were against

Lawrence and Ella Holley, at home, November 1977 (Bill Griggs)

drinking alcohol or smoking cigarettes,'' says Mrs. Holley, ''and Buddy didn't hold to that strictly. When he started smoking, he'd do it on the sly, thinking I didn't know, and finally I said, 'If you're going to smoke, don't bother hiding it, just come out here in the living room and do it there.' He drank, but not too much; at least I can only remember him being drunk once. It was when the Hank Thompson band came to town once in 1956. Buddy had toured with them a few months before, so some of the fellows rang him up and got him out of bed and told him to come on down. And when he came back it was pretty clear that he was drunk and he just said, 'Mom, I'm sorry.' I wasn't really mad at him—I was mad at those fellows in the band.''

She adds, ''I didn't always see that much of Buddy—he was always on the go, running around with his friends. But when he came in at night, I'd fix up some peanut butter-and-jelly sandwiches, and we'd sit in the kitchen and talk about things—we called it our 'jam session.' '' Is this all just the way a mother wants to remember it? No, it doesn't seem so—Buddy's friends still describe his parents with affection, and never fail to mention the Holleys' close relationship with Buddy. (It's strange that while rock 'n' roll is associated with adolescent rebellion in everyone's mind, many top rock 'n' roll singers received strong support from their families—for starters, take the cases of the Everly Brothers, Jerry Lee Lewis, and, especially, Elvis Presley.) But there is another side to the story, too. It's hard to pin down—it's not obvious in anything Buddy said or did—but one does get the impression, from following Buddy's story, that he shared the teenager's fear that his parents did not really understand his hopes and concerns. One boyhood friend of Buddy's offers this explanation:

''Buddy was never really convinced that his parents cared about what he was doing; he felt like he had to prove himself to them, over and over. And I guess that's the way he was about a lot of things. He could be confident, even arrogant; but really, he was so determined to be successful because he was so afraid of failing. He wanted to be liked—it wasn't just a matter of making a lot of money. And so every record had to be a hit, and when he had one, he had to try for another and prove himself again. He could never be sure. Funny how his songs are like that, too.''

Physically as well as emotionally, Buddy matured late. His physical appearance always led people to underestimate his age. His high school senior picture makes him look closer to sixteen than to nineteen years in age. As a boy, he had been of average build, even overweight at times; but by the time he graduated high school, he was thin and lanky, though he had not yet reached his adult height and weight: an inch under six feet, and only 145 pounds. He had a boyish face and voice, and brownish-black hair that was just beginning to curl. (Holly's hair was naturally dark. Album covers that show him with light hair are either touch-ups of black-and-white shots or color photos taken with filters.)

And of course, he wore eyeglasses. Though boyhood pictures of Buddy indicate that his eyes were weak, his nearsightedness was not discovered until he was about fifteen, when a routine school eye exam showed that he needed glasses badly. His wearing of glasses became a bit of an issue when he began to perform as a rock 'n' roll singer before young audiences. After all, who had ever heard of a singing star with glasses? For a short period in the early part of 1956, Holly tried contact lenses, but found them uncomfortable and awkward. On one tour later that year, he did attempt to perform without glasses, but that experiment ended one night when he dropped his pick and had to get down on his hands and knees to search for it. Thereafter, Holly was willing to take off his glasses for publicity photos, but he stubbornly spurned the advice of those who suggested that he remove his glasses when he sang. He told his mother, "They just want me to fall right off the stage, that's all. If people are going to like me, they'll just have to like me with my glasses on." And by the time Holly was through, he had made his glasses such a distinctive feature that some singers even tried to look more like him by wearing glasses that they themselves didn't need.

There was school, and there was music—and there was a girl named Echo. The two had met when Buddy was about fifteen and had dated steadily through high school. Although they had planned to get married after high school, they found themselves moving in different directions as their high school days were ending. Echo respected Buddy's interest in music, but was not personally comfortable with it. She explains, "I came from a very conservative church background, and I didn't even dance. So when Buddy would play for dances, I did not go. He accepted that as the way I was, but it was a separation between us."

In the fall of 1955, Echo began to attend a Christian college in Abilene. She

Holly, Larry Welborn, and Bob Montgomery, at the KDAV studios, May 1955 (Dave Stone)

and Buddy continued to see each other on weekends, but she gradually came to realize that his life as a musical performer was not one she could be happy sharing. She says, "Deep down inside, I probably knew it was the type of life I couldn't be a part of. When he started to make records and become known as a musician, I shared in his excitement, but I think I realized that this was going to come between us. I could see the direction that he was going in, and it just wasn't what I wanted for myself. It wasn't that I loved him less or fell out of love with him; I think I still loved him, but I couldn't see myself in that position."

Echo transferred to a college in Nebraska in 1956. She and Buddy continued to correspond, and he came to Nebraska once to see her; but by late 1957, she had become engaged to a classmate, whom she married in early 1958.

Country & western, western swing, bluegrass, blues, rhythm & blues, black and white gospel music—all these had a place in Buddy Holly's musical background. It may seem a long way from the Louvin Brothers or Flatt and Scruggs to the music of the Crickets; and yet, such was the music Holly was listening to and playing with Bob Montgomery, even while the two were adding rock 'n' roll tunes to their repertoire. It is reasonable then to think that even Holly's later styles were influenced by the music with which he had grown up.

As a solo vocalist, his early style owed much to both country and blues performers. Hank Williams was an important model. Williams's quavering tenor voice and his distinctive country habit of rising to a required pitch instead of sounding it cleanly had their influence on Holly's own style. Holly's famed "hiccup" is really related to Williams's yodelling technique, which Holly had been fond of imitating. Of course, other country singers shared these traits, so Williams may not have been the only one to influence Holly. Hank Snow was another favorite of Holly's; the pleasant strong tone of Snow's singing, the fast tempo of his rhythmic train songs, and the guitar playing featured on his recordings made Snow another considerable influence on the development of rockabilly artists. And the self-confident lyrics in such Snow songs as "I'm Moving On" and "Golden Rocket" ("You trifling women can't keep a good man down....") found their echo in such Crickets classics as "That'll Be The Day" and "Think It Over."

Hank Williams and other country singers were themselves so influenced by the blues that it is hard to say just where their influence on Holly leaves off and that of black blues performers begins. Holly was quick to imitate the styles of blues and rhythm & blues singers, and did so long before he ever heard of Elvis Presley—in fact, the first time that Larry Holley heard a Presley recording, he turned to his wife and said, "You know something? That boy sounds a lot like Buddy!" According to Larry Welborn, Elvis's example did influence Holly to use a blues style on such fast-paced tunes as Presley's "That's All Right," in addition to the slow and medium-paced songs ("Work

With Me, Annie" as an example) which Holly was already singing in that manner.

Holly never explained what lay behind his music, or how he developed the sense of rhythm and texture that characterized it; but bluegrass undoubtedly had a lot to do with it. Although in Holly's rock 'n' roll recordings the vocal harmonization and instrumental ensemble style of bluegrass are not evident, yet something of the spirit of bluegrass remains. The fast, driving rhythms, offbeat chordal shifts, and country-based harmonic patterns of Holly's songs (and the bar-by-bar chord changes often involved) owe much to bluegrass. Though the steady, flowing guitar effect typical of Holly's songs has no particular parallel in bluegrass, it did aim at the same feeling of unrelieved rhythmic excitement that is created in bluegrass performances. KDAV announcer Ben Hall, with whose country band Holly sometimes played in those years, remembers that Holly was then already using the driving rhythm guitar sound of "Peggy Sue" when he played rhythm guitar on fast-paced bluegrass and fiddle tunes. The full texture of Holly's songs likewise has its precedent in the polyphonic effects of bluegrass music. As in bluegrass, Holly's music does not rely on sudden shifts between loud and soft passages to create excitement; instead, tension is built through the conflict of rhythmic patterns and the varying blend of voices and instruments. This is not to say that Holly was imitating bluegrass consciously; rather, some of it simply rubbed off on him.

One influence which Holly was apparently not exposed to was Mexican music. It has been thought that the unusual rhythmic patterns found in some of his songs were derived from a firsthand exposure to Latin music. However, Lubbock is several hundred miles from the Mexican border, and the culture of the Chicano community in Lubbock itself was isolated from that of the whites. Spanish instrumentals were part of the repertoire of western swing bands at the time; but while Holly's parents do recall him playing such tunes occasionally, they don't remember him showing any deep interest in Mexican music. The calypso and "chalypso" (cha-cha plus calypso) sounds which fed into the popular music world in 1956 and 1957 and the various Latin dance beats popular earlier in the decade probably had more of an influence on Holly's rhythms.

The term "Tex-Mex sound" often used to describe Holly's recordings was therefore rather misleading. The term had been used before the rock 'n' roll era to categorize Spanish language music of the Texas-Mexico border areas. As applied to Holly's recordings, though, the abbreviation stood for Texas and New, not Old, Mexico. It was a convenient way of categorizing Holly, who didn't seem to fit the existing categories, and it did suggest that there was something distinctive to the brand of rockabilly played in the area. However, while there are still country musicians there who can play excellent rock 'n' roll when given the opportunity, they do not play the same way Holly did. Holly's environment was important to the spirit and style of his music—it did make a difference that he was born and raised in Lubbock, and not New York City or Pittsburgh. But even those who played with Holly and who grew up surrounded by the same musical influences are quick to give Holly the credit for the innovative quality of his music. "It just came from inside of him," they say, unable to explain its derivation otherwise. They are the first to admit that Holly's style was unique, and not just an example of a broad regional sound.

In 1954, such questions of rock 'n' roll style still lay in the future. Holly, Montgomery, and other young musicians played their country music and, if they had high ambitions, waited for the break that would give them a chance to become recording stars. Meanwhile, change was coming to the music industry. Before Holly had graduated from high school, a demand had been exposed, one which was gradually filled by the type of singer Buddy Holly was and the sort of music he was able to play.

Interlude:
"My Autobiography"

(The complete text of an assignment Holly wrote for his sophomore English course in the spring of 1953.)

I was born one fall day, a certain particular one, because it was Sept. 7, 1936 and school for that year was starting. It was also the first Monday of the month and Dollar Day, and also Labor Day, so you see, it was very eventful in more ways than one. Mr. and Mrs. L. O. Holley were the happy parents of this bouncing, baby boy, or so I'm told, because I was a little young then to be remembering it now.

My life has been what you might call an uneventful one, and it seems there is not much of interest to tell. I was born here in Lubbock and except for a year and a half when I moved to the Roosevelt School District, I have lived here all my life so far. I don't remember too much of this period of my life up until the time I started to go to school at Roscoe Wilson when I was seven. Since then I remember most of the more important events of my school days. It was during the 4th grade that I moved to Roosevelt and continued to school there until I finished the 6th grade. I then moved back to the Lubbock School Dist. and started to Junior High School at J. T. HUTCHINSON. It was great to be back among my old grade school friends and everything clicked right off. It was really a joy to me to become a westerner of Lubbock Senior High School. Little did I know what the last nine weeks of my sophomore year held in store for me. This will make the second time I have given my English theme for my test; I got kicked out of Plane Geometry class in the last week of school; I am behind with my Biology work and will probably fail every course I'm taking. At least that's the way I feel. But why quit there? I may as well go ahead and tell all. My father's out of town on a fishing trip, and he is really going to be proud of my latest accomplishments when he gets back. As of now, I have these on the list. When I was driving our pickup Sunday afternoon against a hard wind, the hood came unfastened and blew up and now it's bent so that it won't fasten down good. Before I got home, I stopped at a boy's house and he knocked a baseball into the front glass, shattering it all over me. As if that wasn't enough, I had an appointment to apply for a job with a drafting firm yesterday afternoon and when my mother came after me, she let me drive on towards town. I had bought a picture of the choir and she was looking at it. She asked where I was, and I pointed to my picture. Just as I looked back up we hit the back of a Chrysler and tore the front end of our car up. So you see, I hope my father gets to catching so many fish that he will forget to come back for a little while.

Well, that's enough of bad things for awhile. I have many hobbies. Some of these are hunting, fishing, leatherwork, reading, painting, and playing western music. I have thought about making a career out of western music if I am good enough but I will just have to wait to see how that turns out. I like drafting and have thought a lot about making it my life's work, but I guess everything will just have to wait and turn out for the best.

Well, that's my life to the present date, and even though it may seem awful and full of calamities, I'd sure be in a bad shape without it.

FINIS
FINALE
In other words,
THE END

*Buddy Holly, probably at Owen Bradley's Nashville studio,
November 1956 (Maria Elena Diaz)*

3. To Nashville and Back

By 1954, a pop station in Lubbock (KSEL) was playing rock 'n' roll regularly, for an hour in the afternoon after school let out. The audience was largely white, but the songs which were played were mostly rhythm & blues recordings by black performers. Lubbock's white teenagers favored the original versions of rock 'n' roll hits by black artists over the cover versions by whites which often captured the market for the songs elsewhere. Joe Turner, Little Richard, and Fats Domino had hit records and successful personal appearances in Lubbock when their audiences were more limited nationally and their songs were providing hits for Bill Haley and Pat Boone. Black vocal groups like the Clovers and the Drifters were also early favorites in Lubbock.

None of this, by the way, had the social implications one might expect. It's true enough that the popularization of rock 'n' roll and the growth of the civil rights movement both occurred in the years after 1954, and it's tempting to think of this as more than just a coincidence. But this may just be wishful thinking, or a natural inclination of those who have always supported racial equality to assume that anyone who liked black music lost his prejudices against blacks in general. That didn't happen in Lubbock, nor did it happen elsewhere. Unlike some other cities in the South, Lubbock's auditoriums did allow integrated seating, and shows by black artists were attended by large numbers of whites. But one disc jockey remembers that, even at such shows, whites usually sat together in the orchestra, while blacks watched the show from the balcony.

As more young whites turned to rock 'n' roll, the Buddy and Bob Show began to attract a larger audience. At first, the boys' listeners had been mostly young adults and older country fans; now, requests were coming too from teenagers, and Holly performed rhythm & blues tunes more frequently. The show even became a live attraction. On Sunday afternoons, the KDAV studio, located in the open country south of the settled parts of town, became a gathering place for Lubbock teenagers, who would drive down, park their cars in front of the station with radios playing, and watch the performers through the studio windows.

By 1955, Buddy was getting requests to sing the material of another white singer—Elvis Presley. Billed as "The Hillbilly Cat," Presley became popular

The Cotton Club in Lubbock, May 1978 (John Goldrosen)

in the South and Southwest a year before the rest of the nation discovered him. Even in these areas where country music was popular, it took a while for him to catch on. Actually, since teenagers didn't listen to the country & western stations which were playing Presley's records, it was the older country audience which first "discovered" Presley, before most of the area's teenagers had heard of him. Presley's first single, "That's All Right"/"Blue Moon of Kentucky," was released on Sun Records in August 1954, and became a sizable hit on such country stations as KDAV.

Early in 1955, KDAV booked Elvis into the Cotton Club, Lubbock's leading country dance hall. For this appearance, Elvis got thirty-five dollars—out of which sum he had to pay his sidemen, Scotty Moore and Bill Black. Hipockets Duncan remembers that appearance:

"To a lot of the people there, Elvis was a novelty—a country singer performing black music, and doing all those motions too. And so maybe they thought it was funny at first—but if you looked at the women, well, you could see that they were eyeing Elvis and they knew what it was all about; and I think that even made some of the men a bit jealous. But you know, he was just a quiet, polite kid. A bit later, one of those Hollywood magazines paid some writer a few thousand dollars to come up with a story about Elvis's trips to Lubbock, and that writer invented a pack of lies—said Elvis had been caught making love to the police chief's daughter, and had had his Cadillac firebombed by the girl's boyfriend on his next trip to Lubbock, and so on— every bit of it completely fiction. Elvis didn't even smoke or drink when I knew him then. Between sets that night, he just sat in a corner, drinking a Coke. And Buddy and Bob were there that night—I don't know what the age limits were there, but they came down all the time to see the shows. And so they went over to talk with Elvis. Later Buddy said to me, 'You know, he's a real nice, friendly fellow'—I guess Buddy was surprised that Elvis was so normal and would talk to him so easily; because Buddy thought of Elvis as a big star, and really admired him. Elvis was enough of a star to be paid to play at the grand opening of the local Pontiac dealership the next day. Buddy and his trio played there, too. And when the next KDAV Sunday Party rolled around, Buddy was singing Elvis's songs.''

It was still a while before Presley's popularity among teenagers began to match his appeal to adults. He soon began performing on the Louisiana Hayride and touring on country package shows, but these attracted primarily adult audiences. On his next visit to Lubbock, Elvis appeared on a show with Ferlin Husky. Buddy, Bob, and Larry opened the show, and Elvis was the next act—the first of the touring acts to come on stage, and hence the least important. Larry Welborn recalls, "After the show, we had to help Ferlin Husky climb through a dressing room window to get away from all the autograph hunters. But Elvis had no trouble just walking right out of the auditorium." In fact, when the tour bus had come into town that afternoon, Montgomery and Holly had met it at the edge of town and driven Elvis off in their car for a guided tour of Lubbock; a year later, that might not have been too safe to do.

Led by Presley, the country-rock sound of Sun Records was gaining in popularity. Dave Stone and Hipockets Duncan boosted Elvis's records on their station. To them, Presley was country, and they could sense that his style was the coming thing in country music. Stone even added a daily "Rock 'n' Roll Hit Parade" to the KDAV schedule. Buddy and Bob steadily performed more rockabilly, both on their radio show and in the other engagements they played. Their calling cards now read "Buddy and Bob—Western and Bop,"

"Buddy and Bob" business card, 1955 (John Goldrosen)

BUDDY HOLLEY   LARRY WELBORN   BOB MONTGOMERY

♪ *Buddy and Bob* ♪

"WESTERN AND BOP"

BUS. MANAGER   KDAV BOX 1319
HI POCKETS DUNCAN   LUBBOCK, TEXAS

Dallas Sportatorium, formerly the site of the "Big D Jamboree," as it looks today (John Goldrosen)

and it was more of the latter they were called on to play at both teen-age shows and country dates. Once, they played intermissions at the Cotton Club during an appearance by Hank Thompson and the Brazos Valley Boys. The trio played all rockabilly—apparently, the audience was ready to accept this new dance music alongside the older western swing of Hank Thompson.

Holly and Montgomery were now out of high school—and still looking for their break. During 1954 and 1955, they cut several "demo" (demonstration) records with the hope, Montgomery says, of interesting a record company in offering them a contract. They gave the demos to a local promotion man for Columbia, who promised to "send them to some people." Whether he actually did or not, nothing ever came of that. The boys were a bit ignorant about the whole process, anyway. Montgomery explains, "We thought if you got a record contract, you were automatically rich. We had seen the country artists come through in their Cadillacs with Tennessee license plates and we thought all you had to do was to get on a record and you had it made."

Holly and Montgomery also took advantage of the contacts they had with other musicians and lined up appearances on shows outside the immediate Lubbock area. Once, they appeared on the Big D Jamboree, the live country music show broadcast over KRLD in Dallas. Sid King, a Dallas country musician about the same age as Holly who had a band called the Five Strings, recalls how that came about:

"We worked Lubbock several times, and we got to know Buddy. When we'd play the Cotton Club, he used to come up and sit in with us, him and Bob Montgomery and Larry Welborn. We were recording then for Columbia and our records were being played; and of course, he hadn't even made a record, so he thought we were big deals. A couple of times, he invited us for dinner, over to his house. Now, we were regulars on the Big D Jamboree, so one time I said, 'Well, Buddy, why don't you come on up, and we'll get you on the Jamboree.' And we must of told him what week we'd be on, 'cause we didn't play every Saturday, we only worked there once a month. Well, you couldn't say something like that to Buddy, 'cause he'd be there the next day. And that's kind of what happened—he didn't even call us or anything, he just showed up, him and the others. He came in on Friday night and he spent the night in my house. And so I introduced him to Johnny Harper, who was the talent coordinator on the Jamboree, and they put Buddy on the show that night. He did two or three songs, and I think he encored."

Larry Holley remembers that the trio sang "Down The Line" that night, and Sid King confirms that Holly performed rockabilly on the show. King says, "He was on an Elvis Presley kick—he just idolized the guy. And I mean, he sounded exactly like him. He did the Presley things on the Jamboree."

Holly did not get paid for the appearance on the Big D Jamboree, but it was the exposure that he wanted. King remembers another long trip Holly made, just for the chance to play:

"Me and my band had done a show in Wichita Falls. We told Buddy about the show, and darned if he didn't drive up there the very next week. Now, we hadn't gone back there, because the promoter was supposed to send us some money, but we never did get paid. Well, Buddy went up to the promoter, and he said, 'Sid King told me to come down, said you might use us on the show.' And the guy said, 'Well, Sid and his boys didn't show up, so we'll just let you play in their place.' And Buddy said, 'Will I make the same money they did?' And the guy said, 'Yeah.' Which was zero!"

Another time, Holly, Montgomery, and Welborn drove all the way to Shreveport, Louisiana, in an unsuccessful attempt to get on the Louisiana Hayride. When Elvis Presley had come to the Cotton Club, he had told the boys that if they came on down to the Hayride, he'd be sure to get them on the show. "Of course, we had always dreamed of appearing on the Grand Ole Opry and the Louisiana Hayride," Larry Welborn recalls, "and so one weekend, we decided to take Elvis up on his offer. But there was one little thing we forgot to check out. We drove all the way to Shreveport and went to the show and told Horace Logan, the Hayride program director, that 'Elvis sent for us.' But Elvis was out on tour that weekend. Heck, we couldn't even get in the door."

Months later, though, the dream actually came true for Buddy Holly—a record contract with one of the Nashville majors. The details of how Holly won his first recording contract are colored by legend and obscured by the subsequent deaths of several leading figures involved.

Contrary to popular legend, it was not a show with Elvis Presley that led to

Buddy Holly's first contract. According to KDAV owner Dave Stone, neither Elvis nor Colonel Tom Parker had anything to do with it. The decisive event was instead an appearance Holly made on a show which KDAV booked into Lubbock on October 14, 1955. Bill Haley and the Comets headlined the show; also on the bill was country artist Jimmy Rodgers Snow, Hank Snow's son. Travelling with the show was Nashville talent agent Eddie Crandall. Stone thought that putting Buddy, Bob, and Larry on a bill which included both country and rock 'n' roll artists might impress upon Crandall the range of Holly's talents and possibilities. On such shows, Buddy sang some rock 'n' roll tunes solo and did country duets with Montgomery as well, so that Crandall would get to hear the variety of Holly's style. Where the story involving Presley and Parker originated is anyone's guess. Presley appeared in Lubbock the night after the Haley show, and Hipockets Duncan recalls struggling successfully to get Buddy's trio placed on the already crowded bill (which, according to a newpaper ad, included country artists Jimmy Newman, Bobby Lord, Floyd Cramer, and "sensational new star" Johnny Cash). Parker was not yet Presley's full-time manager, however, and it seems doubtful that the Colonel was in Lubbock that night. The proximity of events would explain, though, why some thought that the show with Presley had been the one that brought Holly to the attention of people in Nashville.

Eddie Crandall got to see Holly perform even more just two weeks later, when Marty Robbins, whom Crandall managed, played Lubbock at the end of October. Larry Welborn remembers that the Buddy and Bob trio opened the show and also joined Robbins and his group afterwards for an all-night jam session at the Cotton Club; Welborn believes that Crandall was there that night. Crandall was indeed impressed by what he had seen of Holly during these two visits to Lubbock. When Crandall returned to Nashville, he set out to do what he could for the young singer. On December 2, he wrote to Dave Stone:

> *Dave, I'm very confident I can do something as far as getting Buddy Holly a recording contract. It may not be a major, but even a small one would be beneficial to someone who is trying to get a break. And he's got to get a start somewhere. Anyway, I'll see what I can do. . . . Marty Robbins also thinks Buddy has what it takes. So, all we can do is try. . . . O.K.?*

The next day, Crandall sent a telegram, asking Stone to have Holly make four demos and send them to Nashville. Crandall thought to add an instruction: "Don't change his style at all."

Crandall spoke with Colonel Tom Parker, but the Colonel was busy— Parker had just become Presley's official manager, and was in the midst of negotiating the sale of Elvis's Sun contract to RCA Victor. Crandall also spoke with Jim Denny, who had for some time been a booking agent for the Grand Ole Opry and was now moving out on his own as a talent agent and a music publisher. Denny agreed that Holly had potential, and he took on the task of getting Holly a contract. At the time, Decca, RCA Victor, and Columbia were the three major record companies with country & western divisions in Nashville. Denny had no luck with Columbia, which was then uninterested in rockabilly, but found a more receptive listener in Paul Cohen, Nashville A & R (Artists and Repertoire) director for Decca. With RCA Victor having just signed Presley, Decca was open to the idea of giving a contract to a similar rockabilly singer.

One night in mid-January 1956, Denny called Dave Stone's home. Stone was out, and so Denny spoke to Stone's wife, Pat, about Holly's physical appearance and personal habits. Satisfied with what he was told, he asked Pat Stone to find Holly and have the singer call him; Decca was ready to offer Holly a contract.

Holly was of course elated at the offer—but there was one hitch. Decca was interested in him only, and not in the Buddy and Bob duo. When Buddy asked about bringing Montgomery to Nashville, too, Denny told him, "Well, you can bring him along if you want, but he can't sing on the records. We want one singer, not two."

The development should not have surprised Buddy. During the previous year, he had been singing more and more solo rockabilly numbers whenever the trio performed. Still, for years, he and Bob had played together, planned together, and thought of winning a contract together. At first Buddy thought of turning down any offer which did not include Montgomery. But Montgomery soon talked him out of that; Bob argued that since a recording contract and a career in music was what they had hoped for, for so long, Buddy should seize the opportunity given him. Mrs. Holley recalls, "Bob said, 'You've got your chance—now go ahead!' And so Buddy did."

The contract offer did lead, though, to the break-up of the trio and the end of the Buddy and Bob Show. Bob undoubtedly felt that he would now do better on his own. His voice was suited for country and not rock 'n' roll. And he did not want to be just a sideman. In the early days of the Buddy and Bob team, they had performed about three country duet tunes (on which Bob normally sang the solo passages) to every blues tune (on which Holly sang mostly solo); but now Buddy had developed into a solo artist, and Bob's role could only have been a limited one. Larry Welborn perhaps didn't want to choose between the two; anyway, he was a couple of years younger, still in school, and not ready for the travelling life of a professional musician which Holly now envisioned. Welborn went off on his own and began to play lead guitar for a young local rock 'n' roll group, the Four Teens. All three remained good friends. Montgomery did in fact go with Holly to Nashville once to watch a session, and the two later wrote several songs together; and Buddy lent his own lead guitar to Welborn for him to play when he was starting his new group. When the trio was dissolved, Hipockets Duncan ended his formal relationship with Holly, too. He simply called the boys together one day and tore up their contract, as he had promised to do when their activities began to expand beyond the Lubbock area.

As was mentioned before, Buddy had never limited his playing to the appearances of the trio, but had also played gigs with several local country bands. Holly now drew on the area musicians he had known for some time to accompany him on his first Nashville session. On the Sunday Party and in playing with Ben Hall's band, Holly had met Sonny Curtis, a talented musician just a year or two older than Buddy. At that time, Curtis was playing the fiddle a lot, but he was also a fine guitar player, familiar with the Chet Atkins guitar style which had influenced Scotty Moore's lead guitar playing on the early Elvis Presley records. Holly was impressed with Curtis's playing; indeed, Larry Welborn says that Curtis was a more proficient guitarist than Holly at the time, and that Holly owed much of his technique, though not his "feel," to what he learned from Curtis. Holly asked Sonny to play lead guitar on the upcoming recording session. For a bass player, Buddy turned to Don Guess, a musician about Holly's age with whom Buddy had played off and on since their junior high school years.

Also part of Holly's new group was a drummer, Jerry Allison. Allison actually joined Holly in late 1955. The original Buddy, Bob, and Larry trio had fittingly, if inadvertently, matched the instrumental line-up in Elvis's original band. Once Presley's recordings began to include drums, Holly was quick to move in the same direction. Jerry Allison was two years younger than Buddy and still a senior at Lubbock High. The two were long-time friends, having first met when Allison's family moved to Lubbock in 1950 from nearby Plainview and Jerry entered Buddy's junior high school. Allison now had several years experience playing drums in all sorts of dance bands— jazz, pop, and country. Like Buddy, his tastes ran to rhythm & blues and rockabilly, and Allison was as ready as Holly to form a band playing their own kind of music. Holly and Allison practiced together often in the winter of 1955-1956—"Jerry's drum set sat in our living room for the longest time, it was almost part of the furniture," says Mrs. Holley. "Of course, they needed a place to play, so we didn't mind." Unfortunately, when Buddy went to Nashville in late January to cut his first records, Allison was unable to go along, since he was still in school.

Before going to Nashville, Holly bought some new equipment for himself and his band. During his high school years, he had bought a small amplifier and a pick-up for his Gibson, and in 1954, he had purchased an inexpensive electric guitar. Now that he was going to Nashville, he was determined to go first-class. Larry Holley recalls Buddy's reasoning:

"Buddy came to me and asked me for a loan so he could buy a new guitar and amplifiers. Well, I had my own business by then and I was doing all right and had the money, so I was glad to help him out. I asked him how much he needed, and he said a thousand dollars. I didn't mind giving him that much, but I wondered if it was wise to spend money that way—I think six hundred dollars went for the guitar alone. So I questioned him about it, and he said, 'No, I know what I'm doing. I'm going to be a star now, and everything I do has got to be the best, and my guitar has got to be the best.' And I gave him the money—I didn't doubt that he'd be able to pay it back eventually, when he got big. That was when he bought that Fender Stratocaster, the one he used on all his records and in his concerts."

"As I remember," says Sonny Curtis, "we left for Nashville in a bit of a hurry. Buddy was driving a new Oldsmobile then; his family had traded in their old car and sort of given him this new one as a graduation present, but he was supposed to make the payments on it. So he was trying to stay one step ahead of the collection agency, and I think that's why we left so quick. There was Don Guess and Buddy and me, and we strapped Don's bass to the top of

Holly's
Fender Stratocaster
guitar
(John Goldrosen)

the car. It was a long trip; and on the way back we were practically broke. I remember we stopped at an aunt of Buddy's in east Texas, so we could get a decent meal."

When the Texans arrived at the Decca studio in Nashville, Holly found that although Decca was willing to let him use Curtis and Guess on the session, they did not want Holly to play his own rhythm guitar—they argued that the instrument would feed into the vocal microphone and interfere with the quality of the recording. Nor did they think that a rock 'n' roll style of drumming was necessary on the session.

Buddy accepted Decca's decision. He was ready to do whatever was asked of him, and whatever it took to get started in the business. It was reasonable for him to assume that the people he was working with knew what they were doing and what was proper for his recordings. Decca was a major label, and had for years been a leader in the country field with such acts as Red Foley, Ernest Tubb, and Kitty Wells. Paul Cohen had been one of the pioneer A & R men in Nashville, and Owen Bradley, Holly's producer, was a primary figure in the growth of the Nashville recording scene.

But that was just the problem. The company and the men who were in charge of Holly's first recordings were involved in country music too deeply and too successfully to cope with rock 'n' roll. Decca's one rock 'n' roll star in the fifties was Bill Haley, and he was not connected with the Nashville office of the firm. The other country-based rock 'n' roll stars had started with Sun Records in Memphis, two hundred miles and a world away from Nashville, or with more obscure labels in Texas and Louisiana. Some, including Jerry Lee Lewis, had been turned down by the Nashville companies they had first sought out.

The world of country music offered a mixed reception to rock 'n' roll. On one side were some younger musicians like the Sun artists who considered their music to be an extension of country music or a mixture of it with other forms—but not a wholesale abandonment of country music. On the other side, though, were the established record companies and some major artists, who saw the new music related to country music only in the way that heresy is related to orthodoxy. Certainly, part of their opposition was a matter of self-interest—they had dominated the field for some time, and new artists and independent record companies were a threat to their security and prestige. The split in Nashville lingers to this day. Some remember the late fifties as a disastrous time for country music; but at the same time, many of those prominent today in country music came to Nashville after beginning their recording or producing careers in rock 'n' roll. I once found myself in a Nashville office with two men—one, an important producer and publisher who had been an independent rock 'n' roll producer in east Texas fifteen years before; the other, a "picker" who, when asked for *his* memories of rock 'n' roll, answered, "Remember it? I'm still trying to *forget* it!"

Country music fans were also split. Elvis Presley was the first center of controversy—"Letters to the Editor" columns in country music fan magazines were filled with attacks upon, and defenses of, Presley's credentials as a country singer. When someone didn't sound like a traditional country singer but sold records in country markets and was a hit with country audiences, what was he? Elvis, at least, was given a mark of approval by being invited onto the Louisiana Hayride and the Grand Ole Opry; but later, there were rockabilly stars who had number one hits on the country charts but were not allowed to appear on the Opry. Amid this confusion, the record companies, producers, and artists attempted to come up with recordings that would sell to both country and rock 'n' roll audiences—and sometimes created tunes that were not enough of one or the other to sell in either market.

Although Holly's recordings on Decca have since been described as country & western, they were not really intended to be so at the time—at least, they were intended to appeal to rock 'n' roll audiences as well. This was 1956, not 1953; Presley was having his first million-sellers on RCA Victor, and rock 'n' roll was becoming a national pheomenon. Holly was already well familiar with the songs of Presley, Domino, Little Richard, and other rock 'n' roll performers. Decca apparently wanted Holly to be a rockabilly artist, along the lines of Elvis Presley—that is, such was the intent, if any attention at all was paid to the question of Holly's potential appeal. His records received little promotion of any sort in any market.

The confusion was not eased any by the tense and uncertain atmosphere at the sessions. Nashville was a closely-knit society, and teenage rockabilly musicians from west Texas were not part of it. Decca personnel were not deliberately unfriendly—after all, Holly was under contract to them and any success he gained would have been to their profit. But Holly and his friends could easily sense what the unspoken attitude was: they were inexperienced, "hick" musicians with nothing special to offer a large, old, sophisticated record company. The cultural gap could not have been much wider if the boys had gone to Los Angeles or New York to make their first recordings. Jim Denny was astonished when he discovered, shortly before the first session was about to begin, that Holly and his comrades did not belong to the musician's union—a requirement for anyone playing on a recording session in Nashville. Holly, for his part, was young and brash and overconfident, not yet aware of the difference between having a record contract and having hit records. He rubbed some people the wrong way. At Cedarwood Music, the publishing company founded by Jim Denny, a secretary will tell you bluntly, "All I remember about Buddy Holly is that I didn't like him."

Sonny Curtis offers his memories of those sessions: "In Nashville, we just stayed at the motel and didn't hang around with anybody. Just sort of hung with ourselves. Or hung up at Marty Robbins's office and chased chicks. I don't think anybody there was really very interested in Buddy. I don't think they thought about him being a big star, or wanted him to go in any particular direction. They just made a contract and were going to record him. Best I remember, nobody messed with us at all, or told us how they wanted it to sound—they just turned on the mikes and let us go. They weren't really into rock 'n' roll, and they didn't know what to do—they knew it was happening, and they just wanted a rock 'n' roll artist. And they didn't have a clue as to how rock 'n' roll should sound, because everything in Nashville was still basically country—this was even before those Nashville guys got into rock 'n' roll. So they wanted a rock 'n' roll group and they left it all up to us, but we didn't know anything about how you did it, about how to make a recording.''

Jerry Allison, who made it to the next session, adds, "Back on those dates, I don't even remember which guy was Paul Cohen and which guy was Owen Bradley or who the engineers were. It was like, they were biggies and we were just dips. We didn't groove with them or anything. We were sort of just afraid of them.''

Owen Bradley, the producer of Holly's Nashville records, offers his explanation of what happened at Holly's sessions: "When Paul Cohen sent Buddy over, Paul said he wanted it country—at least, that was my understanding. And it was my job to please Paul Cohen. We had been very successful with a country formula; we were all into country, and it's hard to

Owen Bradley, in Nashville, July 1978 (John Goldrosen)

change patterns. Buddy couldn't fit into our formula any more than we could fit into his—he was unique, and he wasn't in a pattern. It was like two people speaking different languages. Or you could say it's like comparing different flavors of ice cream. Buddy was an unusual flavor that we just didn't understand. Our musicians were fantastic at what they were doing, but they just didn't know how to do what *he* was doing. I remember Buddy wanted the drummer to do something, and the drummer (it would have been Faris Coursey then) just couldn't do it. Buddy was trying to make sort of a rock 'n' roll record, and he should have had guys with a black feel—our guys had a country feel.

"He was a very nice guy, very easy to work with. I think we gave him the best shot we knew how to give him, at the time. But it just wasn't the right combination; the chemistry wasn't right. It just wasn't meant to be. We didn't understand, and he didn't know how to tell us."

Nashville just didn't know what to do with Buddy Holly, and even if it had been ready to listen to Holly's own suggestions, Buddy probably could not have explained to them just what they *should* do. He had not yet arrived at his own distinctive style, nor did he understand the commercial complexities of the record industry. Playing live at west Texas dances was one thing; making a record that would catch the ears of disc jockeys and listeners was another. Besides, despite his brash exterior, Holly was self-conscious and uncomfortable in the presence of the more experienced producers and musicians. Whenever Holly had a clear idea of how he wanted something done, he could be very stubborn about insisting upon it. But at the time of that first Nashville session, he did not have enough confidence in his own judgment to demand that things be done in a certain way—or maybe he just realized that he did not have the power to do so anyway. He was somewhat awed by the reputations of those with whom he worked and occasionally followed their advice too readily. For example, because singer Webb Pierce told Buddy that the way to be successful was to sing in a high voice, Holly sang above his own range on some recordings and wound up out of pitch.

Holly was allowed some leeway in the material he chose to record. Paul Cohen and Owen Bradley determined the arrangements for the sessions and decided what was to be recorded and released, but they did choose most of the songs from tunes offered them by Holly and his group. The arrangement suited all, since Holly got to sing songs of his own choice, while Jim Denny could have the new songs published by his Cedarwood Music publishing firm. Anyway, no established songwriter would have wanted to waste songs on an unproven artist if the tunes could be saved for bigger names.

Holly was starting to write some songs himself, but for his first recordings, he turned as well to the efforts of other musicians and songwriters. When Holly got word of his record contract, he called KDAV disc jockey Ben Hall to ask him if he had a song Holly could cut on the upcoming session. As a happy coincidence, just a couple of weeks before, Hall had written a song with Holly's style specifically in mind, hoping that Buddy would get the chance to record it. "Blue Days, Black Nights" became Holly's first recording and his first release.

Looked at in isolation, "Blue Days, Black Nights" is not a bad record. The arrangement is simple and uncluttered, and Holly has the vocal choruses to his own. The melody is country, but with blues inflections (particularly in the refrain phrase), and is a good vehicle for the vocal slides and stops which already marked Holly's style. Still, there are flaws, especially when the record is considered in relation to the markets of the time. The recording falls into a curious gray area between older country and the developing rock 'n' roll forms. The unrestrained vocal goes beyond country standards, but the beat is not emphatic enough for rock 'n' roll—although Don Guess's bass playing lends an emphatic rhythm to the tune, it is under-recorded by rock 'n' roll standards. What drumming there is on the record is almost inaudible, and the absence of rhythm guitar makes it impossible to accent the rhythm enough. Only Holly's vocal contrasts with the bass rhythm. The lead guitar solo by Sonny Curtis is technically perfect but lacks the drive of guitar breaks on the early Sun recordings of Elvis Presley, Carl Perkins, Roy Orbison, and others. The use of echo doesn't help the recording. While on the recordings made at Sam Phillips's studio in Memphis, the use of echo serves to give the impression of a live recording in a dance hall or club, Decca's echo was based on a tape-delay system rather than a "live" echo chamber and hence sounds more artificial. The echo on these recordings is so distinct as to emphasize, not de-emphasize, the fact that the sound has been studio-recorded. Overall, the record lacks the immediacy of Holly's later recordings. He puts feeling into the vocal but he remains remote, performing before the listener without truly communicating with him.

The flip side of the single, "Love Me," was written by Holly and Sue Parrish, another local Lubbock songwriter. It is one of Holly's less memorable recordings. The material was inferior to begin with—Holly still had a lot to learn about songwriting. With a rocking band, he could have given some excitement to the song by working the rhythms of the lyrics against those of the band; but here, he is left stranded, and there is little to the song. The recording does at least demonstrate that some of the marks of Holly's style were developed well before the Crickets recordings that made them famous.

Two other tunes, "Don't Come Back Knocking" and "Midnight Shift," were recorded at this same session. "Don't Come Back Knocking," like "Love Me," was written by Holly and Sue Parrish. It was a stronger and less cliché-ridden effort than "Love Me," with a blues-based melody, a vocal that delivered the hurt but defiant tone of the lyrics, and a stronger accompaniment—thanks to the addition of Nashville veteran Grady Martin on rhythm guitar.

"Midnight Shift" was, for many years, as obscure in America as most of these Decca recordings were (in England, the song was released as a single in the spring of 1959 and made the top thirty). More recently, rock critics have given it much attention, one describing the recording (in particular, Holly's vocal) as "early Dylan." The song was written by Luke McDaniel, an Alabaman, who had himself recorded as a country and rockabilly artist for

King (he later did one session as well for Sam Phillips at Sun). McDaniel wrote the song in late 1955 and took it to Nashville, where he made a voice and guitar demo of it for Buddy Killen of Tree Publishing. McDaniel never met Holly; it was Killen who somehow got the song to Jim Denny. Sonny Curtis remembers Denny playing the demo for Holly at the session: "Some old boy just had his acoustic guitar and sang on the demo. It was a really good demo, and we all just loved the song."

McDaniel meant for "Midnight Shift" to be done in a rockabilly style. "I started off country," recalls McDaniel, "but I was doing rock on my flip sides, even before Elvis came on—except we didn't call it rock, it was just the old-type Saturday night blues that we had been doing." The name of the woman in the song was not intentionally derived from Hank Ballard's "Annie" songs; McDaniel says, "I did not have any other song in mind, at the time that I wrote 'Midnight Shift.' I was just picking up things of what women would do when they begin to slack off from a true marriage—you know, things begin to pop up in your life, and so I put them into the song." If McDaniel's

Holly in 1956 (John Beecher)

name seems unfamiliar to even the most devoted Holly record collector, it's because McDaniel used a pseudonym, "Earl Lee," on the song. "I was under a writing contract to Acuff-Rose Publishing at the time," he explains. "And of course, they didn't handle that kind of material—they were strictly country, heartbreak country, if you know what I mean. So I used another name, and put the song into Tree Publishing." The second name on the song, "Jimmie Ainsworth," was also a pseudonym, for a friend of McDaniel's named Jimmy Rogers, who did not actually participate in writing the song. "We were travelling in his automobile," says McDaniel, "so I put his name on the song."

Holly's first single was released in April 1956. Although it was not a complete flop, it didn't exactly blaze up the charts, either. A few months later, Decca estimated sales at nineteen thousand copies, but that estimate was undoubtedly optimistic. Holly was obviously straining to be positive when he wrote to a booker, "I have talked to some friends that were travelling up around the northeastern part of the country, and they said my record was very popular around Washington, D. C. and through Missouri." Sonny Curtis and Jerry Allison remember the thrill everyone got when they stopped at a bar on the way to Nashville for their next session and found "Blue Days, Black Nights" on the jukebox.

The uncertainty of the record's classification didn't help its success. Whatever Decca's original intention in signing Holly, his record was treated as country; *Billboard* covered it in its "Reviews of New Country & Western Records" column. The reviewer gave the single a good rating and added an offhanded sort of compliment in his comment: "Cedarwood succumbs to rock 'n' roll, too. If the public will take more than one Presley or Perkins, as it well may, Holly stands a strong chance." The record was not close enough to rock 'n' roll to be played on pop stations; programmers were unlikely to pay much attention to records which did not readily seem to fit the musical categories of their stations, especially when the artist was an unknown. Anyway, there was little or no promotion of the record, and due to the independent character of Decca's Nashville division, it is unlikely that the single was even distributed to other than country stations.

For Holly and his friends, getting out on record was quite a thrill, at least until the realization sunk in that the record was going nowhere and they were still broke. Only Ben Hall recalls Buddy ever expressing any dissatisfaction with the recording; Hall remembers that Buddy thought the absence of Allison on the recording had weakened it considerably, and hoped to re-cut the song with Allison present before putting it on any intended album.

Twice during 1956, Holly managed to get booked on extended package tours travelling outside his native area, and thereby gained some needed experience in facing the public. In April and May, Holly and his band toured through the Southeastern states on a show which included Sonny James, Faron Young, Tommy Collins, and Wanda Jackson. Holly, Curtis, and Guess opened each program, doing a short set of their own tunes before stepping back to act as sidemen for the acts on the tour which lacked their

Holly in 1956 (John Beecher)

own road bands. "We were a little 'green,'" Holly later wrote a friend in a bit of understatement. "We were pretty terrible," says Sonny Curtis more directly. "Our portion of the show was very amateurish—we couldn't get it together. We opened the show, and they'd open up the curtain, and Buddy would have his back to the audience and be messing with his amp."

In the fall, Holly made another three-week tour, accompanied this time by Curtis, Guess, and Allison; this show was headed by Hank Thompson and included Cowboy Copas, Hank Locklin, Mitchell Torok, Wanda Jackson, Glen Reeves, and George Jones. On such tours, Holly and his band had to vary their style of accompaniment, depending on how close the lead singer came to their own rockabilly style. At times, there was some rivalry with the more strictly country acts—especially George Jones, then just beginning to gain prominence in the country field, and steadfast about staying in it. Jones made no secret of his dislike for the dress and style of Holly and Glen Reeves; Curtis recalls, "Reeves was into rock 'n' roll and he wore green coats and all that—sports coats instead of cowboy boots. Turned George Jones right off." Holly's group would sometimes retaliate by breaking into a rockabilly beat while backing up Jones. "You'd like it if you could do it," they said before one show; and so Jones went on stage that night and performed nothing but rockabilly, in fine fashion. Or so the story goes.

The tours taught Holly something about stage manners, and gave him and his companions a welcome taste of what it was like to be professionals. Don Guess recalls, "On our early tours, we were wide-eyed youngsters from Lubbock and the music business was just fantastic to us. Actually, we could not really absorb what was happening to us on these tours. We had Buddy's car, and we carried the bass fiddle right on top of it—and I remember, one of those guys that was touring with us, Faron Young, we pulled into some town in Florida, and he was out in the street, and he said, 'Gee whiz, look at those hillbillies.' It sort of tickled us, and it was a compliment, too, actually."

But the first record hadn't created much of a stir, and bookings were few and far between. Hipockets Duncan had recently left KDAV and moved to Amarillo to run a club and a restaurant there. "One day," he remembers, "I got a call from Buddy—'Hipockets,' said Buddy, 'we're hungry.' Their record wasn't doing too much, and they just weren't getting bookings. So I booked him into my club, the Clover Club, for Friday nights for a teenage dance—we closed down the bar. I couldn't pay him much, but of course we had the restaurant so the boys would eat there and get a good meal. They'd come up on Friday and play and stay overnight, then go back to Lubbock. And we had maybe a thousand teenagers there on the average after it got going.

"There's a lot of people think Buddy just skyrocketed to fame overnight, and that's just not true—there were plenty of hard times to go through before that. But he wouldn't let it stop him—on a number of occasions he could have said, 'Well, I quit,' because of things that happened to him. But he didn't give up; and he didn't forget other people either—he had a big heart, and he was a buddy to a lot of people. Once up at the Clover Club, a young man named Earl Sinks came in to see me, and he wanted to know if there was any chance

Holly in 1956 or early 1957 (From the Buddy Holly Memorial Society Collection)

that he could sing with Buddy's band—to get a little recognition for himself. So I went up to talk with Buddy about it, and he said, 'Tell him to come right on up, he's welcome.' So that was his attitude, even though he was still trying to make a name for himself. And by coincidence, this fellow Earl Sinks later sang lead with the Crickets on a few records after Buddy got killed."

At the Amarillo dances, Holly and his band could play rock 'n' roll exclusively. They also began to play rock 'n' roll more regularly in Lubbock on Saturday nights at a youth center's teen dances. Before this, there had been little opportunity for Lubbock teenagers to dance to their own music. The town did not provide any place for them to use, and dancing was prohibited at rock 'n' roll concerts in the town's auditorium and coliseum.

The dances brought Holly and his friends their first mention in Lubbock's newspaper, the *Avalanche-Journal*. "Oh yeah, I remember that," says Jerry Allison. "They talked all about knife fights or something; and I think it said, 'while three young musicians frantically belabored "Hound Dog."' I think that's how they put it, about what the band was doing." Sonny Curtis adds, "It had the kids doing the dirty bop, and it had their eyes all blacked out—I remember that. There was a picture and an article and everything."

Mrs. Holley also remembers it well: "Buddy came home one day all excited and said that the newspaper had sent a reporter down to the youth center to do a story on Buddy and the boys. And I was sort of suspicious, wondered what they were up to. Sure enough, when the story came out, it was really slurred— they just wanted to put the boys down and play up any trouble they could find at the center. Which wasn't fair, because it was the first place the kids had had for their own; and when Buddy was playing there, if there was any trouble, like fights or beer being brought in, he'd take charge a bit and tell the kids, 'Look, we've got to stop this or the police will be coming in here to shut us down.' Anyway, that article made me really mad, and I wrote the paper a letter. I said that they wouldn't have reported any of these things if they had happened at the country club. And I told them that Buddy and his friends were just poor boys trying to make it all on their own, doing the best they could to work their way up in the world. And that's what this country is supposed to be all about, after all. Well, they did send another reporter over to do a more factual story on Buddy, telling about his contract and all. But even when he was a big national star, the rich people here never paid any attention to him."

The rock 'n' roll Holly was playing at the time comes across best on the recordings he made with his own full band at his second Nashville session, in July 1956. Decca did not release these cuts until a year later, after Holly had left Decca and become a success with the Crickets. Holly's Nashville recordings were then rushed out in an album with the deceptive title *That'll Be The Day*—deceptive because the version of the song on the Decca album was not the hit version which had sold several million singles by the time the Decca album came out. On this album, Holly's band was labelled the Three Tunes; actually, his band had no set title at that time. On the springtime package tour, the two band members who had accompanied Holly were called the Two Tones. Most of the time, however, when the act appeared on its own, it was just billed as "Buddy Holly." Just as Buddy and Bob had chosen their duet title after other country acts of the day, and Holly was later to use the group title of the Crickets when group titles were popular, so in 1956, when stars like Domino and Presley went by their own names, Holly's band didn't require a title.

The July session almost didn't come off. Holly drove to Nashville with Curtis, Guess, and Allison, now out of school. The one item the group lacked was a bass. Guess, who had played acoustic and steel guitar before joining Buddy, had never actually bought a bass. As strapped for cash as the rest of the group, he had instead rented one from the Lubbock school system for about six dollars a year. Now it was July, the school year was over, and Guess had lost the use of the bass. Curtis and Allison recount what happened:

Curtis: I remember Owen Bradley real well 'cause he gave us a big hassle—

Allison: About getting that bass. He wanted to go waterskiing—and he gave us twenty minutes to round up the bass.

Curtis: We were gonna use somebody's bass, but when we arrived at the session, it wasn't there. It was up at WSM—Lightning Chance's bass, he's a big old bass player in Nashville. And we had to go up there real quick and get that bass. Or we weren't going to get to record that day.

Allison: Or the next day, I don't think.

Curtis: Or ever again!

The engineering on Holly's first single had at least been technically proper, even if it failed to match the earthy rock 'n' roll sound Sam Phillips was producing at Sun. By contrast, the production of the five July masters was poor by any standard. Obvious flaws in the recordings were allowed to stand, instead of being corrected in additional takes. Instruments are poorly balanced and the echo effect is extremely overemphasized. All the same, Holly's early rock 'n' roll sound still comes through better on these masters than on those cut at his other Decca sessions.

Probably the two best of the Three Tunes recordings are "Ting-a-Ling" and "Rock Around With Ollie Vee." The first, written by Atlantic producer Ahmet Ertegun, had been a rhythm & blues hit for the Clovers in 1952. Holly's version is quite different from the original. At the same time as he moves the tune forward into the rock 'n' roll era, he actually gives it more of a basic blues sound than it had had on the Clovers' version. Jerry Allison comments:

"We used to sit around and listen to blues pickers like Lonnie Johnson. Like there was that song called 'Jelly Roll,' and the style of guitar that Buddy played on 'That'll Be The Day'—that was the sort of guitar that that old blues picker played. So that's probably how he got that; and I think he played exactly the same lick on 'Ting-a-Ling.'"

"Rock Around With Ollie Vee" was written by Sonny Curtis and features him on lead guitar. It is faster in pace and equal in excitement to 'Ting-a-Ling;'' Holly's vocal has the freedom and variety of his finest recordings. Allison's drumming provides the emphatic beat that is so lacking on the songs recorded with Nashville musicians. "Ollie Vee" is not far removed from the frenetic performances of "Oh Boy!" and "I'm Looking for Someone to Love," recorded by the Crickets a year later.

Somewhat similar in tempo but closer to country melodic and harmonic patterns was a song written by Holly, "I'm Changing All Those Changes." "Girl On My Mind" (written by Don Guess) has the slow but emphatic beat of rock 'n' roll ballads; its major flaw is Holly's strained vocal, an instance of his unwisely following the advice and example of others on how to sing. He was too ready at this point in his career to imitate Elvis Presley or Tony Williams (lead singer for the Platters) instead of adapting songs to his own style. Sonny Curtis played lead guitar on both of these tunes.

The fifth song recorded at this session had been written by Holly and Allison, with an assist from John Wayne. In 1956, Wayne starred in the Western *The Searchers*. Wayne's catch phrase throughout the picture was "That'll be the day!", which Wayne snarled in disagreeing with the opinions or threats of other characters. The saying became a byword among those who saw the movie, including Holly and his friends. Eventually, Buddy and Jerry constructed a song around the phrase, a song which embodied the toughness, cynicism, and bluster that Wayne had put into the line.

"That'll Be The Day" became the first hit for the Crickets on the Brunswick label in the summer of 1957; the earlier recording of it is quite different and definitely inferior. The Decca version lacks the ease and the humor of the Brunswick recording. The beat is more rigid. Holly's vocal, harsh and a bit overbearing as he compensates for the lack of background voices, is pitched too high for his own voice. His guitar solo is inadequately supported by the rest of the band, which is underrecorded. Finally, the echo effect is way overdone.

Despite the flaws, Buddy and the others were convinced from the start that they had a potential hit song in "That'll Be The Day." Others present had different opinions. Jerry Allison says, "It seems like Owen Bradley said that that was the worst song he'd ever heard." Sonny Curtis adds, "Yeah, all the engineers thought that was the worst one. But there was this one kid there, swept up the studio, I think. And we got that kid out in the alley and said, 'Hey, which one did *you* like?' and he said, 'Man, I like "That'll Be The Day"!' And we said, 'Yeah, you're so right.' I remember when it was number one in the country, Owen Bradley had a record out of 'White Silver Sands' that was number one hundred, and I went ahhh!"

Much to Holly's disappointment, Decca did not release any of the July masters, and seemed in no hurry to release anything of his again. Holly apparently thought that he could come closer to the sound Decca wanted if he did a session using all regular studio musicians. Sonny Curtis explains, "I think Holly went through a period there when he was kind of in awe of all those studio musicians. He wanted to get that type sound. I think he thought, 'Boy, if I had that really good slick band behind me, it'd really sound good,' And then after it happened, he changed his mind."

Decca agreed to cut Holly once more, and Buddy went back to Nashville in November for the Disc Jockey Festival (the ancestor of the current October DJ Convention) and for a last session with Decca.

Three songs were recorded. One was a remake of "Rock Around With Ollie Vee," done this time with a studio band whose guitars and saxophones lent the recording a Bill Haley sound. (This version of the song was released on a single the following year, but was never put on an American album.) The other two songs, released in December on Holly's second single, were both written by Don Guess. The "A" side, "Modern Don Juan," is a happy up-tempo tune along much the same lines as "Blue Days, Black Nights," but is superior to the early recording in several ways. Overall, it has a more unified sound, with repeated identifying riffs on saxophone (played by Boots Randolph) and lead guitar (Grady Martin). Holly's vocal is enthusiastic and shows a developing sense of timing. "You Are My One Desire," the slow ballad on the flip side, provides a dramatic vocal which is free of the strain shown by Holly on "Girl On My Mind." Both songs are a bit closer to rock 'n' roll than the first release had been—closer, but still not there. Compare the instrumental accompaniments on "You Are My One Desire" and "Girl On My Mind," or the two versions of "Rock Around With Ollie Vee," and it is obvious that the Decca studio musicians, for all their skill and experience, could not match the rock 'n' roll feel of Holly and his band.

The new single, released around Christmas time, followed the course of "Blue Days, Black Nights": "Modern Don Juan" received an acceptable review from *Billboard*, was treated as a strictly country & western disc, got no promotion, and did not sell. By then, Decca was only going through the motions anyway, since it was about to drop Holly's contract. Like most artists signed by major record companies at the time, Holly had a five-year contract with Decca, with the company having the option each year of continuing or dropping the contract; Decca could see no reason to maintain Holly on its roster.

Holly was probably just as happy to be leaving the label. There was some personal animosity involved. Holly got along well with Owen Bradley and Jim Denny, but he clashed with Paul Cohen. Cohen told Holly that the Texan didn't have the voice to be a singer and should forget about a musical career; according to Norman Petty, the producer who was to handle most of Holly's future recordings, Cohen called Holly "the biggest no-talent I have ever worked with." Producers and musicians who recorded with Holly generally describe him as easy to work with at sessions, but it all depended on who was involved—sometimes, sparks could fly. Don Guess remembers, "Buddy was very temperamental at times. He definitely wanted his own way. He did make suggestions at the sessions—he told them what he wanted and how he wanted it to sound, and sometimes they disagreed with him. Jim Denny and his wife, Dollie, had a lot to do with holding Buddy down as far as his temper was concerned in sessions."

"Holly was likely to get in a hassle with somebody," explains Jerry Allison. "He always knew just what he wanted—and if somebody didn't do it like he wanted it done, there would be a conflict. Buddy wasn't ever meek."

Now, Holly was waiting for his Decca contract to expire, but he didn't have anything better to look forward to. He had received some encouragement from artists he talked to at the November country music convention. "They told him to try again," says Mrs. Holley, "but they said he had to get out of Nashville, because they just weren't ready for him there." If he had learned anything during the course of the year, it was that the road to success for a young Texas singer did not necessarily run through Nashville.

The association with Decca was an unsuccessful and unhappy one for Holly. However, looking at it now in the light of his subsequent career, it was actually for the best that he failed with Decca. He was to have much more independence with Norman Petty and Coral Records than he would ever have had with the more conservative and tradition-bound Decca and its producers. Besides, the year's delay was beneficial to Holly. Too often, a young and inexperienced artist has been pushed before the public too quickly, before he has fully developed his musical abilities or mastered the art of holding a live audience's attention and sympathy. During 1956, Holly gained some experience he badly needed, in singing as a solo artist and in performing on stage before unfamiliar audiences. The year gave Holly time to play different sorts of material and blend different styles in the songs he wrote and performed. He could see now that it was one thing to sing before a small audience, and another to arrange and record a song so as to make a hit record out of it. By 1957, he had developed a more distinctive style and had started to write his own songs, instead of relying primarily on others for his material.

While Holly was maturing as a performer, he was also losing his youthful naiveté about the music business. His experiences with Decca taught him much about the capricious nature of the recording industry and the people involved in it. He knew now a little better how to deal with such problems in the future. He had also matured as a person. His temper and occasional overconfidence had been cut down to a more reasonable level, but his will was unbroken. From this point on, he could direct his course more surely. Had he become a sudden star in 1956, Decca or Jim Denny could have claimed the credit for Holly's success, and he would have had little basis on which to protest the judgment of others as they charted his career. Now though, he was less likely to be trapped in such a position.

All that can be seen in retrospect. But for Buddy Holly, the late fall of 1956 was the most discouraging time of his life. He had had his chance to become a recording star, the chance he had dreamed of through adolescence. Now, a major record company had pronounced him a failure, and he had no evidence to contradict that.

Before long, though, Holly rebounded from his discouragement. The advice of those who had told him to give up his career only caused him to try harder. Singing was his chief joy, what he most wanted to do in life. Observes one Lubbock acquaintance: "Buddy was a pretty intense person—and moody. I think his music helped him get 'up'—it was a release for him." Larry Welborn adds, "Offstage, he was quiet—not wild at all. But he was very uninhibited when he performed. He didn't worry about how he looked to an audience. Not that he didn't care, I don't mean that—what I mean is, he didn't hold anything back. And that was what made him so good."

Music was more than just a career to Buddy Holly; it was his way of proving his worth. He could not give it up yet; and he was not to be deterred by the pessimists, such as one Lubbock adult whom he overheard saying, "That Buddy Holly will never amount to anything!"

Within weeks after his last session in Nashville, Holly drove up to Clovis, New Mexico, just ninety miles from Lubbock, to see Norman Petty.

The CRICKETS

Jerry Allison   *Buddy Holly*

The high flying Crickets hail from Lubbock, Texas, and the group consists of Leader Buddy Holly on guitar, Joe Mauldin on bass, Jerry Allison on drums, and Niki Sullivan on guitar. They were organized in Lubbock by Holly.

Buddy Holly was born on September 7, 1936, in Lubbock, and his musical career started at the ripe old age of eight at which time he started taking violin lessons. However, several squeaks later, Buddy decided his interest should be changed to the guitar. At the age of 15 this change was made and Buddy began singing while accompanying himself on guitar at various clubs around the Southwest. He then went to Nashville, Tenn., where he was signed by Decca Records and recorded a few Western tunes.

After this, he visited the Norman Petty Recording Studios in Clovis, New Mexico, where with the help of Petty, who, incidentally, had a hit record of his own in "Almost Paradise," Bud recorded a few of his own compositions. Petty took the demonstration records to Murray Deutsch of the Southern Music Publishing Company in New York, who in turn brought them to Bob Thiele of Coral and Brunswick Records. Thiele signed Bud Holly and The Crickets to a recording contract with the Brunswick label, a subsidiary of Decca Records.

When Impresario Irvin Feld first heard them, he and his assistant, Allan Bloom, started telephone wires singing (humming) to sign them up for the Fall Edition of "Biggest Show of Stars for '57." We feel sure that The Crickets will prove one of the reasons that "Super Enterprises" shows are the SHOWS of STARS.

Niki Sullivan   *Joe Maulden*

Page from the souvenir book for the Show of Stars tour, September 1957 (Ralph M. Newman, Time Barrier Express *magazine)*

4. The Crickets

Thanks to his association with Buddy Holly and some lesser rock 'n' roll artists, Norman Petty is recognized as one of the independent producers who were so important to the recording of early rock 'n' roll. Petty, born in Clovis, New Mexico, in 1927, played the piano and other instruments from a young age. As a child, he was exposed to folk, country, and western-swing music, and later became familiar with pop and classical instrumental music as well. During his high school years, he worked for a local radio station and gained the technical know-how which he used later in constructing his own studio and producing records. Petty married in 1948; a year later, he and his wife Vi, a classically trained pianist, began to devote more of their time to music. The Norman Petty Trio was formed, with Petty as organist, Vi Petty as pianist, and a friend named Jack Vaughn as drummer. His band featured the sort of sweet instrumental mood music played at country club dances and similar affairs, with little resemblance to either rhythm & blues or country & western. Besides performing in person, the Trio began to make recordings. Their version of "Mood Indigo" was a moderate hit in 1954, while Petty's own composition, "Almost Paradise," brought him sizable returns in 1957, both from the Trio's recording and from the writer's royalties on the very successful version by Roger Williams.

Soon after the success of "Mood Indigo," Petty had established his own studio. His original purpose was to free his group from dependence on other studios and producers. Soon, though, he found that there was a demand in the area for a well-equipped studio. Petty had the equipment, musical training and ability, and technical competence to make good records. Before long, he found that his recording work was more than just a sidelight to the Trio's activities. In addition, he established a publishing firm, Nor Va Jak Music (the title being formed from the names of the Trio members; Jack Vaughn later dropped out of the picture). Petty gradually increased his activities as a publisher and producer, recording new artists, publishing their songs, and selling the masters to established labels.

By 1957, Petty had connections with major music firms. His trio was under contract to Columbia Records, and Petty was friendly with Columbia's A & R director, Mitch Miller. Petty had a tie as well with Murray Deutch at Peer-

Offices of Nor Va Jak Music, Clovis (John Goldrosen)

Southern Music, the firm which had published Petty's "Almost Paradise": Petty had entered into an agreement whereby Peer-Southern acted as Nor Va Jak's selling agent, giving Petty the benefit of Peer-Southern's worldwide operations. Thus, unlike many independent producers, Petty was known and respected in the New York music business, and had less difficulty than others in finding someone to listen to the masters which he had produced and wished to sell.

Aspiring musicians in the area knew about the quality of Petty's equipment and the extent of his connections. They were attracted, too, by Petty's policy on studio rates. While most studios charged by the hour, Petty instead charged a group for a session or a record, without setting time limits on the studio work involved. His theory, as he explains it now, was that a group would produce a better record if the group could take as long as it needed—and what Petty was most interested in was a record that would sell well enough to establish the song as a standard in his publishing catalog. He was willing to take a loss on the studio (usually just a paper loss, since all that was involved was his own time) in exchange for the large returns on publishing royalties for the original record and later versions of the same song.

Petty's casual studio procedures meant that the sort of routine record-keeping of a strictly ordered, union-regulated studio was never made at Holly's Clovis sessions. As a result, there is no easy way to determine accurately just who played on what sessions, and when each recording was made. The story of the recordings must be pieced together from the accounts of the participants, whose memories are sometimes contradictory. In some cases, dated demos exist; otherwise, only an approximate date can be offered, and even that is just my judgment based on the varied guesses of the musicians involved. The release dates of singles are not decisive, since the songs were sometimes chosen from a stockpile of recordings made six or nine months before.

Buddy Holly was not the first rock 'n' roll performer to make recordings with Norman Petty. In late 1956, a west Texas group called the Rhythm Orchids came to Clovis and recorded some masters, which they eventually sold to newly-formed Roulette Records. Roulette put out two separate records under the names of the two different vocalists in the group, and wound up with two million-selling singles—Buddy Knox's "Party Doll" and Jimmy Bowen's "I'm Sticking With You." Petty was involved in the Bowen and Knox recordings only as a producer; the deal with Roulette was made by the Rhythm Orchids on their own.

Petty's studio had been one of the three or four studios used by Holly and his friends for cutting demo records in 1955 and 1956. Petty and Holly became slightly acquainted at the time; by late 1956, Petty was aware of Holly's impending departure from Decca. When Holly came to see Petty to discuss making some professional demos, the producer told Buddy to go back to Lubbock, form a group and rehearse some songs, and then return to make the demos.

"My first impression of him," Petty later told an interviewer, "was of a person ultra-eager to succeed. He had the eagerness of someone who has something on his mind and who wants to do something about it.

Norman Petty, in his studio, May 1978 (Bill Griggs)

"He wore a T-shirt and Levis. Really, he was unimpressive to look at, but impressive to hear. In fact, businessmen around here asked me why I was interested in a hillbilly like Holly, and I told them I thought Buddy was a diamond in the rough."[1]

Many fans have wondered why Holly never sought out Sam Phillips at Sun Records after the year with Decca—or before that. (There have even been rumors that Holly did in fact make records with Sun, but in fact that never happened.) One explanation is that Clovis is a lot closer to Lubbock than Memphis. Perhaps if Petty had been unable to do anything, Buddy would next have made his way to Memphis.

Larry Welborn offers an explanation of why this didn't happen earlier: "Buddy may have thought of going to Sun Records—I really don't know. But at least back when I was playing with him, he wouldn't have thought of going to Memphis himself to seek a contract. You see, there was this idea everyone had at that time, that you just didn't do something like that—you waited for someone to discover *you*. You just kept playing and hoped that there was someone out there in the audience noticing. Which, after all, was the way Buddy got his first contract with Decca."

By the end of 1956, Holly had the problem of putting together a new band. Don Guess had dropped out shortly after the fall tour with Hank Thompson. The circumstances are forgotten now, but Jerry Allison thinks it had to do with Don's unwillingness to buy his own bass. Not long after, Sonny Curtis also left the group. Allison explains:

"The reason that we changed people was usually personal things—like Sonny didn't particularly like to play rhythm guitar, he liked to play lead guitar. So when Buddy got to wanting to play lead, Sonny said, well shoot, I don't want to play rhythm, so I just won't play those gigs."

Sonny Curtis points out another reason:

"I wasn't getting along with Holly that well—we sort of had a conflict of personality. But the main reason I quit was because we weren't making any money. So I was playing around with different people, just whoever needed a guitar picker. I got a gig with Slim Whitman, and then one with the Phillip Morris country music show down in Nashville. And then I moved from there to Colorado Springs and picked in a club, and that was about the time Buddy and the Crickets made it with 'That'll Be The Day.'"

As in the years before 1956, Holly's band had not been a set group. "There wasn't really any steady group," Jerry Allison explains, "it was just whatever came up and whoever was hanging around at the time and was available to play." Buddy was ready enough to practice or perform with anyone who asked him. As a result, there are dozens of people around Lubbock who claim to have played with Buddy Holly, and most of them are telling the truth. For some time in late 1956 and early 1957, though, Holly and Allison performed regularly at the Lubbock youth center without any other accompaniment—just a solo vocal backed by an electric guitar and drums, rockabilly down to

[1]Norman Mark, "The Life and Legend of 'This Unforgettable Texan,'" Chicago *Daily News* "Panorama," April 15, 1967.

the bare essentials. Holly and Allison were good enough to pull it off, and the experience forced the two to develop the intuitive teamwork that characterized their later records. Sonny Curtis recalls, "Boy, that was some good stuff, when Allison and Holly were just picking by themselves—that really felt nice. And that's how they got to picking together so good—they simply had to fill up every hole." "Sure made the money go farther, too," adds Allison— and that may have been one good reason why Holly and Allison didn't search immediately for another guitarist or a bass player.

By January, though, the two were looking for other musicians and vocalists to join them on the demos which they were now planning to cut at Petty's studio. One person they met was Niki Sullivan, another Lubbock resident who was a year younger than Holly. Sullivan played rhythm guitar, and had much the same musical interests as Buddy. (Strangely enough, Holly and Sullivan were third cousins, but only found this out when a number of their mutual relatives showed up for a Crickets appearance in Waco, Texas, in late 1957.)

Sullivan traces his own interest in music back to 1949, and Hank Williams's "Lovesick Blues": "I listened to that song *all* the time. My father had a guitar around the house that I had never touched, but when that song came out I was so intrigued by it, that I asked my father how to play the guitar, and he showed me about four or five chords so I could sing and play along to 'Lovesick Blues.' And then I got involved with steel guitar, and took some lessons. My parents sent me to a steel guitar school here in Lubbock, but I detested reading music, and so I dropped out of the school and eventually drifted away from steel guitar, and went back to the rhythm guitar."

Sullivan remembers that he lost interest in music for a time in favor of golf. It was rhythm & blues and rock 'n' roll that rekindled his interest in music: "I started listening to rhythm & blues in high school. I can remember in my junior year, the Midnighters were very popular—where I ate lunch, they had those records on the jukebox, like 'Work With Me, Annie.' And we listened to KWKH in Shreveport, Louisiana, and XERF in Del Rio, and by 1954 or so, there were radio shows on KSEL. And then when Elvis Presley came along, I was just awestruck by Presley. That's when I started to pick up the guitar again. And I started standing in front of a blank wall—I didn't have a mirror in my room—and I imitated Elvis Presley in my imagination, playing the guitar. I borrowed all of his Sun recordings from my friends. Now, Buddy was the closest thing to Elvis Presley we had. I can remember him sitting in a black car parked on the west side of the high school, playing his guitar. And he'd burn a little rubber with some of his friends, making the circle around the drive-ins. He would stop and have a Coke or a hamburger, and there would always be a crowd of people over at the car, listening to Buddy play. So then *I* started riding around with friends, and we'd go to the Village Drive-In, which was close to the Hi-De-Ho Drive-In where Buddy liked to hang out, and I'd sit out on the car and play, to get out and be seen."

Sullivan's involvement with Holly and Allison seems almost to have been a matter of accident. One day in late 1956, a mutual friend named Bobby

Peeples who was on his way over to Holly's house with a tape recorder asked Niki to come along, and suggested he bring his guitar. "When we got there," says Niki, "Bobby mentioned to Buddy that I had a guitar out in the car, so Buddy said, 'Well, why don't you go ahead and bring it in,' so I did. Jerry was there, too, and we jammed around." (The answer is no—nobody knows what happened to those tapes.)

Sullivan kept practicing with Holly and Allison, off and on. "It was sometime early in February," he recalls, "that Buddy explained to me that he wanted to try something in Clovis. I don't remember Buddy ever suggesting that we actually form a group—so much of everything was just off the cuff, just 'Let's do it.' It was just put to me that we were going to go over to Clovis and make some demos."

Holly and Allison did not plan to have Petty arrange a contract for them: they believed they had their own contact with Roulette Records in New York. Jerry Allison goes through the complicated story: "Donnie Lanier was Buddy Knox's lead guitarist, and Lanier's sister worked for Roulette. She had this cousin in Lubbock named Gary Tollett, and she wanted to see if she could get him on Roulette, just like she did Buddy Knox and Jimmy Bowen and the Rhythm Orchids. So there was this other sister who lived in Lubbock named June Clark, and she called Sonny Curtis, and told him that she wanted to cut some demos with this cousin of hers, and asked, do you know a good drummer? And so Sonny said, yeah, call Jerry. So she called me and said, Sonny Curtis told me to call you; I want to cut some demos with this cousin of mine to send to New York, and do you want to play on this? And I said, yeah—but you shouldn't use Sonny, you ought to use Holly. For guitar. And so that's how that thing got started. And so Sonny and I—I mean, we live across the street from each other, and we're still real good old buddies, and have been for twenty years. But Buddy and I were rock, and he was kind of singing just country, and we played together some, but just had different musical tastes or whatever. So we got together to rehearse with this cousin, Gary Tollett, and to cut some demos with him. And we said, hey, if we cut some demos we could use someone to send ours to. And June Clark said, sure."

Allison remembers that he and Holly did play on some demos for Tollett which were cut in Clovis and at KDAV, but that nothing was ever done with those records. As best Jerry remembers, those demos were later lost.

Clark, Tollett, and Tollett's wife Ramona were recruited to sing the background vocals with Niki Sullivan for the upcoming session. Holly still needed a bass player, and he invited his old friend Larry Welborn to play on the recording date. Welborn accepted.

Niki Sullivan remembers the practicing that preceded the trip to Clovis: "We worked on 'That'll Be The Day' several times, just for me to learn the parts and everything, because I had never heard it played publicly. Everything we played was in the key of A. Buddy decided on the vocals and the arrangements—he was in total charge of everything. Whatever changes were made from the way it had sounded in Nashville, Buddy made those changes. The last night, we were over at June Clark's house; we worked on background vocals especially."

Sullivan recalls that "I'm Looking For Someone To Love" was written that last night of practice, to provide a flip side for "That'll Be The Day." It was just a few days later that the group went to Clovis for its session. Sullivan says, "I was working at the time, delivering flowers, and I called in sick so I could go up to Clovis. It seems to me we went in Buddy's car, that black and white Oldsmobile. We stopped on the way to visit someone's relatives, and then went on to the studio; we got there in the evening."

The date of that first session was February 25, 1957. Each of the participants remembers it a little differently. Larry Welborn remembers the work that went into the record: "We had worked on 'That'll Be The Day' for a long time, along with those singers. But even when we went up to Clovis, it seems to me like we spent twelve hours on it—just recording it over and over. Buddy had worked out the arrangement ahead of time—he was responsible for that. But Norman Petty had us run through it again and again, trying to make sure it was perfect. He'd stop us when he heard a bad note, or if he thought Buddy was a bit off-key."

By contrast, Allison recalls having a relaxed attitude about it: "We were cutting 'That'll Be The Day' just as a demo to send to New York, to see if they

The building which housed Norman Petty's original studio—the one in which Holly and the Crickets recorded. The Nor Va Jak offices and echo chamber were in a separate building to the right of the one in this picture (Photograph taken in 1978) (John Goldrosen)

liked the sound of the group—not for a master record. So we just went in and set up and sort of shucked through it. I think we cut it two times. And of course, all of it at one time, voices and instruments—it was mono. So we just cut it and said, that's good enough for a demo. And we didn't try to get it perfect, because we never suspected that record would come out."

Niki Sullivan agrees with Welborn that it took some time, but remembers above all the good feeling that prevailed: "It did take two hours, maybe three—it didn't take that long to do the actual song, but there was a little problem in setting up and getting the balance and everything right, to where it would sound like a decent demo. I was standing with the other singers, with Gary Tollett on my left, and June Clark and Ramona Tollett facing me, all singing into one microphone. I was playing rhythm guitar, but it wasn't miked, so if it had been picked up at all, it would have been through our singing mike. And I don't remember how we got in the mood, but I definitely remember it being a very fun thing, laughing and cutting up, and I know even when we were singing background, we smiled a lot."

Sometimes Holly's songs were recorded in just one or two takes, but there were times when Petty and the Crickets spent hours on a single song. The sound and "feel" of the tune were either worked out in advance by the Crickets at practice sessions back in Lubbock or quickly determined at Petty's studio by running through the new song a few times. Then, the group played the song over and over again, repeating it in almost identical fashion to make sure that the balance was right and there were no mistakes in the performance. Sometimes, in the opinion of the musicians, Petty sought to "polish" the sound of the group more than was necessary or desirable— Petty's metaphor for Holly, "a diamond in the rough," might indicate how he conceived his role. But Petty disputes any impression that he imposed his standards on the groups which recorded for him.

"I don't recall anybody being forced to do anything over and over. Most of them would say, 'Well, what do you think?' They were uncertain and relied on my better judgment. If I felt that they could actually do better, we tried it, harder and longer, and they usually came out much better. But it was not at my insistence. I don't recall anything being done over and over until *I* felt that it was the best. It was usually either that mistakes were obvious, or the musicians got tired and would go back and start again. I wasn't really 'polishing' Buddy. It was the others who would have problems getting with what Buddy was trying to do. I was just paid for sessions—if a group was satisfied with two takes, 'bye,' because I was paid the same whether it was an hour or just fifteen minutes."

In any event, Petty's trained ear and open-ended studio schedule prevented any obvious flaws caused by accident or haste. But the apparent spontaneity of the recordings was not just an illusion. The few songs which Holly cut in New York in 1958 with Coral music director Dick Jacobs were recorded more quickly. "On the songs I produced," says Jacobs, "we cut two or three takes at the maximum—and as far as Holly's performance went, we could have stopped after the first take."

Even if those first Clovis recordings were meant only as demos and not as masters (and Holly probably sensed the distinction less than Jerry remembers), the two cuts were among the finest to come out of Holly's Clovis sessions.

"I'm Looking for Someone to Love" follows a twelve-bar blues pattern. However, like such other Holly recordings as "Peggy Sue" and "Oh Boy!", this tune has a bright, happy sound which makes it blues in form but something else in spirit. The lyrics are a bit autobiographical. Like the singer in the song, Holly had been "playing the field" since breaking up with his early girlfriend, Echo.

Mrs. Holley reluctantly mentions: "After Buddy and Echo split up, Buddy seemed not to care who he went with much. He just decided to get him a girl. Of course, he was starting out singing, and getting pretty popular around here by that time, so he could get a lot of girls, you know. But, I'm sorry to say, he went with quite a few that weren't just—you know, he met them at these dances and places like that, and they weren't—they didn't have too good a reputation, maybe. I wouldn't have wanted him to marry them, I know that."

The singer's confident tone does not disguise his disappointment over the turn of events. Though he says, "Well, if you're not here, baby, I don't care," the slant of the lyrics casts doubt on his proclaimed indifference:

> Staying at home,
> Waiting for you,
> Just won't get it
> 'Cause you say we're through,
>
> > Well, I'm looking for someone to love,
> > I'm a-looking for someone to love,
> > Well, if you're not here,
> > But baby, I don't care,
> > 'Cause I'm looking for someone to love.
>
> Playing the field
> All day long,
> Since I found out
> I was wronged,
> > Well, I'm looking for someone to love....
>
> Caught myself
> Thinking of you,
> You can't love me
> And another one, too,
>
> > Well, I'm looking for someone to love....[2]

The remaining verse was just for fun—"Drunk man, street car, foot slip,

---

there you are!'' was a saying of Mrs. Holley's, and Buddy decided to put it on a record.

The whole recording is an excellent example of the Crickets' "total sound." Jerry Allison's drumming perfectly accents the melody and the vocal, while the vocal background functions as an instrument in itself. Holly takes two full instrumental choruses, after the second and third verses, playing figures which he sometimes had simply picked up from other guitarists in the rhythm & blues and country fields, but which had not yet been presented so thoroughly in rock 'n' roll recordings. His vocal has hints of the hiccuping style used more dramatically on "Peggy Sue." The catch in the voice was an effect common to many vocalists with country backgrounds—not *everyone* who sounded like Holly was imitating him—but when presented to new audiences in Holly's controlled fashion, it was a novel and attractive sound.

Like many of Holly's flip sides and album cuts, "I'm Looking for Someone to Love" might have been a hit record on its own; but it was a definite "B" side when coupled with "That'll Be The Day." Holly's and Allison's faith paid off. With a careful arrangement, a proper balance of instrument volume levels, and a natural unstrained vocal performance, the new version was free of the flaws in the earlier Decca recording. As with the flip side, the sound can be summed up as "unified." According to Norman Petty, when Buddy liked or disliked something strongly, he said it gave him "the all-overs"—an accurate term expressing the spirit and effect of his own recordings. It isn't just Holly's vocal or the melody or the lyrics or any one instrument, that makes "That'll Be The Day" a success. What is most important is that all the elements mesh so perfectly—as they had not on the Decca recording. Consider just the instrumental chorus: first there are the blues runs of Holly's treble strings, falling in pitch and then returning upwards in the fourth bar to a crescendo which Allison supports with a heavy triplet rhythm on drums and cymbals; then the sound subsides for four bars, while the stand-up bass, bass drum, and bass guitar strings dominate the sound. And at the expected moment, Holly's treble lead guitar comes back to the fore for the perfectly timed and syncopated phrases of the last four bars. The chorus builds and captures all the excitement that is dissipated in the Decca recording.

Jerry and Buddy still had to decide what name to put on the records with which they hoped to win a new contract. It seemed at the time that the name "Buddy Holly" would, if used, get them in trouble. Although Holly's option had not been picked up by Decca, the company had not yet formally granted him his release. Besides, there was a standard provision in the contract forbidding Holly from re-recording for another label material he had already recorded for Decca, for a period of five years. This clause, of course, covered "That'll Be The Day," even though Decca had not released their master of the song and had no inclination to do so. According to Allison, Holly actually called Paul Cohen and asked permission to re-record the song, but Cohen refused. Holly and Allison were determined to make "That'll Be The Day" a hit, and were prepared to go ahead and ignore the prohibition. Obviously, though, the records could not carry Holly's name until things were straightened out. And so, the two decided to come up with a group title to disguise the personnel on the record.

There are several legends about the naming of the Crickets. One of the incorrect stories is worth telling—although it is not the true explanation for the origin of the title, the story is at least based on an actual incident. Later in the spring of 1957, while the group was recording "I'm Gonna Love You Too," Norman Petty heard the occasional chirping of a cricket on the sound returning from the echo chamber. Several takes were ruined by the cricket before all present put down their instruments and searched the chamber for the insect. When Petty and the musicians entered the room, the cricket stopped chirping, and no one could find the insect. The session was resumed, but once again, the chirping interrupted the takes. After another unsuccessful search, Petty and the boys went ahead and recorded the song a few times anyway. In playing back the tape, Petty noticed one take where the cricket only joined in at the very end of the song, chirping four times at the right tempo as the record faded away. Petty decided to leave the chirps on the record, as a sort of gimmick; and so, the legend goes, the Crickets got their name.

Actually, while the incident just described did happen, the name had been chosen before then. There was nothing so dramatic about the choice. Early rock 'n' roll groups offered myriads of titles based on birds, jewels, astronomical objects and flowers; perhaps thinking of an earlier rhythm & blues group, the Spiders, the group decided to consider an insect for a name.

"We were at Jerry's house," says Niki Sullivan, "and everything we thought of had been used or didn't fit. So Jerry got an encyclopedia, and somehow we got started on insects. There was a whole page of bugs. We thought about 'grasshopper,' and quickly passed that over. And we did consider the name 'Beetles,' but Jerry said, 'Aw, that's just a bug you'd want to step on,' so we immediately dropped that. Then Jerry came up with the idea of the Crickets. He said, 'Well, you know, they make a happy sound, they're a happy type of insect.' I remember him saying too, 'They make music by rubbing their legs together,' and that cracked us up. So we kept going and tried some other names, but finally we settled on the Crickets. You know, though, we really weren't happy with that name. In fact, at some point, we were laughed at—might have been the Cotton Club, just after our record was released. People kidded us about the name, about how dumb it was."

The Crickets themselves developed an attachment to the name and the creature that inspired it. "We were on tour down in Corpus Christi in the fall of 1957," says Niki, "and we got to this motel about two or three in the morning. Well, we walked into the motel room, and I had never seen so many crickets in my life. There were about fifteen million, in the beds, under the pillows, on the floor, everywhere. So we immediately closed the door and went back to the office, but they said, 'Sorry, nothing we can do about it—it's just that time of year.' And that was the only room they had. So we went back to the room, and it was Jerry who said, 'Don't kill any of the crickets! It'd be a bad omen.' So we swept the crickets out the door, or put them on a sheet and threw them outside—just anything to keep from killing them. But I know that when we finally got to bed that night, I slept with my mouth closed.''

Shortly after making the first two Clovis recordings, Holly and Allison found their permanent bass player—Joe B. Mauldin, then just sixteen and still in school at Lubbock High. Joe had known Jerry in school, but not Buddy. Actually, though, Buddy had unknowingly influenced Joe to become a rock 'n' roll musician.

"When I was very young," Joe B. recalls, "my mother started me taking piano lessons, and I took lessons for about six years. It was a drag the whole time because I didn't enjoy it at all. Of course, she had me studying classical music. And after I got into junior high school, I guess I was thirteen years old, I wanted to play steel guitar, so my mom bought me a steel guitar, and I took lessons for awhile. And kinda faked it for awhile. And I took some trumpet lessons while I was in junior high, and tried to get involved with the school band. But that never panned out either—I think I lost my trumpet or something. And then I was out of music, outside of singing at school functions and what have you. I had liked pop music more than country— Johnny Ray was my idol—when I was in grade school. And then I got interested in rhythm & blues, and I listened to Stan's Record Review—came on at 10:30 at night, and we could just barely tune it in on our car radios. But the little group of guys that I ran around with, we used to always make sure that we'd listen to Stan's Record Review.

"I had known of Buddy and seen him play when it was just Buddy, Bob, and Larry. This was back before I had any conception that I might be a musician or get into the record business. And I remember one day, my mother and I were walking down the street in downtown Lubbock—this would have been in the fall of 1955—and we passed a tire store. Buddy, Bob, and Larry were doing a show there, a promotion thing for this tire store, and were up on a big trailer truck playing. And as we walked by, my mother said, 'Look, there's Elvis Presley!' So I had to explain to Mother who it really was. So she wanted to stop and watch for a few minutes, and we did. And I guess that's what got me really interested in music. You know, seeing a hometown boy playing the kind of music that I liked myself. And I happened to think right then, 'Boy, wouldn't it be fun if I could get in his group—wish I could play an instrument good enough.'''

Not long afterwards, Joe B. met a young singer and rhythm guitarist named Terry Church (who later recorded under the name Terry Noland), and Church showed Mauldin how to play a few notes on a bass fiddle. Church and Mauldin soon joined with Larry Welborn and a drummer, Brownie Higgs, to form the Four Teens. Joe was still bass player for this group when he was approached by Allison and Holly.

"Buddy and Jerry came by one day," he recalls. "They had a job in Carlsbad, New Mexico, to play a dance, and they needed a bass player for that night, and so I accepted the job, and went to Carlsbad with them and played the dance. And on the way back, Buddy asked me if I wanted to play regular with him. And become one of the Crickets. One of the things that Buddy laid on me to play with the group, he said, 'We've cut a record called "That'll Be The Day," and it's gonna be a stone hit. And we're gonna get rich.'

"Well, I'd heard this a million times before, from all kinds of people. So I said, 'Man, what makes you think that? It's not even out yet—how do you know it's going to sell?'

"He said, 'Oh, that's all right, it'll be a hit. And we're gonna get rich.'

"And I said, 'Well, how long do you think *that's* going to take?'

"And he said, 'How long did it take Elvis?'

"So I laughed at him. But the next day, I agreed to play regular with him."

The Crickets, now a full foursome, returned to Clovis and cut two more tunes to send to Roulette—a simple rock 'n' roll ballad which Joe and the Four Teens had written called "Last Night," and a loosely-paced version of "Maybe Baby," a big hit for them a year later after they revised the arrangement and beat and recorded the song again. (The unusual demo version has never been released in the United States, although it has appeared in England.) They saw no point in re-recording "That'll Be The Day" or "I'm Looking for Someone to Love" just because Mauldin had joined the group on bass. As a result, Larry Welborn actually played on the Crickets' first record. "Of course, all I got back was my expenses up and back from the session, which Buddy paid," Welborn remembers with a laugh.

While waiting for a reply from Roulette, the Crickets tried to gain a spot on Arthur Godfrey's *Talent Scouts*, a nationally-broadcast television showcase for amateur talent, with the idea that this would help their chances of winning a record contract. Joe B. explains, "We were thinking that this was a good chance for some network exposure, television exposure. It seemed as though anybody that was on one of those big talent shows—Arthur Godfrey or Ted Mack—they always got record deals." The Crickets drove up to Amarillo, the nearest place they could audition for the Godfrey show.

"We got on the audition," says Mauldin, "and I think we played a Little Richard song, and some of our own stuff. When we finished, the guy that was in charge of the audition said, 'Oh my gosh, what is music coming to.' So we kind of knew right away that we weren't going to get on the show."

(The Godfrey show did not exactly have its finger on the pulse of American pop music: in 1955, Elvis Presley had flunked *his* audition for *Talent Scouts*.)

Despite their contacts at Roulette, the Crickets were turned down by the record company, which apparently felt it already had what it wanted in Buddy Knox, Jimmy Bowen, and Jimmie Rodgers. Roulette, Allison remembers, was more interested in the songs on the demos. "Buddy Knox and Jimmy Bowen, and I think the guitar player Donnie Lanier, were going to record the songs. Of course, we were in touch with them because of Lanier's sister. And we said, please don't record the songs, because we're trying to get a deal ourselves. So they didn't put them out."

At some point, Norman Petty became involved in trying to land the group a record contract. Holly and Allison certainly knew that Petty had contacts with Peer-Southern Music and Columbia. Petty says that his efforts were made at their request. "They asked me to take it into New York to sell," says Petty. "I didn't say, 'Well, I'll take it in for you.' They said, 'Will you take it in?'" Whether or not Petty knew of the Roulette connection, and whether he began his efforts before or after Roulette turned the group down, is disputed. The Crickets say that Petty knew that they planned to submit the record to Roulette—that was, after all, the reason for making the demos in the first place, to take advantage of their supposed "in" with the company. They say that Petty offered to try to place the record, even while the approach to Roulette was being made. Petty remembers it differently: "I didn't know they were even considering the Roulette angle at all. That was not my impression. Had I known they wanted to do that, I would not have taken the record. Because it's always a difficult thing to do, to have five people working on the same thing."

According to Petty, he personally took the tape of "That'll Be The Day" to New York and played it for Bob Thiele, A&R director for Coral Records, at a meeting arranged by Murray Deutch of Peer-Southern. (Coral was a subsidiary of Decca—a coincidence which Holly would later recall with some amusement: "They kicked us out the front door, and so we went in the back door.") Thiele and Deutch remember the sequence of events differently; Thiele, in fact, does not remember even meeting Petty until a trip which Thiele and Deutch made to Clovis several months later.

Deutch offers his account: "Norman sent me the tape of 'That'll Be The Day,' and I went nuts about it. I don't know quite what it was, it was just my instinct—the song had an intonation I had never heard before. Now, on 'Almost Paradise,' we had set up a deal whereby the publishing rights were split fifty-fifty between Peer-Southern and Nor Va Jak, and our firm acted as the administrator. So I made a deal with Petty: if I could get Holly and the Crickets a record contract, then he would give Peer-Southern fifty percent of the publishing on 'That'll Be The Day.'

"But then, I couldn't sell anybody on what I believed in. I went to Jerry Wexler at Atlantic, Mitch Miller at Columbia, Joe Carlton at RCA— everybody turned it down. So then I tried Bob Thiele at Coral. Dick Jacobs, the music director at Coral, had had a hit the year before with one of our songs, 'Petticoats of Portugal.' But Bob turned me down for two weeks. Finally, I asked him, as a favor to me, to press just a thousand copies, just so I could get the publishing rights to the song. Because I was sure it could be a hit."

Thiele's delay was actually caused by opposition within his own company. "I liked the record from the start," says Thiele. "I was excited about it. In those days, the A&R director got a budget from the company and could then spend the money as he wanted to—of course, if you didn't have hits, you didn't work there anymore. But if you wanted to sign a new act, you had to get the approval of the top executives at Decca. At the time, Milton Rachmil was the president and Leonard Schneider the vice-president. When Murray kept on me about the song, I went to the executives and told them I wanted to buy this master and put it out. Well, they turned me down. They felt the record was junk—they thought it was a joke. At the time, Coral was having success with artists like Lawrence Welk, the McGuire Sisters, Teresa Brewer, and Steve Lawrence. Rachmil and Schneider thought 'That'll Be The Day' was so bad that it would hurt the image of Coral.

"To this day, when I believe in something and I get turned down, I fight even more. So I kept after them. Now, at the time, I had been putting out jazz on the old Brunswick label. Brunswick was the label for the people I wanted that the company *didn't* want. So I finally convinced them to let me put out 'That'll Be The Day' on Brunswick, where it wouldn't hurt Coral's image, as they saw it. I really believe they did it just to amuse me—sort of, 'Let Bob have his kicks,' you know."

On balance, the Crickets give Deutch primary credit for getting them their record contract. Niki Sullivan says, "If anybody was responsible for getting us placed, it would have to have been Murray Deutch. To us, the man was a genius." Joe Mauldin comments, "I've always felt like Murray Deutch was the one who was responsible for getting us our record deal."

The resulting arrangement left Holly contracted to an autonomous subsidiary of a major record company, with his recording activities in the hands of an independent producer. This gave him the advantages of both worlds. Major companies had advantages over independents in promotion and distribution, but were often so concerned with making records palatable to a broad audience that they diluted the style of rock 'n' roll musicians who came under their control. Independent labels were sometimes run by men closer to the artists and more attentive to new styles; but many such labels, financially weak and apt to lose good artists to the more prestigious majors, had short life spans, regardless of their artistic success. Holly was now contracted to a major, but only indirectly, through Petty, an arrangement which gave Holly the artistic freedom of artists on independent labels.

It was just a matter of accident, not cleverness or calculation, that Holly signed with a subsidiary of the company which had held his first contract—and which had a right to prevent him from re-recording "That'll Be The Day" for anyone else (even if it had no intention of releasing the song itself). Petty, Deutch, and Thiele say they did not know of the prior recording of "That'll Be The Day" at the time the Crickets were signed to Brunswick. Deutch and Thiele knew that a singer named Buddy Holly was the lead singer of the Crickets, but they did not know that Holly had previously had a contract with Decca. In the loosely-knit world of Decca, Paul Cohen was not involved in the decision to sign the Crickets for Brunswick, since he was responsible solely for country music on the Decca label. He did not find out about Holly's connection with the Crickets, it seems, until after the Brunswick record was already out. It was fortunate, though, that the Crickets did land with Brunswick, and not with another company, for Decca was hardly likely to sue itself (that is, its subsidiary Brunswick) over the re-recording of "That'll Be The Day." Not that that stopped Decca from *threatening* to sue: before Decca would formally release Holly from the old contract and agree not to enforce the prohibition on re-recording material,

Holly had to waive any royalties due him on sales of the version of "That'll Be The Day" which had been recorded for Decca in Nashville.

A more serious legal dispute involved the question of who was entitled to hold the copyright on the song, Nor Va Jak or Cedarwood. When Holly had first recorded the song on Decca, a contract had been prepared by Cedarwood, but through an oversight on someone's part, Holly had never signed the contract. Nevertheless, when Jim Denny found out that the song had been issued on Brunswick and published by Nor Va Jak, he threatened a lawsuit. (This might have been of more interest to Paul Cohen than the academic issue of the multiple recording contracts at Decca: Paul Cohen had an unpublicized financial interest in Cedarwood.) To avoid one of the lengthy legal battles so common in the music industry, Petty flew to Nashville and worked out a settlement with Jim Denny. Nor Va Jak got the publishing rights to "That'll Be The Day," while Cedarwood was granted the rights for a future release—which turned out to be "Think It Over." Denny, of course, retained the publishing rights for the other compositions Holly had recorded in Nashville during his year on Decca.

It was always understood that Holly was the leader of the group and its principal figure (the identifying sign on Allison's drum actually read "Buddy Holly and the Crickets"). Even before "That'll Be The Day" became a hit, the decision was made to release records under Holly's own name in addition to the releases bearing the name of the Crickets. Norman Petty may have been responsible for coming up with this idea; Deutch and Thiele would certainly have been agreeable, since both saw Holly as the key figure in the group. In this way, whatever popularity the group gained could be used to the utmost: disc jockeys might not be willing to play two records by the same group at the same time, but they would play one by Buddy Holly, and one by the Crickets, if there was enough variety in the material and the group could come up with a consistent stream of good songs. Thiele got Holly a separate contract on Coral (the earlier Decca contract only affected the re-recording of material: it didn't limit Holly's freedom to sign a new personal recording contract). In the past, singers had sometimes left their own groups to seek a solo career (Thiele, for instance, was about to sign Jackie Wilson of the Dominoes to a solo contract), but this may have been the first time that an artist was to have solo releases while still recording with his group. Holly, therefore, was a forerunner in this, as in so much else; a decade later, Frankie Valli of the Four Seasons successfully followed Holly's example.

Buddy was thus both an individual artist and just one member of a foursome. Even if the first role was more significant than the second, he still insisted on treating the members of his group as more than mere sidemen. He took much less than what might have been considered his fair share of the income.

"Buddy was the most giving person to the people around him that I've ever known," comments Joe Mauldin. "Other stars kept their musicians on salary but Buddy said, 'No, man—share and share alike. You're as much a part of this group as I am. If it wasn't for you guys, I couldn't perform the show that I put on.' When we started out, and it was Buddy, Jerry, Niki Sullivan, and me, Buddy wanted to split everything four ways flat—twenty-five percent for everybody. And Norman said, 'Hey, wait a minute. You're the star, they're sidemen. Put them on salary.' And Buddy said, 'No, I wouldn't do that to a dog.' You know, in so many words."

Sullivan agrees, "We divided everything equal shares, twenty-five percent apiece, the records and the touring. Buddy did insist on that. I can remember Norman saying, 'Buddy is the singer, the leader, and he's entitled to a larger share.' And Buddy at that point said, 'No, I want it equal. I'd rather have it that way.'"

Petty denies that he put things in quite this way, but his own explanation does shed light on how he viewed the contribution of the Crickets: "I

Allison, Holly, and Mauldin in Lubbock, 1957 (Lawrence and Ella Holley)

suggested the four-way split on the gigs, but not on the records. I said, 'When you're on the gigs, it makes sense, you're participating equally. You're each going through the same amount of discomfort and displeasure on the road, so you should all split it. I didn't say anything about salary, or 'You're the star' but I told Buddy at the time, 'Why have a four-way split on the records, when most artists will go in and hire studio musicians and pay them scale, and that's it—the musicians don't participate in the record.' So I said, 'You're being overly generous,' but I added, 'You boys, set up what you want, what you feel is right.'''

When Niki Sullivan left the group at the end of 1957 (by which time the success of "Peggy Sue" had made Holly well-known in his own right), the split on the income from personal appearances was changed to 50/25/25—Buddy got half, Joe and Jerry each got a quarter. On record royalties, Holly got a bigger share, about sixty-five percent. The arrangement held for all records, both the Crickets releases and the records issued under Holly's own name. In fact, Jerry and Joe were entitled to claim this share even on records they did not play on, like "Early In The Morning" and "It Doesn't Matter Anymore." However, when the contracts were redrawn after Holly's death, they specified which songs they had not played on and refused to collect royalties on them. Mauldin explains, "I had a percentage of them, legally; but if I didn't perform on them or have anything to do with them, why should I be entitled to receive anything?"

Of the singles released under Holly's own name, only "Rave On" had any male vocal accompaniment for Holly's own vocal, while all of the Crickets' recordings did include such vocal additions. Actually, with the exception of Sullivan's background vocals on "That'll Be The Day" and "Not Fade Away," none of the Crickets ever sang on the records—it was always local vocal groups which sang accompaniment. (The vocalists used on most of the cuts on the *Chirping Crickets* album were the Picks: Bill and John Pickering and Bob Latham. In early 1958, the Picks stopped working for Petty and were replaced by the Roses: Bob Linville, Ray Rush, and David Bigham. This group sang on "Think It Over"/"Fools Paradise" and "It's So Easy"/"Lonesome Tears.") After "That'll Be The Day," though, many fans thought that the Crickets did indeed sing, and thus it was almost mandatory that future Crickets releases include such backgrounds. It was also natural that recordings supposedly by a solo artist should have little or no vocal additions, and so the Buddy Holly records rarely had vocal accompaniment. However, the policy was not a clearcut one in the beginning. One pair of early demos tentatively coupled "Peggy Sue" and "Oh Boy!" under the Crickets label, while "Everyday" was paired with "Not Fade Away" under Buddy's name. On the eventual releases, though—after the success of "That'll Be The Day"—"Peggy Sue" and "Not Fade Away" exchanged places.

That obvious distinction between the Crickets and Holly releases was the only intentional difference between them. The records were not designed for different audiences, nor was it planned that the two sets of records should offer different images of the lead singer or follow different themes. "When we started to record something," points out Jerry Allison, "we didn't know if it was going to be a Crickets record or a Buddy Holly record." The background vocals were usually dubbed in later, not recorded at the same time, as had been done on "That'll Be The Day." Therefore, Petty and the Crickets could consider what was "in the can," pick the next single, and add vocals if the record was going to be released under the name of the Crickets. They may have considered whether a record would sound better with background vocals added. But Petty confirms that he and Holly were not trying to create two contrasting series. Petty says, "Every time that we would record, there would be some songs that would be conducive to just being a solo, and some that needed backing." Bob Thiele agrees that there was no attempt to appeal to two different audiences.

The contracts with Coral and Brunswick called for Holly and the Crickets to receive a royalty of five percent (that is, five percent times ninety percent of the retail price of records sold). This was favorable by the standards of the time: some rock 'n' roll artists were getting just one or two percent (or, too frequently, nothing at all); three percent was considered normal. At the time the contracts arrived, the four Crickets, at Petty's suggestion, made an unusual decision: to take forty percent of their record royalties on "That'll Be The Day"—the difference between the three-percent royalty rate they had expected and the five-percent rate they actually received—and to donate that "extra" amount to their respective churches. Niki Sullivan recalls this decision: "When the contracts were being brought out to be signed, Norman suggested, in so many words, that since God had seen fit to give us this break in show business, it would only be fitting to donate forty percent of the royalties on our first record to our own churches. We were all Baptists, I believe; Buddy and Norman were the most religious, but we all did attend church at one time or another. Since we were very happy to have what we had, we readily agreed. And it was a very well-meaning thing—there was no phoniness to it. Before we signed the contracts, we held hands in prayer. And it was a very moving moment."

While waiting for "That'll Be The Day" to be released, the Crickets recorded about fifteen songs at Petty's studio—at a time when they did not even know if their first record would have enough success to warrant a second. "Buddy just loved to record," explains Petty. Real costs were minimal. Petty was not so heavily booked that he had to turn down other business to spend so much time with the Crickets. And the Crickets were not being paid as session musicians, nor were they paying Petty for his time.

Most of Holly's recordings were made late at night or early in the morning, when Petty could be sure that there would be no interruptions from visitors or telephone calls. Holly himself preferred to record at night. He didn't explain his preference, but one would guess that Holly just felt more relaxed or creative at night—a common enough feeling. The sessions themselves usually had a relaxed and easy feeling to them, even though everyone involved in the recordings was completely professional when it came to the work which had to be done. Adjoining the studio itself were several smaller rooms with kitchen facilities and some beds. And so, if a session was proving difficult or Petty and the musicians were tired, they could take a break for dinner (or breakfast), and then start again. Occasionally, the Crickets would take advantage of the beds and spend two or three days at Petty's studio instead of driving back and forth between Lubbock and Clovis, a two-hundred-mile round trip.

There were three rooms to the studio itself: the control booth, the main studio, and a smaller studio with windows facing on each of the other two rooms. Sometimes, all the musicians were placed in the main studio, but often, Holly performed separately in the small room—so that Allison's loud drumming would not overwhelm Holly's singing or rhythm guitar playing. On one occasion—the recording of "Peggy Sue"—Allison played in the small room instead.

Petty used a live echo chamber to produce the effect on the records. Normally, the sound produced in the studio was fed through a speaker in an empty room above an adjoining garage, picked up by a microphone in the same room, and channeled back to the control room. This gave a much more realistic sound than the tape-delay echo method used on Holly's Nashville recordings. Petty's method of recording the string bass might be considered unusual. He placed a small microphone between the strings and the body of the bass to pick up the percussive effect of the instrument; then, other microphones were used to pick up the tones themselves. (The Fender electric bass was only introduced about 1958. Mauldin played electric bass on one tour in October 1958, but on all the other tours, and on all the records, he played stand-up bass.)

Beyond that, the quality of the recordings depended solely on Petty's equipment, his talent at placing and balancing microphones and instruments—and the talent on hand. Petty himself limits the credit due him for the success of the Crickets recordings. He has said, "Many people give me credit for creating Buddy Holly. I didn't. I exaggerated or captured the various peculiar and natural things he did."

Niki Sullivan credits Norman Petty with establishing an atmosphere at Clovis that contributed to the success of the music the Crickets produced there. He says, "The one thing Norman did for us was just to let us ramble. If there was an idea there and we had it worked out in song form, then we could go into the studio and work on it until we got it the way it sounded good to everybody. Norman just let us keep going; however long it took, it didn't make any difference. There was never any pressure at Petty's studio, and Buddy felt relaxed. Buddy felt he could do what he wanted to; we could experiment. Buddy was able to sing natural. The songs just came natural; ideas came natural. And Norman never stood in the way—he might offer a suggestion here or there, or want to add this or take away that, but he never pressured Buddy to hurry up, or to change what Buddy was trying to present."

Holly only came into his own as a songwriter at the time of these Clovis recordings. Before his association with Petty, Holly had relied on his music partners, Bob Montgomery, Sonny Curtis, and Don Guess, for most of his songs. Those which he himself had written were usually heavily blues-inflected and closely related to the rockabilly sound of Elvis Presley and other Sun artists. (For example, compare Holly's "I'm Gonna Set My Foot Down" with Roy Orbison's "Ooby-Dooby.") These early songs lacked the variety of his later compositions; they were imitative, rather than novel and trendsetting, as so many of his Coral recordings were. Holly's new role as a songwriter was not a conscious change in policy, nor was it simply caused by the exit of the earlier songwriters from Holly's group—after all, everyone still remained friends and associated with each other in Lubbock. But as Holly matured as an artist and as a person, he was learning more about music and what went into the making of a good song, and gaining a more experienced vision of life. And he began to have more confidence in his own tastes and intuitions.

On many of Holly's songs, others are listed as co-writers—Jerry Allison sometimes, Norman Petty almost always. Before discussing how much any song reflected Holly's own thinking, then, the question of just who wrote what must be confronted.

Petty has said, that, usually, Holly wrote the music for a song and brought it to Clovis, where he (Petty) wrote the lyrics. In at least several instances, this is clearly untrue. It's not even necessary to rely on the Cricket's own memories to come up with evidence for this. For example, the hit version of "That'll Be The Day" lists Petty as a co-writer, even though Allison and Holly had written the song and recorded it for Decca before recording it with Petty. (In fact, on the Decca album which included the original Nashville recording, Holly and Allison were listed alone as the writers of the song.) "I'm Looking for Someone to Love" is another case. Although Petty's name is on the song, his contribution to it must have been small, since even before going to Clovis to record the song, Holly had written out the words in a notebook almost exactly as they appear on the recording. On the sheet music for the tune, an extra verse appears which was not used on the recording: "Looking for love, searching for fire, finding true love is my desire...." These lines bear Petty's touch and may be the basis for his credit as co-writer—but the sheet music was only drawn up after Holly had recorded the song. A third instance where Petty's claim to part-authorship is apparently false is the song "Down The Line," a Buddy and Bob recording on the album *Holly In The Hills*—the pair wrote the song and were performing it before Holly had ever met Petty. Likewise, "Last Night" was part of the Four Teens' act before Mauldin joined the Crickets, and yet Petty is listed with Mauldin as co-writer of the song.

As more direct evidence, the Crickets have their own accounts of how things were done. Jerry Allison says, "I wasn't real happy about Norman putting his name on 'That'll Be The Day.' I remember him getting to see us in the control room and saying, 'O.K., now, I'm going to put my name on the record, but it won't be on the contract, or on taking the money. The reason I'm doing this is because I'm popular with the disc jockeys.' 'Almost

Paradise' he had had out, and 'Mood Indigo' was a hit record for the Norman Petty Trio; and Norman said, 'We'll get more plays.' And I didn't want to do it at the time. I wasn't really thinking about the money, I was just thinking, 'Well, that makes it look like I wrote a third of the tune, instead of half.' My ego was involved. And Buddy said, 'Man, what difference does it make— forget it.' He just didn't want to hassle him, you know. But of course, as far as money and all this, it made a lot of difference. And the idea of it all still really irritates me.''

Joe Mauldin adds, "We all contributed ideas to the arrangements. I can't say any one specific person did the arrangements, but I guess Buddy and Jerry would receive more credit than I would. I didn't contribute all that much, but I did throw in a few ideas that stuck sometimes. Norman would come up with ideas when we went to Clovis; and even on some of the songs that we had written, Norman would come up with lyric changes or chord changes—you know, musical changes. And as to what he changed on which songs, I wouldn't dare try to even say, because I don't think I could remember. But I felt like it was minor. I didn't feel like it warranted equal writer's credits. But that was one of Norman's big ideas. He said, 'I'll just take a manager's fee of ten percent, but let's put my name on the songs, because the jocks know me and they'll see my name, and that'll get you a few plays, and help the records a little bit.' And we said yeah. And then somehow or another, just before it came time for money, there was a little disagreement or argument, and Norman would say, 'Well, we'll just split the money like the contracts read.' And he had an equal share on all the contracts. So, you know, what could we do?''

Niki Sullivan also minimizes Petty's songwriting role. "I really don't mean to put Norman down,'' he says, "but I honestly do not remember Norman making any serious changes that even stick out in my mind. I cannot remember any songs that Norman definitely had a hand in. Norman did contribute by altering what we had said—you know, the grammar, he might have changed a 'but' to an 'or,' or what have you. And he did write out the sheet music on the songs, but that's not co-authoring. There were times when Norman felt he should have a share of the songs, and I think all of us readily agreed. We weren't going to argue. It wasn't important then, because we didn't even have a hit record at that point. We didn't know what the hell we were doing. We didn't care.''

Corroborating evidence is furnished by other songwriters whose tunes were published by Nor Va Jak. Bill Tilghman and Sonny West wrote two of Holly's biggest hits, "Oh Boy!'' and "Rave On.'' Tilghman says that he wrote the words and West the music to those songs; they are still writing songs today, in the same fashion. Petty's name is also on both "Oh Boy!'' and "Rave On,'' but Tilghman says flatly that Petty did not have any role in writing the songs.

Petty maintains that he only received credit for those songs to which he actually contributed. He says, "That can be backed up by people who were in here before and afterwards. If I made a major change, my name went on the song; if I didn't, if I just changed a word, I didn't put my name on the song." As for "That'll Be The Day," Petty says he put his name on the song at Murray Deutch's suggestion, as compensation for the legal and personal expenses Petty incurred in settling the dispute with Cedarwood over the copyright to the song. And it was Bob Montgomery's idea, says Petty, that Petty put his name on "Down The Line," "for doing what we were doing—to put the thing out [on *Holly In The Hills*]."

Murray Deutch categorically denies that he suggested that Petty's name be put on "That'll Be The Day." "That is not true at all, whatsoever," he states emphatically. "Never, in thirty years in the business, did I ever suggest anything like that to anybody."

Mr. and Mrs. Holley say that when Buddy wrote a song, he usually worked out the tune first, but with a conception of the lyrics in mind. Though the lyrics might not yet be fully written, the theme and mood of the words affected the music. This is only observation, since Buddy never explained in that fashion just how he went about writing a song. Mr. Holley has offered this memory of Buddy's manner of songwriting.

"Buddy was a peculiar-type songwriter," he says. "He'd leave home in the evening, after we'd have our evening meal, and be gone for an hour, or two or three hours. Then he'd come back, go straight to his room, pick up his guitar, and start to sing it—something he had been thinking about while he was out in the car, by himself."

Though Buddy usually had the original idea for the melody and the themes of the lyrics, the songs were often finished in the company of the other Crickets. Niki remembers, "Buddy was the major contributor, or the originator of the idea of the song. We would all contribute, but it was Buddy who was the basic creator. We did pay attention to the lyrics. Rhyme was not our main concern—meaning was. The rhyming would come one way or the other. I think Buddy taught us that, by taking an idea and just writing a story around it."

To add to the confusion over the authorship of the songs, the persons publicly credited with writing a specific song were not always those who had contributed to it. Joe says he helped write "Maybe Baby," and Jerry wrote a lot of "Not Fade Away," but their names aren't on those songs. Allison remembers that he wrote the bridge in "I'm Gonna Love You Too" ("After all, another fella took ya...."), and that the rest of the song was written entirely by Buddy—and yet, the listed writers of the song are Sullivan, Mauldin, and Petty.

At the time, it made little difference to the Crickets which of their names went on what. Joe B. explains, "Norman said, 'We'll spread it around, and that way everybody will get a little publicity.' And we were all just having such a good time and never paid much attention. We'd say, 'Well, let's put so-and-so's name on that one.' And I don't think Buddy cared, that he might be giving away money this way. I don't think money was that big an interest to him. If it had of been, things wouldn't have gotten as screwed up as they did. We didn't have a lawyer—we just did everything on a trust in each other."

Despite the confusion, the weight of the evidence upholds Holly's primary role in composing the songs written by the Crickets at Clovis.

The next two tunes which the Crickets recorded were "Words of Love" and "Mailman, Bring Me No More Blues," which became the A and B sides of Holly's first solo single on Coral, released in June 1957.

"Words of Love" was not a success as a single. It was, perhaps, too different to be successful—listened to even today, the record seems to bear little relation to its own time, or to any time, a fact which would either have aided its success or worked against it. However, Holly's rendition of his own song never got a full chance to be heard. Shortly before Holly's single was issued, the Diamonds, who had just had a national hit with "Little Darling," issued a cover version of "Words of Love" and it became a moderate success for them. The incident demonstrated the vagaries of the recording industry. By copyright law, anyone can record a published song simply by paying the royalties established by law. Hence, the publisher makes money no matter which rendition of the song sells, and it is to his advantage to push the song to numerous artists. Someone at Peer-Southern Music (perhaps without Deutch's knowledge) "pushed" "Words of Love" to the Diamonds, playing for them a simple demo of the song which Holly had sent to Peer-Southern Music. Before Holly knew what had happened, the Diamonds' version was out. After that, there was nothing to do but to be more careful with demos in the future.

"Words of Love" was Holly's first experience with overdubbing. Although multi-track recording machines were not in use then, it was possible to add voices or instruments to a tape by playing the tape through again while performing new "live" sounds, and recording everything together on a second machine. Fidelity suffered any time this was done, since the final tape was "a generation removed" from the first recording. Of course, the entire procedure was itself more difficult than it is now with multi-track machines, which permit instruments to be recorded at different times and which allow more leeway in balancing and mixing of the sounds. Despite the obstacles, Holly made such dubbed recordings frequently, often first singing and playing rhythm guitar and then adding lead guitar, and occasionally singing in duet with himself through dubbing.

It was Holly's idea to use overdubbing on "Words of Love." Jerry Allison says, "Buddy had two guitar parts worked out, that he wanted to play, before we even started to record that. I don't know just how he got the idea, but he planned to do it that way. It wasn't like he went over to the studio and somebody said, 'Hey, why don't you do this?' Because he had it figured out before." In Norman Petty, Buddy had found a producer who was willing to spend the time on such experiments.

"Words of Love" was recorded one night in April 1957. Holly, Petty, and the Crickets spent at least six hours on the tune, working out the overdubbing by a process of trial and error, and trying to achieve just the balance and sound Holly wanted. On the final master, as far as the ear can tell, drums, bass, rhythm guitar (played by Holly) and one vocal were recorded first; Holly then added the lead guitar part and two vocal lines. Though Holly may not have consciously planned it that way, such an order took advantage of the loss of fidelity caused by dubbing. By the time the recording was completed, the drumming had receded into the background, providing a distant, rolling rhythm which can be felt and heard but does not obscure the vocal or guitar patterns. Similarly, recording the vocal last gave the song a close, intimate feeling, by placing the vocal "in front of" the varying guitar patterns. Petty remembers being quite impressed by Holly's ability to sing along with himself. The technique was experimental then. Les Paul and Mary Ford had worked with multi-track recordings earlier in the decade and the technique had been used sporadically since their efforts, but Holly was probably the first rock 'n' roll artist to use vocal and instrumental overdubbing; it was later artists like Neil Sedaka and Jan and Dean who exploited it more fully.

Technique is just a means, though, and Holly never used it at the expense of content. "Words of Love" succeeds because it is a pretty, entrancing, and almost hypnotic song. The unusual rhythm and guitar patterns were probably suggested to Holly by Mickey and Sylvia's "Love Is Strange"; Jerry Allison remembers, "Buddy would sit around and listen to that song, over and over, all night long." Holly's voice is subdued and tender, but quietly confident, "soft and true," like the words of love whispered in the song. His sincere and appropriate delivery lends an intensely personal feeling to the simple lyrics.

The recording was not finished until sometime around daybreak. Holly was rather worn out from the close attention demanded by such a recording. Still, the Crickets decided to cut a flip side for the record. The song they chose to do was "Mailman, Bring Me No More Blues," a demo of which had been sent to Petty by Murray Deutch with the suggestion that Holly record it. One of the song's three co-writers was "Stanley Clayton" who, it turns out, was none other than Bob Thiele, though only Deutch knew it at the time. Thiele used the pseudonym for writing songs to avoid any seeming conflict of interest with his job as an A&R director. Thiele wrote the song, he says, specifically with Holly in mind; the melody was based on the rolling bass line in the song "Blues, Stay Away From Me." ("Mailman" was later recorded for Coral by Don Cornell.) Murray Deutch says, "We wanted to see how Buddy would sound on that kind of song. I was thrilled when I heard his version."

Buddy and the Crickets listened to the demo of "Mailman," ran through it once, and then did one take of the song, with Vi Petty on piano—and that was it, all in about ten minutes. The lyrics of the tune were not memorable, but Holly gave them an all-out performance—one which, at first hearing, may seem grotesque and over-dramatic, but which after more attention comes to be seen as the saving feature of the recording. The vocal is all the more impressive, considering the circumstances of the recording and the spontaneity of Holly's performance. All else in the recording, including the piano playing, the drumming, and Holly's brief guitar break, is pretty simple and straightforward, since there was no time allowed to work out any more elaborate arrangement.

Through the spring, the Crickets waited for the release of their first single. While they waited, they played some local shows and practiced almost constantly. The Crickets were not just a studio band; they were intent on sounding as good in live performances as on records. By the time their first single began to sell and they found themselves in demand across the country for personal appearances, they were a cohesive unit.

Says Mauldin, "We'd rehearse at my house and Jerry's house. Seems like we rehearsed a few times over at Niki's house, and a few times at Larry Holley's house, in a garage there. And then we rented a little office out on the south side of Lubbock, and set up our instruments out there. And we'd go out there nearly all the time. Any spare time we had, we were either out there just hanging around, talking about how great it was going to be some day, or rehearsing. I think that's one thing that got us so close together, and so tight in our presentations, was the fact that we rehearsed nearly all the time."

Very important to the group's in-person appeal was their ability to match the sound of their records at live shows. Sometimes, when a rock 'n' roll act tried to re-create on stage the sound that had been produced in a studio, fans found the results disappointing. The practice of "lip-syncing" on some television shows was an answer to this gap between recorded and live performances. The Crickets were one group, however, which avoided criticism on this count. Only the vocal accompaniment was lacking at live shows (and Niki Sullivan did sing a bit, to fill in that gap); otherwise, the sound was there. Despite Holly's use of dubbing in the studio, he didn't use any technical trick which would be difficult to reproduce live. Though he did play both lead and rhythm guitars on most recordings, Sullivan could play rhythm in live appearances; though Holly in some cases dubbed on the lead guitar part after the vocal was recorded, he was capable of playing and singing at the same time; and though an echo chamber was used at Petty's studio, it was a live echo which only simulated the sound of a theater or auditorium anyway.

All this was no accident. Holly was very much aware that fans expected to hear the same overall sound at concerts that they had heard on the records (though they would allow for such necessary changes as the substitution of guitar for celesta, a hammer-struck keyboard instrument, on "Everyday"). This was no great problem for Holly in the studio, since he deliberately strove for uncomplicated sounds and songs. "He knew that it would help the popularity of his songs if local bands played them at high school dances and the like," explains guitarist Tommy Allsup, who joined Holly in 1958, "and so he rarely did anything that any little ol' band couldn't play." Or at least *try* to play.

The group reached the point where each member could play what he felt and the sound would fit almost automatically with the styles of the others. Jerry Allison comments: "To talk about what influenced my drumming— Buddy's guitar playing influenced my drumming more than anything. I haven't played with anyone since that I could play with as well, because I learned to play drums with what Buddy played.

"We played together so much, because we used to just sit around and rehearse for no reason, just to be playing. So when a new record would come out—for instance, we were in Wichita Falls for a show when we heard Little Richard's 'Keep-A-Knocking' for the first time on the radio. I think we heard it about three times that afternoon on the radio, and we played it that night on the show. We didn't sit and rehearse it and say, 'Now, it's got to have these breaks in it. . . .'—we just played it. Because however Buddy played, I knew how he was going to play it, and he knew how I was going to play—so we didn't work up 'arrangements.'"

And so, the Crickets practiced and waited, somehow quite confident that their first release would bring them success. Says Sullivan, "The five of us—Norman and the group—just knew in our minds that we had recorded a hit song. Whether or not 'That'll Be The Day' would be a *hit* was not in our control, but we knew that it was a hit *song*." Money was still tight for the boys; Larry Holley helped keep them going by giving them work in his construction business—one of their assignments being to install acoustic tile in Norman Petty's echo chamber. By June, Buddy was growing impatient, wondering why Brunswick had failed to release "That'll Be The Day." He called their offices in New York one day, intending to demand the return of the record if they weren't going to release it. He was told that the record had been released that very day; whereupon he asked, "Well—then how about sending an advance?"

On June 10, 1957, *Billboard* covered "That'll Be The Day" in its "Reviews of New Pop Records"; the magazine gave the record a mediocre 72 rating and a moderately favorable review: ". . . Fine vocal by the group on a well-made side that should get play. Tune is a medium beat rockabilly. Performance is better than material."

The record was no overnight success; six weeks passed before anything happened to it. Just what did happen, eventually, is a mixture of fact and legend. The legend is that a disc jockey in Buffalo, New York "locked himself in the control room and played 'That'll Be The Day' on the air all day long"—and the record took off.[3] The story is based on fact. The disc jockey was Guy King of WWOL. He did play the song an unusual number of times a day—like more than once an hour, and occasionally several times in succession—and undoubtedly, that sort of exposure explains why the northern New York State area was one of the first where "That'll Be The Day" began to sell.

However, Murray Deutch and Bob Thiele credit a different disc jockey with making the record a success: Georgie Woods, one of the top DJ's on WDAS, a popular black station in Philadelphia. "For weeks and weeks," says Deutch, "nothing happened—there were no orders. And then I got a call from Norman Weinstroer, the sales manager for Brunswick. He said, 'Georgie

---

[3]Mark, *op. cit.*

THAT'LL BE THE DAY
THE CRICKETS - BRUNSWICK 55009

I'M LOOKING FOR SOMEONE TO LOVE
THE CRICKETS - BRUNSWICK 55009

Juke box title slip for "That'll Be The Day"/"I'm Looking for Someone to Love," 1957 (Ralph M. Newman, Time Barrier Express *magazine)*

Woods wants to play the record.' And it busted wide open. Woods was the one who broke the record.'' Thiele adds, ''All of a sudden, the record started to sell—the sales department called, and they had one order from Philly alone for 20,000 copies.''

The actual importance of any one DJ is lost in statistics and history. ''That'll Be The Day'' did follow an unusual course. Normally, a new release either moved up the charts quickly and became a success, or else did little, was quickly tagged as a failure, and was soon forgotten as disc jockeys turned to newer records. The Crickets' first record defied this pattern. The record was ignored on the national scene for several weeks, and then began to move in scattered regional markets. The record industry at that time was not as nationally homogenous as it is now, and a record could sell in one part of the country while being ignored elsewhere. One of *Billboard*'s functions was to monitor key regional markets for potential national hits. ''That'll Be The Day'' first appeared on these ''territorial lists'' for Boston and northern Ohio, and a week later, on the one covering northern New York State; this makes it hard to say that Georgie Woods or any one person ''made'' the record. At the time, *Billboard* was keeping separate charts of sales and airplay; ''That'll Be The Day'' consistently did better on the sales chart than on the disc jockey performances list—suggesting that, in the case of this record, the disc jockeys followed the tastes of the record buyers, rather than the other way around.

While the Crickets were in Clovis early in July for a recording session (the one at which ''Everyday'' and ''Peggy Sue'' were recorded), Petty received a telegram from Murray Deutch, announcing that the record had sold fifty thousand copies and was beginning to break. Niki Sullivan recalls the big moment: ''We were at Norman's, asleep. It was early in the morning, like 8 or 9 A.M., and we hadn't been to bed but three or four hours, because we had been working that night before. Norman came in, and he had a piece of paper in his hand. He said, 'Fellows, I have some news for you, a wire from Murray Deutch,' and it said something like '"That'll Be The Day" has reached sales of 50,000 copies, congratulations, prepare the fellows to come to New York.' Norman was ecstatic; but we were so tired, we didn't care. I'm serious—it didn't hit the rest of us that this was any big deal. It hit Buddy—he did get up and look at the telegram. But the rest of us just went back to sleep. I guess we should have started bouncing off the walls, but the timing was just a little off."

It was July 29 before *Billboard* took note of the growing sales for "That'll Be The Day," and listed it as a "best buy": "The record has been out for a while and has suddenly started to move. All of the top markets report that the disc is doing well."

In early August, the single made the Top 100 (the pop listing, called the Hot 100 since August 1958), and within a month it climbed into the top ten in terms of records sold. Simultaneously, the record appeared on the rhythm & blues charts, and was equally popular there. The record hit its national peak on September 23, when it was number one in pop sales and number two in rhythm & blues sales.[4] With their first record, the Crickets had a hit—a million-seller. And soon enough, everyone was talking about the "overnight sensation," Buddy Holly—who, like most overnight sensations, had spent several years struggling along before achieving this sudden success. When success came, luck played some role in it; but only Holly's persistence had kept him in a position to take advantage of the luck.

It was sometime in early July that Norman Petty officially became the Crickets' manager. Petty says that when "That'll Be The Day" began to rise on the charts, offers for tours and other promotions began to come in. He felt that, since he himself was not too familiar with the rock 'n' roll markets and booking circuits and had other commitments, someone else would be better qualified to handle the Crickets' tours. "I did not force myself upon them," says Petty. "I didn't say, 'Hey, I'm going to be your manager.' They asked me; and in fact, I tried to convince them that I really wasn't a manager."

Jerry Allison says, "I don't remember if we asked him, or if he just sort of became our manager. I know we all agreed that Norman *ought* to be the manager. I mean, we were all really tight at the time, and Norman really spent a lot of time with us in the studio. And anything we wanted to do, he was willing to try it. Anyway, at the time, all we wanted to do was play rock 'n' roll music. We didn't want to hear about all the trivials, because we thought everything was straight ahead. Norman was always really good about taking care of things so you didn't worry about it. He always seemed to know the right thing to do, so we let him handle all the business."

Niki Sullivan adds, "Norman never pushed it. As I remember, he asked us who we wanted to be our manager, and either Jerry or Buddy said, 'Well Norman, why don't you be?' And it seems like Norman said, 'Well, I've got a business to run here and I can't travel with you,' and things like this. But Buddy took lead of the conversation and said, 'Well, you've brought us this far, you've done this much for us, and we want you to be the manager.' So when it came to actual agreement as to who was to be our manager, the four of us literally pushed ourselves on Norman—we insisted that he do it."

As manager, Petty was concerned with the appearance and life style of the

---

[4]Was "That'll Be The Day" ever the number-one record on the *Billboard* charts? The answer depends on how "number-one" is defined. The song only reached number three on the Top 100 list, which combined DJ plays, jukebox activity, and record sales. "That'll Be The Day" *was* number one, however, on *Billboard*'s separate list of best-selling singles.

October 1, 1957: the day "That'll Be The Day" was expected to hit the million mark in sales and become a gold record (From the Buddy Holly Memorial Society Collection)

Crickets. Dress was one issue. Back in early 1956, Holly and his group had been apt to dress as they pleased, unless the job really demanded something else. Holly was as likely to wear bluejeans or even bermuda shorts (a favorite of Allison's, too) as to wear a sports coat. Later, Holly began to imitate the loud stage fashions of Elvis Presley. That is how he was dressed when Petty first saw him perform:

"The first time that I saw Buddy on stage, I was quite shocked. I saw him sporting a bright red jacket, bright red shoes, and white trousers. And of course, after I saw that, I decided that it would have to go—because he was playing for some adult audiences, too."

At first, Holly resisted the idea of dressing more conservatively. It was only after travelling with other performers and seeing how they dressed that he went along with Petty's ideas. It was the Everly Brothers who really convinced the Crickets to dress more stylishly. Jerry Allison recalls: "We didn't have it going as far as clothes. Like, we had some suits made, had pants *that* big. So the Everly Brothers finally said, 'Hey, you guys, you got to quit wearing those pleat suits and cuffs, and get you some decent clothes.' So they took us down to a place in New York City and said, get this and this. Helped a lot, too. Because we didn't have a clue as to what was happening."

Soon, the Crickets were dressed in the identical and stylish suits that added to their stage appearance. Off stage, and back at home, Holly was more often dressed in T-shirt, jeans, and sneakers. But he did acquire a taste for "good" clothes, wearing them in public out of choice.

At the end of July, the Crickets flew east from the airport at Amarillo to begin their national career as a performing group. Promoters had assumed that the Crickets were a black vocal group, perhaps because the quartet's name resembled those of such groups (in fact, there had previously been an R&B group called the Crickets, and this might have been the direct source of the confusion). No pictures of the Crickets had yet appeared to show otherwise. As a result, the Crickets found themselves scheduled on week-long black package shows booked for the Howard Theater in Washington, the Royal in Baltimore, and the Apollo in New York—theaters where the audience was rarely less than one-hundred-percent black. Among the other acts on the bill were the Cadillacs, Clyde McPhatter, and Lee Andrews and the Hearts. Jerry Allison remembers being delighted by the "mistake": "It was really great—they were great audiences. And there wasn't any tension at all. I mean, it was really strange to us, coming from Texas where people are really—I don't know just how to phrase this, but...there was a definite barrier down there, but, man, we loved it all. We didn't get there and say, hey what's this. We were really tickled—because black music was what we were into a lot."

Niki Sullivan recalls, "Just to be doing a *show* was a totally new experience to me, so I was happy just to be there. I didn't think about stepping on stage before this black audience. I just knew that we were in Washington, D.C., and when we got to the theater, we saw an awful lot of black people. But everybody made us feel at home."

The Crickets were a hit in Washington from the day they got there; but when they got to the Apollo in New York, the initial reception was frigid, according to Sullivan. "The first time we went on," he says, "it was a weekday matinee. They opened the curtains and Buddy stepped toward the mike, and there was this large black woman in the front row who said, 'It'd better sound like the record!' You could have heard a pin drop. And after we got through, I don't think five people clapped. The same thing on the evening show, and the next day—nothing. The third day, we did our first song, and got no response again. So Buddy turned around and said, 'Let's do "Bo Diddley."'"

Sullivan, Allison, Holly, and Mauldin on stage during the Alan Freed Holiday Show, September 1957 (Jerry Allison)

And we went into 'Bo Diddley,' cutting up and working our buns off. I was dancing around in a big circle, going through a bunch of gyrations, and Buddy was all over the stage, and Joe B. was bouncing that bass back and forth and laying it down, and I've never seen Jerry work harder on those damn drums. And when we finished that song, the people just went bananas. From then on, we were accepted at the Apollo. Funny what it takes to please some people."

After the week at the Apollo, the Crickets made appearances on Dick Clark's *American Bandstand* and Alan Freed's local New York City television show, and then performed on Freed's Labor Day holiday show at the Brooklyn Parmount, before joining a package tour organized by Irvin Feld of the General Artists Corporation (GAC), one of the nation's largest booking agencies. The eighty-day cross-country package tour was billed as "The Biggest Show of Stars for '57." The title wasn't just hyperbole. Back then, touring shows would feature a large number of name artists, and Feld's tour included a bunch: Fats Domino, Chuck Berry, Frankie Lymon and the Teenagers, the Drifters, the Everly Brothers, Paul Anka, La Vern Baker, Clyde McPhatter, Jimmie Bowen, Eddie Cochran, and the Crickets. Of course, no one artist performed for very long. On a two-hour show, even the top acts only had time for three or four tunes. But at least a fan could pay two or three dollars for the best seat in a small indoor auditorium or dance hall for a typical package show and see Bill Haley and the Comets, the Everly Brothers, and Buddy Holly and the Crickets in one night, before

Lobby card for the Alan Freed Holiday Show, September 1957 (Jerry Allison)

intermission. Such all-star touring package shows were possible only because the numerous acts were paid small fractions of what contemporary rock artists now command for solo concerts. The highest fee Holly and the Crickets received for performing on such a show was about one thousand dollars a night.

The Show of Stars opened in Pittsburgh on September 6, and then embarked on its long and wearying string of one-nighters. The artists travelled by bus, hundreds of miles between shows, two-and-a-half months without a day off. One week went like this: Sunday, Spokane; Monday, Moscow, Idaho; Tuesday, Calgary, Alberta; Wednesday, Edmonton, Alberta; Thursday, Regina, Saskatchewan; Friday, Denver; Saturday, Wichita, Kansas; Sunday, Kansas City; Monday, Omaha. . . . The performers would sleep on the bus during the night-long drives—if it was quiet enough to sleep—and get to hotels in the next town with time, perhaps, for a few hours rest—if the promoters had thought it worth arranging for hotel rooms in that town. Then it was off to the theater and on stage, usually for two shows, and then back on the bus again for another long ride. Tired from the grind but often too keyed up to sleep, the young performers would pass the hours with pillow fights, water fights, pulling the pants off someone or another. . . . And in the back of the bus, some of the performers, including Holly, might be singing spirituals, or shooting crap with their night's earnings.

So much for what seemed to outsiders like a glamorous life—fame, wealth, excitement, and so on. Not quite. "It was really a draggy old tour," says Allison. "I think we missed about four states. We'd get on the bus and ride and get off and pick, then get back on and ride." For Buddy Holly, it was just as wearying, but still exciting, and the success the Crickets were enjoying was a dream come true. Holly was as conscious as anyone of the money to be made in the business, but there was something else that drove him on—he simply loved to perform. Whatever shyness he showed off stage disappeared on stage, and his broad grin, good humor, and uninhibited performance made the Crickets as appealing in live shows as they were on record. Guitarist Tommy Allsup recalls how it was when he worked with Holly a bit later: "He was a different person when he was on stage. You'd never know him. When he was on stage, he worked real hard and got through to the kids. He would tear up an audience. When he was off stage, he was quiet. He just liked to sit around with the guys and talk—mostly about music."

Niki Sullivan makes a similar observation about Holly: "I think the *real* Buddy Holly was there, behind the mike. Away from the mike, he was quiet, reserved, businesslike, shy—introverted, if you will. Behind the microphone, he was just like a bolt of lightning. He had to be happy while he was doing it, that's what he always wanted to do. It was one hundred percent, the real Buddy Holly, the minute he walked on stage."

The other Crickets shared Holly's enthusiasm for performing. Says Mauldin, "When we were on the road for a couple of months, we'd get tired of it, and we'd say, 'Let's knock off for two months after we finish this tour, and just hang around at home.' So we'd book two months with nothing to do, and

Sullivan, Mauldin, Holly, and Allison, September 1957 (From the Buddy Holly Memorial Society Collection)

get home, and in just about three days, we'd be ready to get back on the road. So we'd book another tour. The time off was fun, but working was more fun."

Niki Sullivan likewise remembers the weariness, but also the bonds that built up among those on the tour. He says, "My whole life or education seemed to occur, right there on that eighty-day tour. The most outstanding thing to me was the camaraderie—everybody living and working together. Color just didn't come up. The Drifters treated me as kind of a white sheep of the family. If I had trouble, or worry, or loneliness, they would always sit down and talk to me. After we got back to New York, we had our farewell party, and when they all went out and got on the bus to leave, I cried."

As for non-musical pastimes, whatever the desires, time and opportunities were limited. "I don't recall much drinking," says Niki. "We didn't have time—usually we were too tired. As for dope—zero on dope. I didn't even know what marijuana was, until years later. There were girls around, but you know, any time we had to jump on a bus on a show and travel three to five hundred miles, that was out. The musicians on the tour who were veterans, they knew who was waiting for them and where they were going the minute we got in a city; but we weren't veterans, and so for us it could just be a matter of circumstance. To be honest, I don't ever remember seeing Buddy with a girl, or knowing that he slept with one during the tour. I can tell you this, he

Holly, Sullivan, Allison, and Mauldin, in New York, 1957 (From the Buddy Holly Memorial Society Collection)

wasn't looking for guys, either. I think Buddy had enough on his mind, that this was something he could live with."

Mauldin has similar memories of Holly's personal habits. "It was one thing I always wondered about Buddy," he says with a laugh, "he was never hustling girls, after the shows. Every once in a while, he'd have some beer, or go have a couple of drinks, but even that was sparingly. And as for drugs—no, absolutely not, for any of us."

The popularity of rock 'n' roll may not have had the effect on racial attitudes for which it has sometimes been credited, but it did at least point out some striking anomalies. The eighty-day tour brought out one clash between law and popular taste. Several cities in the Southeast had ordinances forbidding black and white performers from appearing on the same stage in the same show. So, when the primarily black GAC tour went to Chattanooga, Columbus (Georgia), Birmingham, New Orleans, and Memphis, the white performers (the Crickets, the Everly Brothers, Jimmie Bowen, and Paul

Anka—Eddie Cochran had not yet joined the tour) had to be dropped from the show. Ironically, at the time of these performances, "That'll Be The Day" and Paul Anka's "Diana" were at the top of the rhythm & blues charts.

To the Crickets, the situation was ridiculous. Joe says, "Buddy felt like it was a little bit much. Because we had no feeling against associating or performing with colored people, I don't think Buddy thought that anyone else should feel the way that the Southern states did about it either. But that's the way it was, so we just had to accept it." Niki Sullivan adds, "I don't think any of us were raised to be prejudiced. We had never been exposed to racism before—not in that vein. It was simply grotesque about those cities where we couldn't play, because the audiences were white, far and away, even in the deep South." Buddy revealed his own attitude well enough in a comment to his mother when he came home after the first tour. She asked him how he was "getting along with Negroes," and he replied, "Oh, we're Negroes, too! We get to feeling like that's what we are."

The Crickets did sometimes find themselves staying in black hotels. Joe Mauldin remembers this happening when they were playing the Apollo. "We were staying at a hotel right across the street from the Apollo, and it was a one hundred percent black hotel. We got a lot of strange looks, and people whispering to each other. We felt a little uncomfortable for a day or two, but everything smoothed out." On the eighty-day tour, says Sullivan, the troupe stayed in integrated hotels north of the Mason-Dixon line, but ran into problems south of the line. "Somebody slipped up, and sometimes the whole tour had been booked into an all-white hotel," he says. "We'd go there, and of course be rejected. So at that point, we said, 'Screw it, we'll just go with you guys from now on,' to their own hotels. We didn't ever have trouble getting into a black hotel; we were accepted."

With the success of "That'll Be The Day," Brunswick was anxious to release a Crickets album quickly, but a few more recordings were needed for the album. The five-day vacation from the Show of Stars tour caused by the restrictions on integrated performances gave the Crickets and Petty a chance to rendezvous and cut some additional sides. The group was due to rejoin the GAC tour in Tulsa, Oklahoma; on one of their free nights, Petty's trio had a job in Oklahoma City, and so the Crickets arranged to meet him there. Petty brought his recording equipment with him in a truck he used for carrying his trio's instruments. His gig was at the Officers' Club at Tinker Air Force Base; after the club closed, he and the Crickets set up the recording equipment in a corner of a room at the club, and the Crickets went to work. By morning, they had recorded four tunes: "Maybe Baby," "An Empty Cup," "You've Got Love," and "Rock Me My Baby." The Crickets then went back on the road, while Petty took the tapes back to Clovis and overdubbed the background vocals in his own studio.

While the quartet was still on tour, Coral released "Peggy Sue," Holly's second single as a solo artist, and by far his biggest under his own name. No other Holly record is so widely remembered, or so decisively fixed in the popular mind as embodying the "Holly sound," as is "Peggy Sue." (In terms of sales, it ran about equally with "That'll Be The Day," each reportedly selling over five million copies.) Strangely enough, like "That'll Be The Day," "Peggy Sue" took a little while to catch on—though released in late September, it was November before it made the Top 100, and late December before it became a top hit.

In terms of long-range effect on rock 'n' roll music, "Peggy Sue" may have been more influential than any other Holly record. The steady and constant rhythm guitar strumming—the rapid, accented drumming of Jerry Allison—the stylized vocal, with its full development of the Holly hiccup—the ringing tones of the guitar solo, and the rhythmic cadence Holly used so often—all these influenced several musical generations of singers, guitarists, and drummers, and found their echoes in records over the next decade and beyond.

Stories differ as to the origin of the song. Petty claims that Holly came to him with the tune early one morning during a session at Clovis, and that he—Petty—wrote the lyrics. Other accounts contradict this. According to the Holleys, Buddy had fairly completed the song in his room at their home when Jerry Allison stopped by to see what he was doing. Holly had written the song as "Cindy Lou," but when Jerry suggested changing the title to name the song after Allison's girl friend, Peggy Sue, Buddy agreed. Petty's only contribution, says Jerry, was the chord alteration in the bridge of the song ("Peggy Sue, Peggy Sue, pretty, pretty, pretty, pretty Peggy Sue"). "I remember when we were cutting it," adds Allison, "I messed it up the first time through, and either Buddy or Norman said, 'O.K., if you don't get it right this time, we're going to change it back to "Cindy Lou."'" But the second time we got it, and it stayed 'Peggy Sue.'"

Niki has his own version of the story. "The song was 'Cindy Lou' originally, and it was done with more of a cha-cha beat. Jerry was in the outer office, in a separate room, and we were in the main studio. After a couple of tries, it wasn't working out. A dialogue got started between Jerry and Buddy over the loudspeaker system, saying, you know, 'This isn't it.' So Buddy suggested that they add paradiddles to it—that practice drum roll that drummers use to rehearse their music. And I think that Jerry agreed to do that if Buddy would instead change it from 'Cindy Lou' to 'Peggy Sue.' Then Buddy started that guitar rhythm, because now the song was a four-four beat. It couldn't have been more than the second or third cut that the song was finalized."

There was no overdubbing on the record, and just one guitar. Holly strummed rhythm while singing the choruses, and played a treble lead in the instrumental break. At first, says Niki, he was playing rhythm guitar too, but there was a problem. "Buddy couldn't switch fast enough from playing rhythm on the chorus to playing lead on the bridge—he couldn't get his hand to the switch fast enough without breaking rhythm and having it show up on the tape." So, says Niki, he put down his own guitar, and the song was recorded with Sullivan pushing the switch on Holly's guitar to go to the bridge and back to the chorus.

Initially, only Allison and Petty were listed as the writers of the song. After Holly's death, Jerry insisted that Holly be given credit and that the royalties on the song be distributed in a more accurate manner. He says, "After Buddy got killed, we all went to New York to straighten things out. So the contract on 'Peggy Sue' said Norman and me, and I said, 'Right, Buddy did write part of "Peggy Sue," and he might be gone and all that, but I'm not gonna set here and say he didn't.' And Norman said, 'Well, you can say what you want to, or you can look at the contract.' And he was sort of saying, leave it like it is. And I said, 'Well, the estate can just take my half right now.' And it finally ended up that I got ten percent of it. At that time I had already gotten eight thousand dollars in royalties. And when I signed that agreement I got ten percent instead of fifty, and the eight thousand dollars came out of my account right on the spot. And of course, all the loot that's come in from it since. If I had to do it again, I'd do the same thing. I don't regret that."

There is at least no dispute that Holly and Allison share the credit for the recording's success. Allison's shifting, rolling drumbeat matches Holly's unprecedented steady guitar rhythm—"I've never seen anyone since who plays it that way," says Allison. "Every other guitar player strums it back and forth with his pick—down-up-down-up down-up-down-up, like that. But Holly did it with just down strokes—down-down-down-down down-down-down-down." Sixteen to a bar, and singing at the same time, of course. Holly's guitar solo shouldn't go unmentioned, either. Its effect is heightened by the contrast between the solo guitar's vibrant treble sound and the lower-pitched roll of the drums and guitar on the vocal choruses. Like many of Holly's instrumental solos, but with more emphasis on full chords, the solo flashes back and forth between the tonic and subdominant chords, and then reaches up to the dominant chord to create a feeling of exaltation that's almost religious in nature. It is all so simple—Holly is only following the blues pattern upon which "Peggy Sue" is loosely based. And yet, it is all so perfectly effective. It is simple, in the most positive sense of the word—it is simple because Holly needs no more to achieve a striking effect.

The flip side to "Peggy Sue" was merely "Everyday," which would undoubtedly have been a major hit for Holly had it been released as a single itself. "Everyday" creates an entirely different mood from "Peggy Sue"—a sweet, quiet, and beautiful one. Even on such quieter Holly songs, though, the rhythm remains steady and insistent. The lead instrument is a celesta, played by Petty. The instrument happened to be in the studio that day; during a break in the recording, Holly began to tinker with it, and Petty said, "You know, that's what this song needs." Holly was always searching for, and willing to try, different sounds—and a celesta was about as different as could be. Now, it is hard to picture the recording without it. (Actually, it was not the first use of a celesta on a rock 'n' roll recording—it had been used on Chuck Willis's "It's Too Late" in 1956.)

Allison's performance on the tune was also a matter of accident. As Holly was playing and singing the song to demonstrate how he thought it should sound, Allison began to slap his hands on his knees in time with Holly's playing. "Hey," said Buddy, "that sounds pretty good." And so, the only "drumming" on the record is the sound of Allison slapping his knees.

To get technical, the melody features a chord pattern found in none of Holly's other songs—the chords in the refrain are built on a new tonic, the flattened seventh of the tonic in the body of the song (i.e., if the song is in C, the chords in the verses are C, F, and G, while those in the refrain are Bb, Eb, and F). Allison credits the melody and most of the lyrics to Holly, with Petty having some role in rearranging the order of phrases and verses.

Overall, the song has the peculiar uncertainty of so many of Holly's songs. Despite its happy, optimistic tone, it is still about love unfulfilled—a love that is "getting closer" but is not yet there, a love which the singer is a bit shy in expressing directly. But in the end, the song is all the more effective for that. Love is pictured as a feeling that does not emerge spontaneously or full-grown; instead, it slowly, but surely, builds—and that is a more hopeful and happy message for those in love who would like to believe, too, that love in return will surely come their way.

> Everyday,
> It's a-getting closer,
> Going faster than a rollercoaster,
> Love like yours will surely come my way—
>   hey, a-hey-hey.
>
> Everyday,
> It's a-going faster,
> Everyone said, "Go ahead and ask her,"
> Love like yours will surely come my way—
>   hey, a-hey-hey.
>
> > Every day seems a little longer
> > Every way love's a little stronger,
> > Come what may, do you ever long for
> > True love from me?
>
> Everyday,
> It's a-getting closer,
> Going faster than a rollercoaster,
> Love like yours will surely come my way.[5]

The vocal is one of Holly's best. The delicate phrasing, gliding tones, and variety of vocal effects give the recording a gentle lilt which has defied imitation in later versions of the song.

"Everyday" was the first song to be released bearing the name of "Charles Hardin" as co-writer. The name was, of course, just a pseudonym for Holly, using his given first and middle names. Jerry Allison explains that the pseudonym was used to hide Holly's authorship of his songs from

---

[5]"Everyday," words and music—Charles Hardin and Norman Petty. Copyright © 1957 by Peer International Corporation. Used by permission.

Cedarwood Publishing at a time when matters had not yet been settled with them. Holly did not have a songwriting contract with Cedarwood requiring that he let them publish his songs; probably, though, he wanted to play it safe, lest they claim the songs on some legal technicality that he didn't know about.

How did Holly feel when he had recorded a song—what did he think of it? And what were his own favorites? Jerry Allison answers: "On those very first sessions in Nashville—it didn't really knock us out, what we had recorded. Because the people in charge weren't all that interested in what we were doing, and we thought we could sure do it better if we had more time. I really can't remember what Buddy thought about 'Blue Days, Black Nights' and those things—at the time, he was pretty tickled just to have a record out, and he took it around to the radio stations and said, 'Hey, listen to this.'

"Later, when we were over at Clovis—after we'd cut something—Buddy was pretty enthusiastic about it all. But you know, after we got started and had those records that did some good, there was never much time to sit around and listen to them. I don't think Buddy had any real favorites. He really liked 'Everyday.' And 'Peggy Sue'—we were all pretty flipped out about that one. We said, 'Man, that's weird. That's different. It sounds good.' My own favorites? 'Everyday' was a good one. 'Not Fade Away.' 'That'll Be The Day' will always be my favorite because that got it all started, and it was the first tune I ever wrote part of. And I always liked 'Tell Me How' pretty good—it was the flip side of 'Maybe Baby.'"

"That'll Be The Day" stayed in the top thirty for a full three months, and the Crickets' second single, "Oh Boy!," was not released until October 27. "Oh Boy!" was written by Bill Tilghman and Sonny West. West was a rockabilly musician in his own right, and had made a record called "Rock-Ola Ruby" at Petty's studio early in 1957; the record had been released on Petty's own label, Nor Va Jak Records. When he and Tilghman wrote "Oh Boy!," they took it to Clovis and made a demo of it. Shortly thereafter, Holly heard the demo, and decided to record it in his own style. "Norman called us," remembers Tilghman. "He wanted us to come over to Clovis. He played us Buddy's version of 'Oh Boy!' Needless to say, it was fantastic—kind of put us both on Cloud Nine."

Juke box title slip for "Oh Boy!"/"Not Fade Away" (Ralph M. Newman, Time Barrier Express *magazine)*

OH BOY!
THE CRICKETS — BRUNSWICK 55035

NOT FADE AWAY
THE CRICKETS — BRUNSWICK 55035

Holly's recording stands out as the best example of his breathless, frantic, rockabilly style—it's a long way from "Everyday" to "Oh Boy!," but Holly was equally adept at both sounds. Allison's drumming is superb, with his driving beat only increasing in intensity as the song progresses. The dubbed vocal obscures Holly's guitar playing on the solo instrumental chorus, but elsewhere, it fills in perfectly. For sheer excitement, "Oh Boy!" is the Crickets at their finest.

The flip side, "Not Fade Away," followed the famed "Bo Diddley Beat," but with a lighter, varied touch and a brighter sound. The vocal shows Holly's sense of variation and control. In spots, his voice illustrates the words, pushing forward and retreating on "I try to show it, you keep driving me back," or dying down on the title phrase. Earlier in his career, Holly had studied Elvis's manner of variation; but by now, he was creating his own effects, reflecting the way he himself felt, talked, and sang. The overdubbed background vocals were by Holly and Sullivan.

The new single was not the monstrous hit "That'll Be The Day" had been, but it did sell close to a million copies. For sure, it proved that Holly and the Crickets were not one-shot artists, as so many groups proved to be. "America's hottest singing sensation," a trade-paper advertisement called the Crickets; and, for the moment, they were just that.

5. Around the World

By December 1957, the Crickets were reaching the height of their popularity in the United States and Canada, and plans were already being made for tours of England and Australia.

After the GAC tour ended in late November, the Crickets returned to New York for an appearance on *The Ed Sullivan Show* on December 1. The quartet performed "That'll Be The Day" in the first half of the show, and "Peggy Sue" in the second. The group had been on Dick Clark's *American Bandstand* the previous August to lip-sync "That'll Be The Day," but the Sullivan show was their first appearance on prime-time TV, and the first time they had had to play their songs live on network television.

How did the Crickets feel, playing for a nationwide TV audience? Jerry Allison talks about it: "I can't speak for everybody, but I was pretty nervous *all* the time. Because it all happened so fast, and it seemed like we went straight from setting tile to being on network TV shows. But I was definitely more nervous on TV than I was on regular shows, and I think Buddy was, too. After all, we had picked plenty—we knew we could play it, and all that. And in front of people, that wasn't any hang-up. But as far as TV, that was something different—an audience that wasn't there. And also, on the first Ed Sullivan show, they had fixed up a big riser for the drums—it was maybe ten feet tall. So I was sitting way up there, and Joe B. was standing on one side of the riser and Niki on the other, and Buddy was out front singing. And of course the amps just went right out front and out the back and I couldn't hear a thing. And when we did the first rehearsal, Buddy said, 'I can't hear the drums good—just take that thing down.' So they struck all that. Because if you can't hear, you can't play together."

"Shock" is the word Niki Sullivan uses to describe his reaction to the Sullivan show. "We were all let down. We expected so many thousands of people in the audience, because that's how it looked when we'd seen the show on TV. But when we walked out there, we just couldn't believe it—it was a very small theater, with only a couple of hundred of people." He too remembers being uncomfortable. "It was the surroundings—the helter-skelter, and rush, rush, do everything on time and be here on time. We just weren't used to that immediacy. And then the night of the show, when we

Sullivan, Holly, Allison, and Mauldin performing on The Ed Sullivan Show, *December 1, 1957 (From the Buddy Holly Memorial Society Collection)*

stood in the wings, the All-American football team was there, and they were giants, every one of them. We felt like ants. Everybody was on pins and needles, all the time we were there, except for the football players—nobody was gonna press *them*."

After the Crickets performed "Peggy Sue," Ed Sullivan unexpectedly called Holly out front for a few brief questions—the Crickets' ages, where they were from, and if they were going to school in Lubbock ("Well, we did until we got out of high school, finally," Holly replied).

"Were you a big hit right from the start?" asked Sullivan.

"Well, we've had a few rough times, I'd guess you say, but we've been real lucky getting it this quick," answered Holly in a soft Texas drawl.

Holly may have been scared at the start of the evening, but he seemed completely at ease talking with Sullivan. When the interview was over, Holly naturally stuck out his hand for a handshake, and it took a second for the startled Sullivan to respond.

After the show, the Crickets flew back to Lubbock for their first visit home since August. The hopeful young musicians who had left Lubbock then with

Sullivan, Holly, and Allison (Mauldin not visible) performing on The Ed Sullivan Show, *December 1, 1957 (From the Buddy Holly Memorial Society Collection)*

one record just starting to climb the charts now returned as established stars; but it made little difference in Lubbock. There was nothing triumphant about the return—no crowds or reporters met them at the airport, and nobody made any speeches about the home-town success stories. You're never as big in your home town as you are anywhere else, the show business line goes—and though their records always sold well locally, the Crickets were never honored publicly by their own community. The local newspaper had printed

Holly performing on the Sunday Night at the London Palladium
television show, London, March 2, 1958 (ATV Photo)

just one item about the group—a small group photo with a caption mentioning their appearance on *The Ed Sullivan Show*. Holly never failed to mention his home town whenever he was given the chance to do so, and it's a pretty good bet that around the world today, Lubbock is noted more for Buddy Holly than for its cotton or its university. But the pride Holly felt for his home town was not reciprocated, at least not by the leading citizens in it.

The Crickets' families, though, offered them strong support; if their sons could be successful playing rock 'n' roll, they saw nothing wrong with it. Joe Mauldin recalls his mother's feelings: "I quit school before I graduated, to play with Buddy. And I hit Mother with the same story that Buddy hit me with when he asked me to play regular with the group. I told her that we were gonna go to New York, and be stars, and make lots of money. So Mother, against her own better judgment, agreed to sign me out of school, because I was too young to pull it off by myself. And I remember when we were at the school, she started crying, and she said, 'I hope you have to work your fingers to the bone the rest of your life, because you're going to regret this someday.' And, you know, it hurt me that she felt that way about it, but I felt like I was doing the right thing. But anyway, after that, Mother just got thoroughly involved. She kept a scrapbook at home, with just about every piece of publicity that was ever put out on us in the United States, like in *Billboard* and *Cashbox*, and with all the publicity pictures that we had. And if we played in Oklahoma City or somewhere in New Mexico or Texas, she and Dad would drive hundreds of miles to wherever we were, just to see us perform."

Shortly after the Crickets returned home, Niki Sullivan quit the group. His decision was sudden and, as he remembers it, unplanned, but it can be seen in retrospect as growing out of tensions and personality conflicts which had built up during the group's four months on the road. It was one thing to rehearse and play around Lubbock; it was another to spend several months with hardly a break, living with the same people continuously in hotel rooms and on buses. Allison and Holly had been friends for some time before the formation of the Crickets, and Joe Mauldin had fitted right in with them, but Sullivan never achieved the same rapport. Looking back on it now, he is able to describe himself candidly:

"Remember, I was an only child, until I was seventeen. An only child who used to play golf by himself just to entertain himself, do a lot of things by myself—I was a loner. And loners quite often can get in certain moods, you've got to reach out and grab them. And that didn't happen. Now maybe they didn't know to do that, or understand the situation. I'm sure they didn't."

Teasing and horseplay were a way of relieving the tensions that built up during the time on tour, but Niki had less tolerance for it than the others did. Joe Mauldin recollects how the Crickets used to blow off steam while out on the road: "We teased each other constantly. Buddy, Jerry, and I teased hard with each other, and then we'd do things to Niki, and he'd do things to us. But I guess Niki just didn't dig that kind of humor, or that kind of funning.

"I remember once when Buddy, Jerry, and I were on the road, we had the night off, and I went to a club, and Buddy and Jerry didn't go. When I got back to the hotel, the lights were out and Buddy and Jerry were asleep, so I thought rather than turn on the lights and wake everybody up, I'd just undress and crawl into bed. Well, I crawled in, and I didn't know what in the world I was putting my feet into. I jumped out of bed and turned the lights on. They'd dumped ash trays, glasses of ice water—they had had food up in the room, and they took the plates and dumped them in there—and so my bed was like a garbage pail. I got so mad I couldn't talk, so I just put my clothes back on and stormed out the door, and didn't show up until the next morning. Of course, they were all apologetic then. They said, 'Oh, we were just playing a joke on you, having fun.' And I got over it. We did things to each other constantly, which I think is only normal with any group of people who are together all the time. But I think that was another thing that kept us knit so close, that we learned to cope with each other's personalities.''

"We all did pick on each other," Niki says, "but it really grated on me. I had never been around that kind of picking, and I took things more personal than the other guys did, and I wasn't prepared for all of that. It wasn't that anyone was trying to drive somebody out of the group, or trying to hurt somebody's feelings on purpose. It was mainly for a release. But the bickering and fighting did get to me, and I had no way to retaliate, except in doing the same thing, and I didn't enjoy it. But it was constant. Like, we'd go to a restaurant, and I might order a waffle, which I like very much, and the rest of the guys would eat steak, which I didn't particularly care for. And they'd pick on me about it, and go on and on and on. And I mean, how long can you pick on a guy for eating a waffle?''

Niki remembers telling Buddy and the others of his decision to leave: "We got back, and I was very tired; we all were. We were over at Clovis, and I just said, 'Buddy, I want to quit, I'm just not happy.' Buddy didn't understand why, but he didn't pursue it; he just said, 'Well, Niki, if that's what you want to do.' So we had a meeting of everyone in Norman's office, and I said, 'Fellas, I enjoyed it and everything, but that's it,' and I walked out and went home.''

Sullivan harbors some regret that nobody tried to talk him out of it. "At no time" he says, "did I ever hold any animosity towards Joe B., Jerry, or Buddy. But my leaving the group could have been resolved, I think, with a night's sleep—just some rest. And Norman did not make any effort to take something that was broken up for the moment and try to piece it back together. A man who is a manager, in any capacity, knows he has employees who have times they're not proud of, and the best thing you can do is say, 'Let's get some rest, let's talk another day.' But that never happened.''

Petty looks at what happened in another way. He recalls that when he was with the group during their first concerts in Washington in August, tension was already building. "The biggest rub was between Jerry and Niki. And Buddy went along with Jerry.'' According to Petty, when the Crickets returned in December, he had separate conversations in which Niki said that he wanted to quit, and the others told Petty that they wanted Niki out of the group. "What was there to patch up?" asks Petty. "I knew that Jerry and Joe

B. and Buddy wanted him to leave, and on the other hand that Niki wanted to leave.''

That version is disputed by Allison. "We never did really have a fight with Niki or say that we wanted him out of the group. Oh, he and I had a good fight one time, when we were playing the Brooklyn Paramount. We got to squirting water at each other, something like that, and we had a fist fight. In fact, my eye was swollen up on the *Chirping Crickets* album cover photo, because he got me good around the eye. But that had nothing to do with him leaving, that was just silly kid stuff. None of us were uptight when he split. He wanted out—it was a mutual thing.''

Mauldin, too, remembers that the decision was Niki's own, and that it arose from Niki's desire to move out on his own. "After about three months on the road," says Mauldin, "Niki on a few occasions mentioned to me that this kind of life was not for him, and that he was going to try to get out and make a record deal on his own. And my response was, 'Hey man, do whatever you think you need to do.' When Buddy and Jerry and I would discuss it, they'd say, 'If he wants out, all he has to do is walk.' Buddy and Jerry never forced or pushed him out.''

Sullivan remembers being of two minds about the idea of becoming an individual artist. "I didn't have any desire to be number one. I had joined strictly by chance, and I was happy to be where I was—it was like fulfilling a dream," he says, while also admitting, "I really kind of did think about stepping out on my own. I did harbor a few feelings like that when we were on tour." Playing rhythm guitar behind Holly was, as others had previously discovered, a role of limited significance. On stage, Niki saw his role as especially a visual one, "moving around and cutting up" (though for a couple of days, during the week at the Howard in Washington, Holly lost his voice and Sullivan had to do the singing). On recordings, Sullivan sometimes played without being miked, and he recognizes the implication: "Buddy's lead style of guitar was rhythm. By my not being miked, that's one microphone less that Norman has to worry about. Because it's all on one track, and if I make a mistake, then we blow the whole thing. So it wasn't necessary. But we went there together, and I think that might have been important to Buddy, to have me sitting there playing, even if I wasn't being miked; Buddy did have a need for people. And anyway," Sullivan adds with a grin, "what else can you do in Clovis, New Mexico at 2 o'clock in the morning?''

Not long after leaving the Crickets, Sullivan did in fact get a contract with Dot Records and had a regional hit with "It's All Over"/"Three Steps to Heaven." (Although Petty has said that this record was made in Clovis and that it was he who sold it to Dot, Sullivan denies this. According to Niki, the recording was made at a Lubbock studio and given by Sullivan to Murray Deutch, who arranged the Dot contract.) Later, Sullivan moved to the West Coast and headed a Los Angeles band, Soul Incorporated, for several years.

When Niki left the group, the remaining trio considered asking Sonny Curtis to join them in Niki's place; but Sonny had other jobs then and was himself about to get a record contract, and so the trio decided to go it alone for a while and see how it worked out. A trio of bass, drums, and one guitar was then unprecedented in rock 'n' roll. But, just like a year earlier when Holly and Allison had performed as a duo, Buddy's ability to play as hard as he sang and Jerry's varied and full drumming filled in the gap at rhythm guitar. The Crickets performed with this three-man lineup for several months and were never faulted for their instrumental performance; fans and reviewers were instead amazed by the Crickets' ability to match the sound of larger combos.

At Christmas, the trio returned to New York for a television appearance on *The Arthur Murray Dance Party*, and then played on the celebrated Alan Freed holiday shows at the Paramount Theater—twelve days of live rock 'n' roll that attracted thousands of teenagers and created waiting lines stretching several blocks. To accommodate the crowds, shows were held about every two hours, six or seven times a day. Like the GAC tours, Freed's shows included many top names; heading the bill on this one were Jerry Lee Lewis, Fats Domino, the Everly Brothers, and the Crickets. Jerry Allison remembers that the Crickets were a bit big-headed over their success—at the time, "Peggy Sue" and "Oh Boy!" were both high in the charts, and "That'll Be The Day"

Marquee for the Alan Freed Show at the New York Paramount, December 1957 (Jerry Allison)

Holly and Mauldin (Allison hidden) on stage, New York Paramount show, December 1957 (Jerry Allison)

Holly, Allison (partially hidden), and Mauldin on stage, New York Paramount show, December 1957 (Jerry Allison)

was still in the top fifty—and the Paramount shows furnished more proof of their popularity.

"That was the high point for me—the New York Paramount show," says Allison. "There were all kinds of people on the show, like maybe twenty acts, and we did better than anyone else, as far as getting encores and all that—like nobody else would get an encore, and maybe we'd get two or three sometimes. That'd get anybody's head—I'm sure I was proud as hell, just sitting there and thinking, well, I'm with a hot group. And Buddy's ego would show a little bit in those days, too."

Just how did success change Buddy Holly? Allison replies, "Of all the people I've ever known, like before they were successful and after, this changes everybody I've ever seen. No matter what—show biz or whatever. And Buddy definitely changed a bit—he got more moody and big-headed, or whatever you want to call it. He sort of got into that—and then he got back out of it. But I remember one trip we were on, where he was the star or the biggest thing on the show, and we were with Danny and the Juniors and Dickie Do and the Don'ts. And we were all kids and fighting all the time; like, I nearly knocked his glasses off one time. And Buddy would say, 'Hey, stop it.' 'Quiet.' 'Quit that pillow fight.' I mean, he wasn't ever really like, 'I'm too big a deal,' but he was a little bit. Oh, as a general rule, he was likeable and all that; and like I say, that sort of passed anyway. But it seemed he didn't want to fool around anymore—it was like he was there to work."

Murray Deutch and Bob Thiele likewise recall Holly becoming more sophisticated and more conscious of his work, but not being changed otherwise by success. Deutch says, "The first time I met Buddy and the Crickets in New York, they were real kids, straight off the farm. They were dressed in T-shirts and jeans, and everything was 'Mister Deutch,' not 'Murray.' Buddy was a very quiet kid who said little until he got to know you. He kept things inside. He never talked too much, but he was a very bright guy: he listened, and it sunk in. He did get more worldly—I mean business-wise, about the record business. But he stayed the same person."

Bob Thiele remembers, "Holly seemed to me to be an extremely sensitive individual. He *looked* fragile—like you could blow him over. And somehow I found myself being aware of his sensitivity, and trying to be careful of how I said things to him. Even with his country talk, he sounded like a gentleman. And he *was* a gentleman."

It was around this time that Buddy adopted a physical appearance that set styles just as his music had. He changed from the thin plastic and metal eyeglass frames he had previously worn to distinctive all-black curved frames. Later, he had squared, thicker frames specially made for him by a New York firm—which thereafter handled plenty of inquiries about the frames from Holly's male fans. Allison had something to do with Holly's new glasses: "I said to him, 'If you're going to wear glasses, then really make it obvious that you're wearing your glasses.' I think Phil Everly had something to do with that, too. I remember that Buddy, Phil, and I went down to a place and rounded up the pair he's wearing on the *Showcase* album—the ones he wore before he got into the square kind."

This was the time, too, when Holly tried to improve the appearance of his smile—already one of his best assets. The mineral-heavy water in Lubbock had left Holly's teeth with a brown stain; now that he could afford it, he decided to have his teeth capped. New glasses, new teeth, new clothes—all this must seem rather vain. But after all, Holly was a performer, and his physical appearance was important to his career. Besides, he had to be concerned not only with how he looked to his audiences, but also how he appeared to business figures who dealt with him—men who were apt to look down on him for his small-town manners and appearance. Coral producer Dick Jacobs, who admired Holly's talent and worked closely with him, nevertheless unconsciously disclosed the importance of Holly's appearance to more urbanized individuals when he once reminisced: "I first met him when he was appearing in Brooklyn. He had silver-rimmed glasses, gold-rimmed teeth, and looked like a hick from Texas. The next time I saw him, he wore a three-button suit, horned-rimmed glasses, had had his teeth recapped, and looked like a gentleman. He was always a marvelous person . . . a sweet gentle soul."[1]

Remember, too, that despite all the protest which seemed inherent in rock 'n' roll, social expectations were often strangely unchanged. To the audiences, rock 'n' roll singers—both white and black—could look like "gentlemen," and even be more popular for it. It was all right to look neat, as long as you didn't seem to be putting on an act about it.

The Crickets never counted on their good looks to win them many fans. "Holly didn't really appeal to girls as far as a teen idol sort of thing," says Jerry Allison. "It wasn't that they didn't dig him; they used to scream just like they did for anybody else. But like if we were doing a show with the Everly Brothers or Eddie Cochran or whoever, and if we were out in the back loading equipment, the fans would come around and get our autographs, and then if the Everly Brothers came out, they'd throw it down and hunt for a bigger piece to get the Everly Brothers' autographs. Compared to Frankie Avalon and all those slick dudes, we were just a bunch of ugly pickers who just picked. But really, that made it all seem better—because we felt like everybody that liked us, liked us because of what we *could* pick. They were fans because of the music, not just because of the emotions or the good looks or whatever. And it seemed too like the boys liked us better—you know, with some of the idol-type groups, the boys would be turned off because their chicks would be saying, 'Oh, look at that!'" Mrs. Holley can also confirm this aspect of the Crickets' appeal: probably ninety percent of the letters she had received since Buddy's death have been from males, even though females make up a large majority of the record-buying audience.

After the Paramount shows, the Crickets made a seventeen-day tour for Irvin Feld and GAC, and then returned to New York for their second appearance on *The Ed Sullivan Show* (January 26, 1958). This appearance was marred by a run-in between the Crickets and Sullivan the afternoon of the show.

---

[1] Norman Mark, "The Life and Legend of 'This Unforgettable Texan,'" Chicago *Daily News* "Panorama," April 15, 1967.

THE CRICKETS *Exclusive Coral Recording Artists*

COPYRIGHT

Autographed picture of
Allison, Holly and Mauldin,
1958 (Lawrence and
Ella Holley)

"It was during the dress rehearsal," remembers Allison. "Joe B. and I were wrestling or goofing around somewhere down in the basement. All of a sudden, they struck the act scheduled before us, and we were supposed to go on. Sullivan announced us, but Buddy just came out alone with his guitar. Ed said, 'Where are the others?' and Buddy said, 'I don't know—no telling!' Finally, we got up there—but Ed Sullivan was turned completely off. I don't remember what all was said—but we were supposed to do two songs that night, and two minutes before the show was over, we were still standing there waiting to go on. So we just got time to do one song. And the lighting was bad—you couldn't even see Joe B. and myself, you could just see Buddy—and the sound was terrible, too, and it was like they did that on purpose. It was really a drag—made us look awful."

The one song they did sing was "Oh Boy!," a choice Sullivan had objected to at the rehearsal, perhaps thinking it too "wild." Holly, though, insisted on performing the song. "I told my friends down in Lubbock, Texas that I was going to sing that song," he said, "and if I can't sing it—why, I don't want to be on the show." Later, Holly turned down an invitation for a third appearance; he'd apparently had his fill of the Sullivan show. Allison says, "I wasn't there when it happened, but I heard that Buddy was at the booking agency when they called the agent, from the Sullivan show, and offered a lot more loot, like twice as much as we'd gotten for the second show. And Buddy said, 'Just tell them to forget it, man, they ain't got enough money.' And the agent said, 'Well, I can't tell them that, you tell them.' So I heard that Buddy got on the phone and said, 'Man, you can forget it, we're not gonna do that.' Well, that's not exactly what he told him—I guess it was a little harsher than that."

American rock 'n' roll was by now starting to capture a world-wide audience. The year 1958 saw overseas tours by those artists who had proved to be most popular with foreign audiences. As "That'll Be The Day," "Peggy Sue," and "Oh Boy!" climbed to the top of the charts in Australia and Great Britain, the Crickets were booked for visits to those countries.

First was Australia. The group flew there with Norman Petty in late January 1958, stopping en route in Honolulu for a show there. The five-day Australian tour consisted of shows in Melbourne, Sydney, and Brisbane. The package also included Jerry Lee Lewis and Johnny O'Keefe, the leading Australian star; top billing, though, went to fifteen-year-old Paul Anka, who had a few months earlier written and recorded "Diana," the best selling record of the decade. Actually, the order of the billing didn't reflect the relative popularity of the performers, but was instead a matter of negotiation: in return for the top spot on the bill, Anka agreed to go on the tour for less than his regular price. Holly, on the other hand, was less concerned with questions of prestige, or with trying to satisfy his ego this way. He wanted something more tangible.

"Buddy was always one for saying, 'The hell with the billing, man, I want the money,'" Joe Mauldin says. "When we played the New York Paramount on the Alan Freed Christmas show, Fats Domino and Jerry Lee Lewis were both billed above us, but I know for sure that we were making more than Jerry Lee, and I think we were making more than Fats. Things like that did go on." According to Petty, whatever Anka's billing, the Australian audiences gave more acclaim to the Crickets and the most of all to Jerry Lee Lewis. (But Lewis himself, in a moment of modesty, once told me, "Buddy was the real star on that one—he just tore them up over there—just drove them wild.")

Holly impressed the Australians with both his music and his demeanor. Whatever the Crickets' antics when they chose to blow off steam in private, in public they were natural, but subdued. This was the first Australian tour by American rock 'n' roll groups, and the Australians were apparently relieved

—16   Newcastle Morning'Herald and Miners' Advocate, Friday, January 24, 1958.

*Advertisement for performance in Newcastle, Australia, January 1958
(From the Buddy Holly Memorial Society Collection)*

by the lack of incidents they had expected would accompany a rock 'n' roll
show—and they were a bit surprised by the normality of their visitors.
Without being ingratiating, the Crickets made a strong off-stage impression
within the music industry. An unusual description of Holly was offered a
dozen years later by Australian record executive Ken Taylor, who wrote in his
memoir *Rock Generation* (page 81):

> *...in the complex world of show business where things are not
> always what they seem...a guy called Buddy Holly was favorite
> and king. Genuine in outlook and unaffected in demeanor, Buddy
> and his group, the Crickets, were the First Gentlemen of Rock and
> Roll....To meet him Buddy was the perfect representation of a
> sombre American parson—ascetic, serious, dignified behind the
> horn-rimmed glasses he perpetually wore. His personality, innate
> decency—and talent—added up to an American legend.*

When Holly and the Crickets returned from Australia, they left behind a
legion of devoted fans who have helped keep Holly's popularity alive in
Australia to this day.

One unusual by-product of the Australian tour was the recording of Jerry
Allison's first—and only—single. Australian star Johnny O'Keefe had
written and recorded a tune called "Real Wild Child"; the Crickets decided

that Jerry should record the song when the group got home. "I was going to try to do it like James Cagney," says Allison, "but that didn't work. So we tried to—well, I forget what I was trying to sound like. Anyway, O'Keefe had done it seriously, and we did it like a joke. But we did one tour, in October of 1958, where we played some places where that record was in the charts, and I sang it on the show sometimes. Buddy didn't like it very much—he thought it was kind of a farce, I think."

The flip side was a rock 'n' roll version of "Oh, You Beautiful Doll," in which Allison demolished the lyrics with a comic mumbling doubletalk he had picked up from Sam Hirt, a trombonist in the Paul Williams Orchestra, the stage band on the Show of Stars tour. There was even a bit of a takeoff, in the instrumental break, on the delicate celesta sound of "Everyday." The result was hilarious, regardless of musical quality.

"At the time," Norman Petty remembers, "the Crickets were so hot that Coral was ready to release *anything* we gave them." Allison's middle name is Ivan (his friends rarely call him Jerry, but instead call him by his initials, "J-I"), and before Petty took the record to New York, Allison decided to put just his middle name down on the disc as the artist. He explains, "I didn't want my name on it. I said I didn't want anybody to know who it was, because I thought it was really atrocious."

The record was in fact a moderate success in some areas and rose to number 68 on *Billboard*'s Hot 100 in October 1958. Allison didn't really have to be embarrassed about it—"Real Wild Child" wasn't a bad record just because it

Holly, Jerry Lee Lewis, and Mauldin, 1958 (Lawrence and Ella Holley)

Holly rehearsing in London for the British tour, March 1, 1958 (John Beecher)

was funny. Allison's flat, nasal, mocking vocal gave the song that ambivalent mixture of identification and self-parody which marked the first-person narratives of Chuck Berry, Eddie Cochran, and Bo Diddley. And besides the humor of a novelty record, the song had a danceable beat and several instrumental choruses offering memorable lead guitar picking by Holly. At the least, the recording showed that, despite the fatigue and tension involved in their performing career, the Crickets could still exhibit a sense of humor on and off stage.

After a short vacation in Lubbock and a brief swing through Florida with Jerry Lee Lewis, Bill Haley, and the Everly Brothers, the Crickets took off at the end of February for a four-week tour of Great Britain. There, the Crickets' records had been even more successful than in the United States—a fact emphasized still more in the months after the tour, when Holly's group and solo singles remained top-sellers in Great Britain, even when they failed to rise high on the American charts.

The reviews in music papers at the time and Holly's influence on British music in succeeding years show that the tour had a terrific impact. Actually, though, it opened on an inauspicious note. On the second day of the tour, the

Holly in London, March 1, 1958 (John Beecher)

Holly in London, March 1, 1958 (John Beecher)

Crickets appeared on the *Sunday Night at the London Palladium* television show, and were not at their best. As was said before, the Crickets were somewhat nervous when they faced television audiences; the major problem on this performance, though, was technical. Microphone volume and balance were poor—the fault not of the Crickets, but of the show's own technicians. This, and the uncertainty of how a British audience would react to their music, increased the group's nervousness. Also, viewers who had thought that the Crickets themselves sang vocal backgrounds on the records were surprised to find that only Holly sang. The British devotion to authenticity provoked some criticism of the Crickets on this count.

After that show, however, the Crickets met little but approval during the rest of their English stay. On tour, where Petty had more control over sound levels and the Crickets felt more at ease and less inhibited in their stage performances, the group won hosts of new fans. Instead of commenting on the lack of vocal background, reviewers remarked how close the group came in live performances to reproducing their recorded sound. As in Australia, critics were struck by the trio's full sound and contagious excitement. Keith Goodwin of the *New Musical Express* wrote:

> *If enthusiasm, drive, and down-to-earth abandon are the ingredients necessary for success in the rock 'n' roll field, then Buddy Holly and the Crickets are all set for a long and eventful run of popularity! They rocked their way through a tremendous, belting 25-minute act without letting up for one moment . . . and the audience showed their approval in no uncertain terms, via handclaps, whistles, shouts, and long bursts of sustained applause.*
>
> *Much of the trio's success can be attributed to the fact that their "in person" sound is almost identical to the sound that they produce on record. . . . But how these boys manage to make such a big sound with their limited instrumentation baffles me! . . . Take my word for it—this is rock 'n' roll like we've never heard it before in Britain!*

Of course, the praise wasn't unanimous; and it's almost as revealing to read an opposite opinion. For example, Peter Holdsworth of the Bradford *Telegraph and Argus* had this to say:

> *Artistry has been kicked out of the stage door and performers who can provide ephemeral thrills are taking its place. Audiences are in search of the momentary gimmick, of which they tire whenever a new novelty is introduced. At least it would seem so from the fanatical reception given to a screeching guitar player and his two colleagues when they headed the bill at the Gaumont Theatre, Bradford, last night. They were Americans Buddy Holly and the Crickets. Unless they had previously read the lyrics or heard them sung by an articulate vocalist, I would have defied anyone in the audience to tell me what seventy per cent of the words were which issued from the lips of this foot-stamping, knee-falling musician.*

GAUMONT IPSWICH

Manager: W. E. SHERWOOD   Telephone IPSWICH 3641

ON THE STAGE FOR ONE DAY ONLY

SATURDAY, MARCH 15th

THREE SHOWS
2.30 - 6.15 - 8.30

LEW and LESLIE GRADE, LTD. presents

THE GREAT AMERICAN RECORDING STARS

BUDDY HOLLY

HIT RECORDER OF **"PEGGY SUE"**

AND THE

CRICKETS

FAMOUS FOR THEIR GREAT DISCS: **'THAT'LL BE THE DAY'** and **'OH, BOY'** etc.

THE PYE-NIXA RECORDING STAR

GARY MILLER

FEATURING HIS HIT RECORD:
"THE STORY OF MY LIFE"

OF STAGE, RADIO AND RECORDING FAME

THE TANNER SISTERS

COMEDIAN WITH THE MODERN STYLE

DES O'CONNOR

BRITAIN'S NEW MUSICAL SENSATION

RONNIE KEENE AND HIS ORCHESTRA

BOX OFFICE OPEN DAILY from 10.30 a.m. to 8 p.m.

Advertisement for performance in Ipswich, England, March 1958 (John Beecher)

Where on earth is show business heading? The tragedy often is that many of the performers, like the trio last night, have a basic talent which they distort in order to win an audience's favor.

The Crickets toured on a package show which was quite different from American rock 'n' roll shows. In England, true variety shows were more common—a rock 'n' roll group might appear with pop singers, jazz bands, comedians, and the like. The arrangement raised rock 'n' roll to the same status level as more established forms of music and entertainment. At the same time, it demanded from rock 'n' roll performers the professional showmanship that the variety show audiences expected. The Crickets had top billing on the tour, and most of those who came to see the show had come to see the Crickets in particular. But since they were the only rock 'n' roll act on the show, the Crickets still had to convey the whole spirit of their music to an audience of mixed ages and interests.

It was a challenge, but the Crickets liked the change from the routine and enjoyed the tour. The tour was not as tiring as American outings, since distances between stops were so much less in England. Even so, the trip was no vacation—the Crickets had no days off during their twenty-five days in Great Britain. Only one feature of the trip really displeased the Texans: the

Allison, Holly, and Mauldin in England, March 1958 (Peer-Southern)

dark, cold wet weather of late winter that greeted them more often than they cared for.

Ironically enough, the triumphant tour ended badly, thanks to some misfiring backstage antics before the group's last appearance.

"Jerry, Buddy, and I were in the dressing room after the first of the two shows that night," remembers Joe Mauldin, "and we were really looking forward to getting back to the States. We had been in England a month, and it was cold, and it seemed like we'd been away from home forever. I had a great big cigar, and I said, 'I'm gonna celebrate, man, I'm gonna smoke this cigar.' Well, it was cold, and all the windows were closed in this small dressing room, and Jerry and Buddy said, 'You're not smoking that cigar in here.' So we started scuffling around a little, and I had the cigar in my mouth, puffing on it and blowing smoke everywhere, and Jerry grabbed my right arm and Buddy grabbed my left arm—they were going to stretch me out and reach up and pull the cigar out of my mouth. I swung around to hit Buddy in the stomach with my head to knock the breath out of him, hopefully, so he'd turn me loose and I could take care of J-I. But when I swung around, Buddy bent down to get the cigar, and instead of hitting him in the stomach, I hit him in the mouth with my head and knocked off two of the caps on his teeth.

Mauldin, Holly, and Allison performing "Maybe Baby" on BBC's Off The Record, *March 1958 (Peer-Southern)*

"Well, you know how it is when you get your teeth knocked out—and Buddy had two big old holes there where he didn't have any teeth. And Buddy said, 'Just bring it to a halt, I'm not performing—I'm not going on again. We'll forfeit the pay or whatever, but we're not going to do the show.' So Norman called us over and soft-talked us, and said this and that. So what Buddy did was, he chewed some gum and then mashed the gum out and smoothed it over his teeth, and I guess from the audience you couldn't tell the difference. I don't know how he sang with a wad of chewing gum up over his lip; but he did it, and we did the complete show. But Buddy was in such a state of mind after this accident had happened that I'm sure the show we put on was hideous. In fact, Norman told us, 'That's the worst show I've ever seen you guys do.'"

The Crickets flew back to the United States on March 25, immediately after this last show. A segment they had taped for the BBC's *Off The Record* TV show was aired two days later, and was a more successful effort than their first TV appearance in Britain had been. The tour had helped to increase the Crickets' record sales there—during one week, Holly and the Crickets had four records ("Peggy Sue," "Oh Boy!," "Maybe Baby," and "Listen To Me") in the British top thirty. And it was probably no coincidence that guitar sales boomed there in the wake of Holly's visit.

When the Crickets arrived back in the United States, they immediately set out on another lengthy tour—this one a six-week show under the aegis of Alan Freed which featured the Crickets, Chuck Berry, Jerry Lee Lewis, Larry Williams, and Frankie Lymon. (This was the tour which led to the famous indictment of Freed on charges of inciting a riot, after violence broke out following the troupe's appearance in Boston on May 3. The charge was dropped a year later.) With such a schedule as the Crickets had been following for the preceding six months, it was fortunate that they had recorded so many tunes in Clovis the year before and at the unusual session in Oklahoma City the preceding fall. These recordings provided the Crickets with their next singles, and with the material for two albums.

"Maybe Baby" was released in the United States in early February and was almost as big a hit for the Crickets as "Oh Boy!" had been. Holly's mother is credited with the original idea for the lyrics of the song. "I had tried to write songs for Buddy before," she says, "but when he'd read them, he'd say, 'Mother, we can't use your songs, they're all too serious—they've got to be more fun.'" However, when Mrs. Holley wrote a couple of lines for "Maybe Baby," Buddy read them and decided to finish the lyrics and write a tune for the song—"But don't put *my* name on it," his mother warned him, and so he didn't. The other Crickets also had a hand in the writing of the tune. In the end, the song had the characteristic ambivalence of many of Holly's songs. The singer has little more than just hope to rely on: *maybe*, baby, you'll be true; and when someday, you do finally want me, I'll be there. But as in "I'm Looking for Someone to Love," the bright melody and happy delivery cast the uncertain lyrics in a new light.

Alan Freed, Larry Williams, disc jockey Ben DeCosta, and Buddy Holly,
April 1958 (From the Buddy Holly Memorial Society Collection)

Both "Maybe Baby" and its flip side, "Tell Me How" (in my opinion, a better record), featured the driving beat and jangling guitar sound of "Oh Boy!" The specific drum beat for "Maybe Baby" was, says Jerry Allison, suggested to the Crickets by Little Richard's "Lucille." The vocal backgrounds copied those on "Oh Boy!" and "That'll Be The Day"; the arrangement on "Tell Me How" is especially well-done, supporting the vocal without ever obscuring the dramatic rendition of the tune.

At the same time as that single was released, another was issued under Holly's own name: 'Listen To me"/"I'm Gonna Love You Too." This release was a commercial failure in the United States; in Britain, it was Holly's only recording before "Early In The Morning" which failed to make the top ten. The timing of the release may have contributed to its lack of success. "Peggy Sue" was still number three on *Billboard*'s Top 100 and "Oh Boy!" was not far behind when the new singles were released. "Listen To Me" was less obviously commercial than "Maybe Baby," and perhaps there was resistance from programmers to the idea of playing four singles by the same group at the same time.

But so much for history. No matter what the sales figures were at the time, "Listen To Me" and "I'm Gonna Love You Too" today rate among Holly's finest songs—"Listen To Me," especially, has endured in popularity.

Like "Words of Love," "Listen To Me" was recorded with some thought to the example of "Love Is Strange"; and like Holly's first solo single, "Listen To Me" made inspired use of overdubbing to create strange, even eerie effects. Throughout the song, the lead guitar sounds hypnotically in the background, as Allison plays a rolling, syncopated rhythm. Holly's double-tracked vocal rises and falls in volume, swaying with its own rhythm, until in the instrumental break, it whispers softly, "Listen...listen...listen to me," followed by the captivating guitar variation running beyond the expected end.

"Listen To Me" provides another example of the mixed atmosphere of Holly's songs. (Though Petty is listed as a co-writer, Allison remarks: "I think 'Listen To Me' was all Buddy's—I think he had that written in Lubbock, before we ever got to hanging around Clovis.") As in "Everyday," there is an ambiguity to the singer's tale, an unsettled character to the love affair. Though the singer proclaims his love absolutely, he must still convince the one he loves by a direct appeal. The tone alternates between faith in the future and pleas for what is still just a possibility—between what will be and what can be:

Listen to me,
Hear what I say,
Our hearts can be,
Nearer each day,
Hold me, darling—
Listen closely to me.

Your eyes will see
What love can do,
Reveal to me
Your love so true,
Hold me, darling—
Listen closely to me.

I've told the stars
You're my only love,
I want to love you tenderly.
Those same bright stars
In heaven above
Know now how sweet,
Sweethearts can be.

Listen to me,
Hear what I say
Our hearts can be
Nearer each day,
Hold me, darling—
Listen closely to me.[2]

As always, the lyrics cannot be separated from the musical setting. It is Holly's vocal, especially, that breathes life into the words, varying and molding the tone of the lyrics, and lending them a tense, urgent emotion.

Holly's vocal on "I'm Gonna Love You Too" is even more graphic, with key words emphasized in unexpected ways—for example, the word "heart" is sighed more than sung. Throughout the song, Holly's vocal habits add to the impact of the lyrics. Although he is singing, he is able to produce the controlled variations in mood, tone, and attitude that color everyday speech. His techniques cannot be better explained in print; they must instead be heard to be appreciated.

As with "Maybe Baby," all the good humor in "I'm Gonna Love You Too" is spent on a song whose lyrics describe a troublesome situation. Since quite a few of Holly's songs follow this pattern, some might argue that the lyrics "don't mean anything"—or else, how could they be sung in this manner? But the situation is not so paradoxical as it seems. It is precisely this characteristic which makes such songs so appealing (and their lyrics so hard to discuss, isolated from the music and Holly's individual performance). Holly's fans, confused by their own hopes and doubts, could find consolation and encouragement in his songs. In his role as a singer, Holly rarely speaks as an outsider merely offering advice to the listener. Instead, he is himself confronted with the problem—hence, it is not so easy for him to provide an answer or retain an optimistic attitude. When he does remain cheerful, and illogically hopeful, in the face of unpleasant reality, he offers a hopeful example to others. If the songs were instead totally cheerful, they would have less impact—because those listeners who needed the encouragement most would be unable to identify with the singer in the first place. Even when Holly cannot see the way out himself, as in such songs as "What To Do" and "Learning the Game," he at least offers the consolation of tragedy: he provides the listener with a friend who has shared his experience and can express it in a general but quite realistic fashion. Holly's songs are uplifting—but not necessarily because they deal with happy situations. So it is with "I'm Gonna Love You Too":

> You're gonna say you've missed me,
> You're gonna say you'll kiss me,
> Yes, you're gonna say you'll love me,
> 'Cause I'm gonna love you too.
>
> I don't care what you told me,
> You're gonna say you'll hold me,
> Yes, you're gonna say you'll love me,
> 'Cause I'm gonna love you too.
>
>> After all, another fella took you,
>> But I still can't overlook you,
>> I'm a-gonna do my best to hook you,
>> After all is said and done,

It's a-gonna happen, someday,
You're gonna see things my way,
Yes, you're gonna say you'll love me,
'Cause I'm a-gonna love you too.

You're gonna tell me sweet things,
You're gonna make my heart sing,
Yes, you're gonna hear those bells ring,
'Cause I'm gonna love you too.

(Repeat chorus)

You're gonna say you've missed me,
You're gonna say you'll kiss me,
Yes, you're gonna say you'll love me,
'Cause I'm a-gonna love you too.[3]

The Crickets' Brunswick album, *The Chirping Crickets*, was released in November 1957 in America, and three months later in Britain and Australia, including tunes which had appeared on the Crickets' first two singles— "That'll Be The Day," "I'm Looking for Someone to Love," "Oh Boy!," and "Not Fade Away"—as well as "Maybe Baby" and "Tell Me How," which appeared on this album and on an EP before being released as the Crickets' third single. The album added three songs cut the previous spring in Clovis ("Last Night," "Send Me Some Lovin'," and "It's Too Late") and three songs which, with "Maybe Baby," had been recorded in Oklahoma City ("An Empty Cup," "You've Got Love," and "Rock Me My Baby").

These last six cuts are generally inferior to other Crickets recordings, mainly because of the overdubbed vocals. The vocal backgrounds are too straight—too "pop"—and sometimes clash with the Crickets' actual performance. The vocal blend of recordings like "That'll Be The Day" or, later on, "Think It Over" is lacking on these six songs. Since the dubbing was probably done in early October, when Holly was still on the long GAC tour, it's unlikely that he was present when the vocals were added. It's a pretty safe guess that the songs would have sounded a bit different had he had a role in the vocal arrangements.

Two of these six songs were rock 'n' roll ballads made famous by other artists: Chuck Willis's "It's Too Late" and Little Richard's "Send Me Some Lovin'." These songs were favorites of Larry Holley's, and Buddy recorded them at his brother's suggestion. Holly himself was a fan of both Willis and Little Richard; Buddy frequently performed such Little Richard tunes as "Rip It Up" and "The Girl Can't Help It" in his own live performances. Excluding the background, "It's Too Late" is an excellent recording; "Send Me Some Lovin'" is slightly less successful, since Holly simply didn't have a voice like Little Richard's. The Crickets' version is slower than the original,

---

[3]"I'm Gonna Love You Too," words and music—Joe Mauldin, Niki Sullivan, and Norman Petty. Copyright © 1957 and 1958 by MPL Communications, Inc. International Copyright Secured. ALL RIGHTS RESERVED; used by permission.

which makes the vocal seem thinner from the start. Also, Holly's vocal is underamplified at just those points where Little Richard's comes on the strongest. A comparison of the two records does reveal, though, just how near Holly tried to come to Little Richard's vocal—and how closely he had studied the original version of the song and Little Richard's vocal idiosyncrasies on that recording. Jerry Coleman, then a disc jockey on Lubbock's KSEL, remembers that Buddy used to come over to the station, pick out records by Little Richard, Fats Domino, Ray Charles, and others, and listen to them in an unused studio with the speakers turned way up. Apparently, he was studying, as well as enjoying the records.

"Last Night," a straight rock 'n' roll ballad, had been cut without background vocals in March 1957 as a demo when the Crickets were trying to get a record contract with Roulette. Holly sings the lyrics in believable fashion, but once again, the dubbed background is jarringly artificial. Two of the songs on the album were co-written by Roy Orbison and Norman Petty. "An Empty Cup" is too maudlin—just the sort of cardboard tragedy that Holly avoided in the songs he wrote himself. Still, between his vocal and his guitar playing he might have saved the song, had not the added vocals pushed it determinedly over the edge. "You've Got Love," recorded as well by its third co-writer, Johnny "Peanuts" Wilson, is a better song; Holly has more fun with it vocally, and offers a guitar break along the lines of those in "Oh Boy!" and "Maybe Baby."

The last of the cuts on the album is "Rock Me My Baby," a novelty tune by songwriters Shorty Long and Susan Heather based on, of all things, "Hickory Dickory Dock." Allison provides a syncopated Latin rhythm to accent the Crickets' typically strong beat. Holly's guitar solo is varied, skillful, and pleasing, and is generally considered one of his finest. For once, the background vocals stay in the background.

Of course, the best cuts on the album are the other six—the ones which also appeared as singles. Most rock 'n' roll albums at the time consisted of eleven filler tunes wrapped around one hit single—the title of which was prominently displayed on the album cover. But that was one more pattern Holly didn't fit. The popularity of his early albums long after his death and the continued demand for packages of his "greatest hits," many of which were never released as singles in his lifetime, reflect the overall quality of his work and not just the success of a few songs.

Holly's solo Coral album, titled simply *Buddy Holly*, appeared in March 1958. It included the "A" and "B" sides of his three solo singles already mentioned, plus six songs not previously released.

Three of the songs on the album had been first recorded by important rock 'n' roll artists. "You're So Square" was performed by Elvis Presley in the movie "Jailhouse Rock"; it was written by Jerry Leiber and Mike Stoller, the team responsible for so many of the Coasters' biggest hits. The attraction of Holly's version lies in the interplay between Holly's rapidly strummed lead guitar and Allison's irregular drum patterns. "Valley of Tears," written and recorded by Fats Domino, is another tune which Holly recorded at the suggestion of his older brother. It has a much cleaner sound than the Domino recording, with Holly's vocal and Petty's organ playing unencumbered by other voices or a lush arrangement. "Ready Teddy," one of Little Richard's greatest rockers, was a tune which the Crickets were fond of performing themselves. On Holly's recording, the beat is modified—from the New Orleans beat of Little Richard's records to the Texas rockabilly sound of Holly's—and the instrumentation is changed, reflecting the use of guitar rather than saxophone on rockabilly recordings; but despite the differences, the versions are comparable in excitement.

Holly was a co-writer of two other songs on the album: "Look At Me," written with Allison and Petty, and "Little Baby," written with Petty and a pianist named C. W. Kendall, Jr., who had come to Clovis to make some recordings with another rock 'n' roll group. The former tune has a sweet and playful air to it, with the lyrics and Holly's voice patterns mixing quiet pleading and audacious confidence. Vi Petty played piano on the cut. "Little Baby," at heart a blues, is dominated by Kendall's heavy rhythmic piano playing and Holly's expressive country-blues vocal.

The one other cut on the album was chosen for Holly's next single, released in late April. To many people, "Rave On" is the most exciting recording the Crickets ever made; the title has become a byword for Holly's frenetic style. Inexplicably, the single was just a minor success in the United States, where it only reached number 39 on *Billboard*'s Top 100 (though it was a top ten record in scattered regional markets). In Britain, by contrast, the disc made the top five on the national charts.

A joyful and driving performance, "Rave On" epitomizes the good feeling of rock 'n' roll. As if to prove this, one "good music" station, in a specially prepared LP attacking rock 'n' roll, chose "Rave On" as one of its "examples" and called it "mood music for stealing hubcaps." The song offers the most perfect introduction to Holly's vocal gimmickry—for who else but Buddy Holly could make a rising six-syllable word out of "well," as he does at the very opening of the song?

The song was written by Sonny West and Bill Tilghman, the same team which had composed "Oh Boy!" Tilghman remembers getting the idea for the song after hearing the expression "rave on!" in another record (probably, Carl Perkins's "Dixie Fried"). "We were driving up and down the street in my home town, Sonny and I," says Tilghman, "and we grabbed onto that title and said, 'Let's do something with it.' First we wrote it as a domestic problem, a disagreement between two people, but Norman turned it down—he told us to bring it back, he wanted us to write a love song out of it. So we worked on it a couple of weeks, to the way it is now, and took it back over." West recorded the song himself at Petty's studio, and the record resulted in a contract for West with Atlantic Records, which released "Rave On" in February 1958; West's version, which never made the charts, had been out for two months when Holly's rendition of the tune was released in mid-April on a single (the album, of course, was out earlier).

Holly's version of "Rave On" was recorded at the Bell Sound Studios in

New York City, probably in mid-January, just before the group left for the week-long Australian tour. Mauldin remembers that the reason given for making the record in New York was the need for one more song to complete the *Buddy Holly* album and the lack of time to return to New Mexico, because of the tight tour schedule; but Bob Thiele says that the New York session came about at his own prodding, and that he in fact produced the record.

"I suggested to Buddy that he record in New York," says Thiele. "I wanted to inject my own ideas, or talent—that was my job. I had pushed for a few months on this. Buddy was for it, Norman was against it. There was some tension at the session, because of Petty's feelings—he was always afraid that he'd blow his hold on Holly. To be honest, though, I think Buddy was more comfortable at Clovis. I don't think any of us really felt this was a great or successful move, to record in New York."

One other song was recorded at the Bell Studios session: "That's My Desire," the 1947 Frankie Laine hit. Holly's recording of this tune was never released in America (years later it was released in Britain). Holly himself would not have wanted the song issued. "We weren't happy with that song," says Jerry Allison. "I mean, we didn't consider it a record. We sort of said, 'O.K., we'll try that later.'"

The flip side of "Rave On," "Take Your Time," follows the same chordal pattern as "Look At Me" and features Norman Petty on organ. Holly's vocal, his strummed acoustic guitar, Allison's varied effects, and Petty's more conventional organ playing provide rhythms that mix and clash to create unexpected patterns. "Take Your Time" was one tune on which Holly, Allison, and Petty did actually collaborate. "We wrote it in the back of Norman's studio," says Allison. "I know Norman had a hand in it, because I remember Buddy not liking the line Norman came up with about 'Heartstrings will sing like a string of twine.'" The lyrics have the patience and confidence in love found in "Everyday," and, in the refrain, mix humor and seriousness:

> Take your time,
> I can wait,
> For all of the love
> I know will be mine,
> If you take your time.
>
> Take your time,
> Though it's late,
> Heartstrings will sing
> Like a string of twine,
> If you take your time.
>
> > Take your time,
> > And take mine, too—
> > I have time to spend;
> > Take your time,

Go with me through
Times till all times end.

Take your time,
I can wait,
For all of the love
I know will be mine,
If you take your time.[4]

The *Buddy Holly* album and the succeeding single showed that Holly was not committed to a guitar sound on all his releases; Petty, his wife, and Kendall played organ or piano on several of these recordings. The use of organ, though, was not Holly's idea, but Petty's. Jerry Allison states, "Buddy didn't like organ at all, on anything. I never heard him say he liked it, and I always heard him say he didn't like it. Sometimes he'd argue about it; sometimes he'd just save the hassle and let it ride." And Petty himself says, "Buddy was very set in his ways as far as having some of his ideas, and we would argue about ideas sometimes. I think that there was one thing that Buddy didn't particularly agree with me on—we used Hammond organ on 'Take Your Time,' sort of against his better judgment, because he felt that organ was to be reserved for church or something or other at the time, but he conceded in the end."[5]

Piano was used on both sides of the Crickets' fourth single, issued in May 1958, one year to the day after the release of "That'll Be The Day." "Think It Over" and "Fool's Paradise" were probably recorded during the Crickets' visit home after the Australian tour. "Think It Over" features one of the better-integrated vocal arrangements among the Crickets' records, the background voices functioning here as both answering chorus and imitation instruments—horns, perhaps. The piano is the lead instrument in the break, but instead of standing out as prominently as on some of the recordings on the *Buddy Holly* album, it is blended with the sounds provided by Allison and Holly. The happy, blues-derived melody is matched with words showing the brand of humor that characterized the songs on which Holly and Allison collaborated. Not that the songs were deliberately modeled on any pattern; their style and tone simply reflected Holly's and Allison's own personalities. Jerry comments: "I never did set and think about it; but a lot of Buddy's songs had a certain attitude—like, 'That'll be the day when *you* say goodbye,' sort of 'I don't need you.' Or 'Think It Over'—you know, 'think it over in your pretty little head—are you sure I'm not the one?' That was his attitude about everything. Because he was really a self-confident, smart-aleck sort of guy, you know. He'd say anything he wanted to—he wasn't ever trying to be really nice to people, he'd just say what he thought. And the same way with chicks—like on the road, a chick would say something like, 'Why do you

[4]"Take Your Time," words and music—Buddy Holly and Norman Petty. Copyright © 1958 by MPL Communications, Inc. International Copyright Secured. ALL RIGHTS RESERVED; used by permission.
[5]Rob Finnis, "Rock's First Singer-Songwriter?", *Let It Rock*, February 1973, p. 31.

Holly, Allison, and Mauldin, 1958 (John Beecher)

wear those big glasses?' or whatever, and he'd say, 'Hey, forget you, you get out of here,' and he'd chase the chick off in a minute."

The swinging rhythm of "Think It Over" was close to that of "That'll Be The Day," even though the Crickets' two intervening singles had successfully featured a steadier, driving beat. The more conservative practice in popular music has been to follow a hit record with a near-copy, hoping for similar success with the second record. The Crickets, though, were never so regimented. "When we were making those records," says Allison, "Buddy was never on a trip about 'What's going to be commercial now?' or 'What will everybody like?' We just played what we could play. I remember on

Norman Petty, Bob Thiele, and Buddy Holly with the gold record for "Peggy Sue," 1958 (From the Buddy Holly Memorial Society Collection)

'Think It Over'—we had used that 'straight eight' beat on several songs, and we started to record 'Think It Over' the same way; and then we thought, 'Hey, that might sound better more like "That'll Be The Day."' The other sound was what was happening, but we thought the song was more fun to play with a swing beat. So we cut it like that. We just did what we wanted to do."

The choice of which songs were to be released as singles was actually the responsibility of the A&R director; in practice, Thiele conferred with Murray Deutch about it, and the preferences of Holly and Petty had a strong influence. "I would talk to Buddy on the phone," says Deutch, "and find out which ones he liked. There were no fights about it." Holly and Allison's disregard for the practice of following a commercial success with a close imitation was, fortunately, shared by Thiele, whose lifelong devotion to the recording of jazz makes him an anomaly in the pop music business. His words, in fact, mirror those of Allison. Thiele says, "This is how I've always operated. I sign artists I like and issue records I like, based on my own personal preference. I've never believed in surveys—I've never tried to be 'commercial.' I just do what I feel like doing."

Besides recording with the Crickets, Holly branched out in other directions during this first year of success. In June 1958, he cut "Early In The Morning"/"Now We're One," the first of Holly's Coral recordings which did not include the Crickets in the instrumental accompaniment. Both tunes had been written by Bobby Darin; Holly's versions were cut in the wake of some complicated maneuvering involving Darin's record contract.

At the time, Darin was under contract to Atco. His contract had only a few weeks left to run before Atco would have to exercise its annual option or release him. Since he had had no hits on the label, he expected that he would be released. He therefore cut the two tunes for Brunswick, in order to have a record ready to sell on a new label when his old contract expired. (The record was produced by Dick Jacobs, who had been music director for Coral under Thiele but had succeeded Thiele as A&R director when Thiele left to go to work for Dot Records in March 1958.) Brunswick prepared to release the single under the group title of the Ding Dongs. Then, the unexpected happened. Atco decided to release one more single by Darin to see if he was worth keeping under contract. They chose "Splish Splash"—which promptly zoomed to the top of the charts, became a million-seller, and made Darin a star. Atco renewed Darin's contract, and when they found out who the lead singer of the Ding Dongs was, they forced Brunswick to pull back its record.

Petty and Holly were in New York at the time. When Petty heard of Brunswick's problem, he suggested that Holly record the two Darin songs for Coral. When asked, Holly quickly agreed to cut the tunes. The session, produced by Dick Jacobs, was held within forty-eight hours, and the record was pressed and released as quickly as possible. Meanwhile, Atco released Darin's recording, labelling his group as "The Rinky Dinks." The two competing singles both made the charts, with Darin's version selling just a bit better in the United States, while Holly's recording, as usual, did well overseas.

On Holly's version of "Early In The Morning," Jacobs followed the exact same arrangement he had used in cutting Darin's original recording. Holly was accompanied by the Helen Way Singers, a black gospel chorus, and by the noted saxophonist Sam "The Man" Taylor and drummer Panama Francis. "Early In The Morning" proved convincingly that Holly could be just as believable singing songs written by others—he was a stylist, as well as a creator of his own material. And he made it all seem very easy. According to Jacobs, Holly listened to the song a couple of times and quickly cut three takes—any one of which would have been suitable for release. The flip side, "Now We're One," is best forgotten. The vocal arrangement is sickeningly sweet, and the lyrics are simply awful; Holly does the best he can with it.

"Early In The Morning" was certainly one of Holly's favorites among his own recordings. He had for a long time admired the mixed gospel-and-rhythm & blues sound promoted on the Atlantic label, and this was his first chance to cut such a record himself. Though his own wild vocal and Taylor's fine saxophone break really made the record, Holly was especially happy over the chance to use an Atlantic-type vocal accompaniment. "He really thought that was an excellent record," Allison recalls. "He liked having the black chorus singing on it. When I heard the record, I thought at the time, 'This is the best record so far.' My feelings weren't hurt by not playing on it—after all, I wasn't even in New York when he cut it."

Around this same time, Holly moved in another new direction and made his first attempt to write songs intended for artists other than himself. Holly had toured with the Everly Brothers on the Feld show in the fall of 1957 and on several later tours, and had become close friends with them. During a visit home in the early summer of 1958, he got together with his old friend Bob Montgomery and wrote "Love's Made A Fool Of You" and "Wishing," hoping to have the Everly Brothers record the songs on a single.

Instead of making a simple, unaccompanied home tape of the tunes to play for the Everlys and their manager, Holly went into Petty's studio and recorded the songs with a full band—providing not just his own versions of the songs, but also his conception of how the Everly Brothers might sound singing them. He then brought the tunes to Nashville and played them for Wesley Rose, the Everlys' manager. Supposedly, Rose told Holly that the Everlys would be crazy to record the songs, since Holly's own recordings, if released, would top any other version. Actually, Rose's response was probably based on other considerations. Besides being the Everlys' manager, he was the head of Acuff-Rose Publishing, for whom Boudleaux and Felice Bryant were then writing their songs. Since the Bryants had written the Everly Brothers' first hits, "Bye Bye Love" and "Wake Up Little Susie," Rose was not in the market for songs by other writers, especially those not writing for Acuff-Rose. (Holly didn't follow a reciprocal course, though; a few months later, he recorded the Bryants' "Raining In My Heart.") Fortunately,

Holly's tapes were preserved and were released on record several years later.

On his demos of the two songs, Holly asked another guitarist to play lead, the first time he had done so since the formation of the Crickets. Tommy Allsup, a native of Tulsa, had come to Clovis a few months before to back up a group on a session, and had been invited by Petty to stay on permanently as a studio musician. Allsup's career had centered on western swing and country music; he had spent several years playing lead guitar in the band headed by Johnnie Lee Wills, Bob Wills's brother. Holly met Allsup at Petty's studio, watched and listened to him play, and soon asked Tommy to tour with him. Once again, the Crickets were a quartet—at least on stage, since Allsup was not mentioned on records or in publicity. Buddy and Tommy alternated playing lead in live shows, depending on the song, while on recordings, Allsup played lead and Holly rhythm on the rest of the Crickets' recordings. Obviously, Buddy didn't feel that he was losing face by sharing the limelight with another. Joe Mauldin explains: "Buddy was a star and he knew it, and he didn't mind anybody else sharing the stardom with him. He loved the way Tommy played; he thought he was a fantastic guitar player. Tommy knew a lot about music, too. And he was a very likeable, enjoyable person. It was just one of those things, where you meet somebody and you really hit it off—it seemed like we all hit it off good with Tommy."

Since "Love's Made A Fool Of You" and "Wishing" were just meant to be demos, Holly also used Petty's other studio musicians on the session; neither Allison nor Mauldin played on these recordings. The drummer was Bo Clarke, who had come to Clovis with the Roses, Petty's studio vocal group at the time. (Clarke also played on the "Ivan" recordings, since Allison was busy with the vocal.) The bass player was George Atwood, a professional musician about twelve years Buddy's senior, and a veteran of several jazz groups, including the Gene Krupa band. In the wake of Holly's success, Petty's studio was attracting enough business from hopeful area musicians to warrant a full-time studio band, and Atwood and Allsup helped fill the need.

Holly's version of "Love's Made A Fool Of You" is memorable for its emphatic Latin-flavored rhythm, folkish sound, and striking lead guitar line. The song is masterfully constructed; Holly's vocal, Clarke's accented rhythms, Allsup's picking and Holly's own evenly-paced rhythm guitar are mixed with perfect timing. The lyrics, with their bemused acceptance of love's pitfalls, are equally memorable:

> Love can make a fool of you,
> You do anything that it wants you to.
>
> Love can make you feel so good,
> When it goes like you think it should,
> Or it can make you cry at night,
> When your baby don't treat you right,
>
> When you're feeling sad and blue,
> You know love's made a fool of you.

You know love makes fools of men,
But you don't care, you're gonna try it again.

Time goes by, it's a-passing fast,
You think true love has come at last,
But by and by, you're gonna find,
Crazy love has made you blind,

When you're feeling sad and blue,
You know love's made a fool of you.[6]

"Wishing" isn't as strong as "Love's Made A Fool Of You," but it too is well-constructed. It features fine guitar work by Allsup, both in the instrumental break and in the background during the vocal refrain, where his guitar playing is along the lines of country fiddle music.

By the summer of 1958, Holly had achieved the stature of an established artist—a star, and not just a one-record sensation. Even he, with his

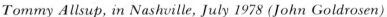

Tommy Allsup, in Nashville, July 1978 (John Goldrosen)

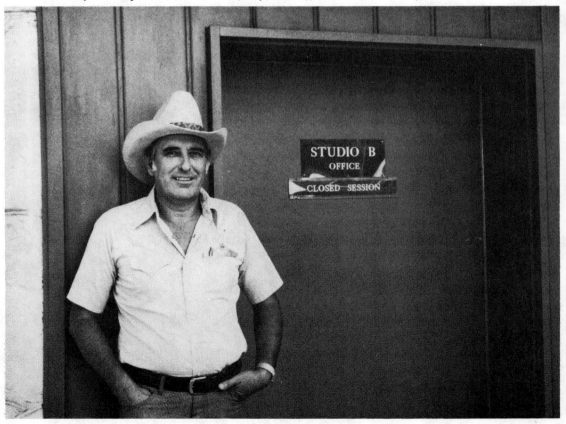

determination to "make it," might never have dreamed of the scale of success he and the Crickets had enjoyed over the previous year. Everyone wanted to "make it," but no one knew just what that meant.

Well, not quite—everyone knew it meant money. And for poor boys in Lubbock, Memphis, or elsewhere, just escaping poverty was the best reward the music world could offer. Actually, Holly, Allison, and Mauldin hadn't yet seen too much of the money; most of what was coming to them was delayed on record company books or in a bank account under the watchful eye of Norman Petty. But there was enough for a few long-desired items. For instance, there was the time the Crickets were returning from a tour by plane; they got off a flight at Dallas and instead of boarding another plane for the last leg to Lubbock, they decided to go out and buy motorcycles and ride them home.

"We had always dreamed of having motorcycles," remembers Allison. "In fact, Buddy had had a Triumph before, because we went and saw *The Wild*

Mauldin, Allison, and Holly buying their Triumph motorcycles in Dallas, 1958 (Jerry Allison)

Ones with Marlon Brando in it, and no time after that Buddy somehow had a motorcycle. Anyway, Buddy was carrying all kinds of cash from the tour we had been on—like, about five thousand dollars. We went first to a Harley Davidson store, but the guy there wouldn't even discuss it with us—we'd say, 'How much is that?' and he'd say, 'Aw, it's too much for you guys.' He was really hateful. So we finally just went out and got a cab and we went to a Triumph place, and the guy there was really nice. Like, we were gonna buy three motorcycles that day, regardless of what happened, but we didn't tell him that. But he said, 'Any one you like the looks of, just get on and ride it around.' He was really a good dude. So Buddy bought an Ariel Cyclone (650 cc.), Joe bought a Triumph Thunderbird, and I bought a Trophy model. And it was a cash deal. Sure was fun." After Buddy's death, his parents kept his bike for a decade before selling it to a Lubbock youth; over the years, they had received many offers for the motorcycle from rock 'n' roll and bike fans around the world. (The bike is now owned by a Holly fan in Austin.)

Automobiles were also of interest to Buddy. When the money began to come in, in the fall of 1957, he bought a Chevrolet Impala for his parents—though when he was home, he used it more often than they did. In 1958, he was able to buy a better car; at the suggestion of his father, he bought a pale blue Lincoln. Within a few weeks, Buddy had become dissatisfied with the car. There were some mechanical problems, and—well, he just didn't like the car, and he didn't feel like putting up with it. So he traded it in (at a twelve-hundred-dollar loss) for a taupe Cadillac Fleetwood. "Buddy always said he'd have himself a Cadillac by the time he was twenty-one," recalls Bob Montgomery. "So he did."

So the Crickets and Buddy Holly had made it to the top—but now the problem was how to stay there. Holly had learned a lot about the entertainment world in the previous year—about recording techniques, stage presentation, and the business aspects to the life of a rock 'n' roll star. He was now beginning to think more actively and creatively about the opportunities open to him and the means of staying in the popular limelight by keeping ahead of the market.

The year had brought other changes, too. When the summer of 1958 rolled around, Buddy was about to be married.

*Buddy and Maria Elena on their wedding day, August 15, 1958
(Jerry Allison)*

6. New Ties Made, Old Ties Broken

Maria Elena Santiago was born in Puerto Rico. When Maria was eight, her mother died, and Maria was sent by her father to New York City to live with her aunt Provi, the head of Peer-Southern Music's important Latin American music division. Despite the family tie, Maria worked at other jobs in New York before joining Peer-Southern Music as a receptionist. The Crickets remember that she was there when they first came to New York in 1957, but Maria doesn't recall having any real contact with Holly until June 1958. She tells the story of their engagement in this way: "One morning the Crickets came into the office to see Murray Deutch. He was tied up just then, so they sat in the outer office to wait. I had never met them before; at least, I don't think I had seen them, and I know I had never been introduced to them. They were joking around, imitating a Spanish accent and changing English words so they'd sound Spanish, and they introduced each other to me that way.

"When Deutch was free, they went in to see him; and when they came out, Buddy asked me when I'd be free for lunch. Well, when you're a receptionist, you're supposed to greet people and be pleasant to them, and not take everything they say too seriously. So I told him I wouldn't be free for a couple of hours. 'O.K.,' he said, 'We'll be waiting for you.' And I thought that was just part of their joking around.

"At lunchtime, Jo Harper, who was in charge of Nor Va Jak business at Peer-Southern, asked me where I was going to eat. I told her I was just going to go downstairs, and she said, 'No, come out with me—let's go over to the Howard Johnson's.' 'Why there?' I asked. And Jo said, 'I've got to bring some papers over to Norman Petty, and he's waiting for me there.'

"So I said O.K. When we went, Norman was there all right, but that wasn't why Jo had insisted on eating there. You see, the Crickets were there too— Buddy had called Jo Harper and set the whole thing up, telling her to get me down there somehow.

"There were two empty seats, and the Crickets were arguing about where I was going to sit. I wound up next to Buddy, on his right. The others were fooling around, playing footsie and grabbing for my hands, while Norman was looking under the table, trying to figure out what was going on. Finally, Buddy grabbed my hand and said, 'O.K. you guys, just cut it out, because I've

143

got her now.' 'But I'll need two hands to eat with,' I said, and he replied, 'Oh, that's all right, I'll help feed you.' And a little while later he said, 'You see this girl? I'm going to marry her. And I'm going to get her to agree in the next two days, before we leave New York.'

"When he took me back to the office, he asked me to go out with him that night—the Crickets were going to record a jingle, and we could go out alone afterwards. Well, I wanted to—I really liked him, I knew that already—but I couldn't say 'yes' right then, because I had to get my aunt's permission first. Being Spanish, my aunt was very strict. I never went anywhere without her approval. I hadn't even dated anyone before Buddy. So I told Buddy to call me back later in the afternoon, because I'd have to ask my aunt first.

"When I asked my aunt if I could go out with Buddy, she said no. The last people she wanted me to be around were entertainers. She thought they were—you know, unreliable and immoral and all that. So when I told her who had asked me out and just who he was, and she heard words like 'singer' and 'musician,' she was dead set against it. I said, ask Jo Harper, ask Murray Deutch, ask Mr. Peer—the president of Peer-Southern—they'll tell you he's all right. But she wouldn't agree. When Buddy called back in the middle of the afternoon, I had to tell him that I was still working on my aunt and I didn't know yet if I could go. So he said that if I could make it, I should meet him at his hotel before 6:30.

"It was after 5:30 when I finally convinced my aunt that it was all right. There wasn't time for me to go home and change. So I went to a store right next to our office building and bought some new clothes on the spot, and changed back in the office where we had a shower. And I hopped in a taxi and headed for Buddy's hotel. The Crickets' limousine had just pulled away as my taxi arrived—but Buddy happened to look back down the street and saw me get out, and he had the limousine circle back to pick me up.

"After the recording session, we went out to eat at P. J. Clarke's. And that was where he proposed to me. I didn't take him seriously at first—I thought he was joking. And he got really upset with me and said, 'No, listen to me—I really mean it.' And so I said yes.

"I guess it sounds crazy, that he should propose and I should accept, the very day we met. But that's really what happened—we just each felt that way, that quickly. The next day I told him, 'Why don't you think about it for a while?' I was sure, but I wanted him to be sure too—everything had happened so fast. But he said, 'I don't have to think it over—I know I want to marry you.' ''

Buddy now had to face the task of telling his family about his bride-to-be. He knew there would be problems with that, if only because of the suddenness of the decision. Besides that, his parents might oppose the marriage on the basis of religious doctrine—racial and (especially) religious intermarriage was opposed by many of the Holleys' fundamentalist Baptist brethren for reasons that mixed prejudice and principle. Unsure about approaching his parents directly, Buddy first called his brother Larry; Larry was not opposed, once convinced that Buddy was really sure about his choice.

Buddy then told his parents, inviting them to come to New York to meet Maria Elena. In the end, Mr. Holley wholeheartedly approved the marriage; he and Maria became very close, treating each other as father and daughter. Mrs. Holley was less happy. The racial-religious question was an issue; but one suspects that, having been so close to Buddy when he was younger, Mrs. Holley would not really have welcomed anyone he chose to marry. The change that had come when Buddy left home to tour with the Crickets was now to be finalized, and it must have been hard to accept. In any case, there was a coolness there and Buddy was aware of it, though he did not make an issue of it if he did not have to. Buddy and Maria had decided to be married once the next round of touring was out of the way. In August, Buddy came home for a visit and told his mother, "My girl's going to come down here and visit about a week. And then we're going to get married." Before Mrs. Holley could say much more than "Oh, no," Buddy stated firmly, "Now, Mother, you might as well not say anything, because I've made up my mind, and I'm going to marry her."

Buddy and Maria decided not to publicize their marriage. (Not until Holly's death did the marriage become general knowledge.) The tenor of the times may have influenced their decision; by keeping the marriage unpublicized, they avoided the possibility of an ugly controversy over a "mixed marriage." It was an era when editors, ministers, and psychologists were alert to any "proof" of rock 'n' roll's bad influence upon public moral

Honeymooning in Acapulco, August 1958: Maria Elena, Buddy, Jerry, and Peggy Sue (Maria Elena Diaz)

standards. Just before Holly's marriage, Jerry Lee Lewis's successful career had been brought to an abrupt halt by the uproar over his marriage to a fourteen-year-old distant cousin—a marriage that was not extraordinary by the standards of the rural South. Under the circumstances, it seemed wise for a rock 'n' roll singer to keep his private life private. Anyway, it was commonly assumed that marriage would lessen a rock 'n' roll performer's popularity. Whatever the influence of these considerations, Buddy and Maria had simply decided that they wanted to keep the news to themselves for a while. However, the marriage was not secret—it just wasn't publicized. "When we travelled on tour," says Maria, "I was supposed to be the Crickets' 'secretary.' But everybody on the tour knew we were married, and Buddy always introduced me to everyone as his wife. So it isn't true to say that our marriage was secret. We just didn't feel like broadcasting the news, not for a little while anyway."

On August 15, Holly's pastor, Ben Johnson, married Buddy and Maria in a simple private ceremony in the Holleys' house attended by Buddy's close friends. When the ceremony was over, Jerry Allison slipped into the next room where the phonograph was and put on the flip side of Buddy's latest single—"Now We're One." Then, it was off to Acapulco for a week's honeymoon—a trip which Buddy and Maria made in the company of fellow newlyweds Jerry and Peggy Sue Allison, who had married a few weeks before but had decided to wait for their honeymoon until the time of Buddy and Maria's wedding.

The fall of 1957 had been completely taken up by the eighty-day tour with the Show of Stars. This year, there were shorter tours and more breaks in the schedule, with more time off for visiting friends in Lubbock and thinking about the future.

In early 1958, radio station KLLL in Lubbock had been acquired by three brothers, Larry, Sky and Ray "Slim" Corbin, and reorganized as an all-country station. Hipockets Duncan had returned from Amarillo to join the Corbins, and Waylon Jennings, a young disc jockey from Littlefield (forty miles up the road to Clovis), had also been added to complete the staff.

Whenever Buddy was home, he would drop in at KLLL and visit with his friends there. Hipockets was an old friend, and Buddy had known the Corbins for a few years as well. Buddy had first met Waylon Jennings at the time of the KDAV Sunday Party shows; Jennings would drive down to attend them, though he apparently did not himself perform then. In the unused rooms at the KLLL studios, Holly and whichever DJ's were not on the air would talk about Buddy's latest tour, or the happenings in Lubbock, or the music scene there or nationwide. And, naturally enough, they would play music—as often old country or bluegrass tunes, as the songs Buddy had himself recorded. On one occasion, Holly taped some promos for the station, strumming his guitar and singing new lyrics to the tunes of his most popular songs, such as "Peggy Sue":

If you knew, what I'd do,
You'd tune our way the whole day through,
To music,
K-Triple-L-uh-L,
Well, it's "Country Clout,"
On K-L-Double-L.

As Holly's associations with KDAV and KLLL indicate, artists like Holly, Presley, Jerry Lee Lewis, and the Everly Brothers were always thought of as country artists in the west Texas area, and their records were played as heavily on the country stations as on pop stations. There's a common assumption that the arrival of rock 'n' roll caused a "depression" in the country music field in the late fifties—but some country DJ's in Holly's home area disagree. KDAV owner Dave Stone remembers, "We thought of rockabilly as just being another kind of country music, so we always played it. And I know *I* did well in the fifties—I bought some other stations in this area, and the size of their audiences kept going up during those years. It seems to me like our decline came in the early sixties, when there weren't so many country musicians involved in rock 'n' roll." Tommy Allsup remembers frequently seeing Holly's records, and those of similar artists, on jukeboxes in country & western nightclubs. Perhaps rock 'n' roll's appeal to adult country music fans has been underestimated.

Hipockets Duncan was still promoting concerts and helping rising young artists. Now, his eye was on Waylon Jennings who, besides working as a DJ, was also performing around the Lubbock area. Duncan pointed out to Buddy that Waylon had potential; Buddy agreed, and set out to launch Waylon's career.

What he did was to arrange for Waylon's first record. It grew out of a session Holly had already set up for himself with King Curtis, the famed rhythm & blues saxophonist featured on the Coasters' records. Holly had become friends with Curtis when the two had appeared on an Alan Freed Paramount show a year earlier. Now, the pair decided to cut a record with Curtis accompanying Holly. (They also planned to record some instrumentals together later on, but this was just one more project left unfulfilled at Holly's death.) Holly paid Curtis's expenses to fly down from New York to Clovis for a session. Buddy decided to record a single with Waylon at the same time; Holly paid the expenses of Waylon's session, produced it himself, and played rhythm guitar on the recordings. Studio musicians George Atwood and Bo Clarke played on the cuts made with Jennings, while Allison and Mauldin backed Holly on the songs he himself recorded.

The song which Jennings and Holly chose for Waylon's first single was the Cajun classic, "Jole Blon." (The flip side was a country tune written by two local songwriters, "When Sin Stops.") The song had come to be a popular country dance tune, and maybe Holly and Jennings found appealing the idea of taking a song like that and giving it a rockabilly treatment. Apparently, the idea had been brewing in Holly's mind for some time; it is said that he had considered recording the song himself.

Before Jennings could sing the song, though, he had to learn the words. Buddy and Waylon spent several days listening to a recording of "Jole Blon" by Harry Choates and trying as best they could to figure out the Cajun lyrics—which, of course, they couldn't understand. And so, on the chosen day, a rhythm & blues saxophonist, a national rock 'n' roll star, and an aspiring country & western singer combined forces to record a Cajun waltz with a west Texas rockabilly beat and lyrics which were now meaningless in any language. Holly got Brunswick to release the record. Unfortunately, this novel and promising conception in hybrid musical forms was a commercial flop. As Waylon himself once said, "A lot of people who heard the results got a lot of laughs out of it."

The two songs which Holly recorded himself that day were "Reminiscing," written by King Curtis, and "Come Back Baby," co-written by Norman Petty and a New York songwriter named Fred Neil; the two cuts were not released until several years after Holly's death. Holly's voice and Curtis's tenor sax make for an unusual combination that works out well on "Reminiscing." Influenced by Curtis's playing, Holly mixes into his more usual vocal style some new effects to match the saxophone sound; the two are performing together, but playfully trying to top each other. An air of ease and simplicity marks the recording, but in fact, it is Holly and Curtis's careful art that gives the tune such a casual sound.

By contrast, "Come Back Baby" is one of Holly's poorest studio recordings—it isn't bad, but it's certainly mediocre when measured against the standard set by his other performances. There's little fervor or drive in Holly's singing—his mind doesn't really seem to be on his material, a comment hardly true of any of his previous recordings. Jerry Allison remarks, "I don't think he was into that tune at all. Norman was probably pushing him to cut it, and he probably just said, 'O.K., I'll cut it,' just to save a hassle." The song itself was second-rate material, and even Curtis's sax playing couldn't spark the recording to life.

Around the same time that Holly was making these recordings with a top rhythm & blues instrumentalist, he was moving as well in a quite different direction—towards the recording of ballads with traditional pop orchestrations.

Ever since Holly and the Crickets had scored their initial successes, Norman Petty had been urging Buddy to move towards the pop music field in his recordings. Petty pointed out to Buddy that the popularity of teen-age singing stars was usually of short duration, two years at the most; when his popularity as a rock 'n' roll star waned, Holly would have to find another style and another audience. Indeed, rock 'n' roll itself might become less important, Petty thought, in which case Buddy should be ready to branch into night-club work as a solo artist and move into the stabler world of pop music.

At first, Holly didn't think much of the suggestion. "Naw, I don't dig it—I don't like it at all," he told Petty firmly. There was no pressing reason to follow this course. Holly's recordings were successful, and there was no visible decline in the popularity of rock 'n' roll; indeed, the arrival of Holly, Jerry Lee Lewis, and the Everly Brothers had marked a resurgence of rock 'n' roll after a period when adult ballads had become more noticeable. (In July 1957, *Billboard*'s top ten records had included only three oriented to the primarily teen-age rock 'n' roll audience: Presley's "Teddy Bear," the Everly Brothers' "Bye, Bye, Love," and Marty Robbins's "White Sport Coat.")

By the fall of 1958, however, Holly had changed his mind about trying some recordings with strings. This does not mean that he had decided to abandon rock 'n' roll, as some have surmised. As the next chapter will show, Holly was considering a wide variety of projects in the last months of his life and did not have the slightest intention of moving on a straight line from his orchestral recordings into the performing and recording world of pop music. When asked if Holly would have gone into night-club work, producer Dick Jacobs says flatly, "It would never have happened."

Holly was not abandoning his field; instead, he was trying to stay on top of it, through constant innovation. This was becoming a more pressing concern in the fall of 1958, when his last few singles had not reached the gold-record-rank popularity of his first three or four releases. (Such was the case in America, that is—in England, it was a different story.) Larry Welborn remembers running into Buddy in Lubbock about this time: "I had been trying to get my own recording career started and hadn't gotten anywhere; and I asked Buddy how he managed to come up with one successful record after another. Buddy kind of grinned and shook his head and said, 'It's getting tougher all the time. You have to keep coming up with something new—something they haven't heard before.'"

Like the Beatles years later, Holly was always trying to come up with a novel sound—not just to satisfy his own creative ambitions, but also to stay one step ahead of the market. Recording with King Curtis was one innovation; using strings was another. It's easy for music critics to categorize styles and expect artists to respect the boundaries, but in fact, they are the last ones to do so—Holly least of all. If he ever had, Holly no longer rejected ideas just because he hadn't tried them out before. It's true that he was under some pressure from his record company to record ballads. Coral was autonomous, but not completely independent—and executives of the parent company, Decca, were passing suggestions down the chain that it would be good for the company's few rock 'n' roll artists to move in the direction of pop music. (The sentiment was not shared by Dick Jacobs, at the time one of the few producers working for a major label who truly *liked* rock 'n' roll.) But the decision was up to Holly, and it was one he made on his own. One day in September, while the Crickets and Petty were at the San Francisco airport, Holly startled Petty with the remark, "Well, Norman, what songs are we going to record on my first session with strings?" It was the first time Holly had mentioned the idea since rejecting Petty's suggestion at least six months before.

The string session was scheduled for mid-October in New York, during an

East Coast swing by the Crickets. The four tunes recorded then were "True Love Ways," "Moondreams," "Raining In My Heart," and "It Doesn't Matter Anymore." Dick Jacobs arranged and produced the session, which was held in a studio at the Pythian Temple.

"True Love Ways" stands out as the best of the ballads. Holly's vocal perfectly expresses the tenderness and calm of the lyrics, and the accompaniment is complete but not ostentatious—the song is never overwhelmed by orchestral theatrics, always a tempting danger in such recordings. Especially fortunate is the use of tenor saxophone to balance the strings and provide an intimate feeling. Moreover, the recording treads the path Holly intended. Despite the orchestration, the ballad is still close to slow-dance rock 'n' roll tunes—the song adopts itself readily to rock 'n' roll triplets, as Tommy Allsup showed on an instrumental version of the song several years later. For examples of what mistakes could have been made and were not, Holly's recording might be contrasted with Peter and Gordon's 1965 hit version, a faithful but overly dramatic rendition of the song. The beautiful melody was based in part on "I'll Be All Right," a black gospel hymn which had been among Holly's favorite tunes since his high school years, when he first heard it on a Nashboro Records recording by the Angelic Gospel Singers. Even the tone of Holly's lyrics—the sense of patience, faith, and acceptance—was related to that of the original hymn.

"Moondreams" was composed by Petty and had been recorded sometime earlier by his trio with Holly accompanying the combo on rhythm guitar. The orchestration of "Moondreams" is heavier, and the overall sound is closer to pop, than is the case on "True Love Ways"; but on both songs, it is Holly's vocal which defies definition as pop. His distinct Texas accent, high voice, and, most of all, country phrasing and sense of pitch (the wavering in tone so distinctive of folk, blues, and country performers) mark Holly not so much as an imitator of earlier pop vocalists than as a forerunner of later country and rock artists who used strings effectively. Buddy Holly's records could have gained some airplay and sales from pop audiences on the basis of such recordings, but it is difficult to conceive of him having become a strictly pop singer, even if he had wanted to—he just didn't have that type of voice. This is not to say that his voice wasn't good enough—it was just different, following different norms than the usual in pop music.

"True Love Ways" and "Moondreams" were not released during Holly's lifetime; "It Doesn't Matter Anymore" and "Raining In My Heart" were instead the "A" and "B" sides of the single issued in January 1959, just weeks before Holly's death. In the years since then, "It Doesn't Matter Anymore" (written by Paul Anka) has remained one of Holly's most popular recordings, remembered not only for its sheer beauty, but also for the coincidence that a song with such a title and such lyrics should have been Holly's last release. Like Hank Williams's "I'll Never Get Out Of This World Alive" and both sides of Chuck Willis's last record, "Hang Up My Rock 'n' Roll Shoes"/"What Am I Living For?", Holly's last single appeared in retrospect to have been strangely appropriate.

Like "True Love Ways," "It Doesn't Matter Anymore" should not be considered as marking a total break with Holly's previous recordings. True, electric guitars and background vocal choruses are replaced by violins; but the ballad is performed at a moderate tempo and with a light but persistent beat. The string accompaniment highlights the tune without overwhelming it; Holly's bright, clear vocal dominates the recording throughout. Once again, his country background is obvious. His distinctive hiccups and vocal slides are used again, with more frequency than on most of his songs; here, they are more than a gimmick, and serve as well to embellish the lyrical melody. His Texas accent is still quite perceptible. In short, Holly's vocal makes few concessions to the standards of pop singing set by the white vocalists who had dominated the pre-rock 'n' roll era. Most of these comments hold true as well for the slower-paced ballad "Raining In My Heart," which has a more elaborate but still restrained arrangement and a distinctive and sincere vocal.

The simplicity of the string arrangement on "It Doesn't Matter Anymore" resulted in part from the last-minute nature of Holly's decision to record the song. Some time before, Paul Anka had asked Holly, "Would you record a song I'm writing?" "Sure, why not," Buddy replied, "let me see it." "Oh, but it's not finished yet," Anka said. "I'll bring it to you when I'm done with it." Anka finally brought the song to Holly on the very day of the recording session. Holly ran into Jacobs's office with the song just two hours before the evening session was scheduled to begin. (As Jacobs remembers it, Holly had originally planned to record something else, but Jacobs cannot recall what the song was. According to Petty, there wasn't any other song: Holly had simply left the fourth slot open for the song which he knew Anka was writing for him.) While Holly played the tune on a guitar and sang the lyrics, Jacobs worked out a quick arrangement. "We had violins on the date, and I had no time to harmonize the violins or write intricate parts," he later told an interviewer, "so we wrote the violins all pizzicato.... That was the most unplanned thing I have ever written in my life."[1]

Holly and Anka had first met when they travelled together on the 1957 Show of Stars tour; they apparently had it in mind to collaborate on songs or to write songs for each other, with "It Doesn't Matter Anymore" being the first effort of this sort. Niki Sullivan dates Holly's friendship with Anka to an accident during that first tour.

"Paul was a brat," says Sullivan. "All the time he was getting into trouble, or doing something wrong. He just couldn't sit still—a thousand, billion volts of energy. We were onstage in St. Louis, and Paul was horsing around backstage, when he kicked the microphone plug out of the floor and all the mikes went dead. We just stood there onstage, helpless. It was just a few minutes, but it seemed like three or four days until the microphones got plugged back in and we could start over. At this point, Buddy was boiling up inside, just ready to explode. When we walked off, the clapping stopped the

---

[1]David Dachs, *Anything Goes: The World of Popular Music* (Indianapolis, 1964), p. 87.

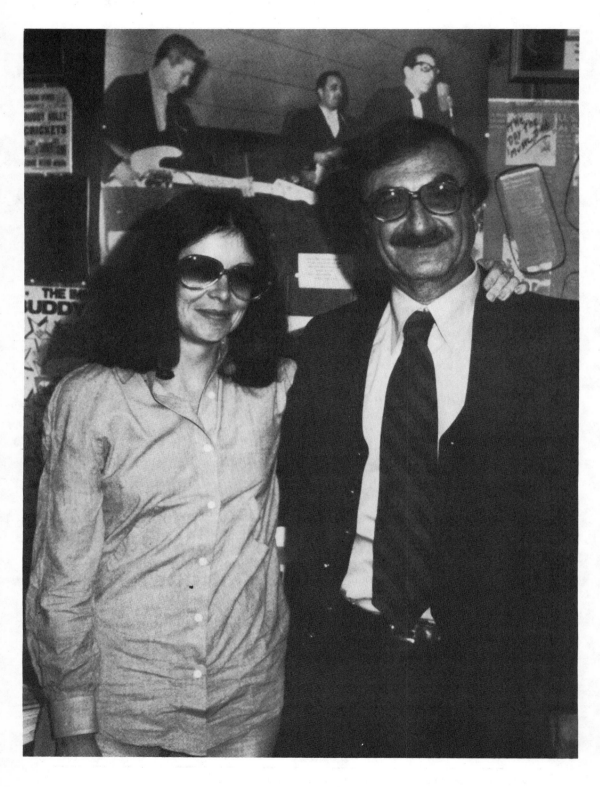

Michelle and Dick Jacobs (taken at the Buddy Holly Memorial Society headquarters, Wethersfield, Connecticut), August 1978 (Bill Griggs)

minute we got offstage, into the curtains—it wasn't a very long clap. So it's totally quiet, and the MC is walking out on to the stage to introduce the next act, and Buddy yells, 'Who in the hell kicked out the goddamn plug?' It rang throughout the auditorium. He calmed down after a bit and went back to the room, and later Paul Anka came back and apologized. And in fact, from that incident, Buddy and Paul became very close, and even rehearsed a few songs together from then on.''

The recordings made with King Curtis and with Dick Jacobs's orchestra were held for future release; the Crickets and Holly singles issued in the fall of 1958 were in more familiar styles, though with innovations. The Crickets' single, "It's So Easy"/"Lonesome Tears," was released in September—and went absolutely nowhere on the national charts. As with other Holly singles of that year, the commercial failure of "It's So Easy" seems inexplicable now, for it is an excellent record in many ways. The song follows an unexpected and novel lyric and melodic pattern—there is little in the way of clear division between verse and refrain. This unconventional structure was repeated years later in some of the Beatles' compositions—two early songs, "Tell Me Why" and "When I Get Home," come first to mind— suggesting that the record had an impact out of proportion to its sales figures. The flip side of the single, "Lonesome Tears," was more conventional. Though a good record, it is below the level of Holly's most famous songs, and it lacks the sparkle of "It's So Easy."

The single marked Tommy Allsup's first appearance on Holly's releases— "Love's Made A Fool of You," of course, had been just a demo not intended then for release. Allsup's country-based guitar playing at times provides a sound resembling that produced by a country steel guitar; this effect is particularly noticeable on "It's So Easy." Allsup's and Holly's styles are distinct, but congenial—the styles are similar enough so that anyone unaware beforehand that Holly did not play lead on all his songs might not guess it from the recordings. This is in fact the case in the United States, at least, where the omission of any mention of Allsup on Holly's albums has made his contribution to Holly's recordings practically unknown.

Holly's solo release, "Heartbeat"/"Well All Right," was issued in November. It was only a little more successful than "It's So Easy," getting only as far as number 82 on *Billboard*'s charts, and barely making the top thirty in England. Why "Heartbeat" was not more of a hit is, again, a mystery. It did lack the pounding beat of "Oh Boy!" or "Think It Over"—but so too did many of the top records in late 1958, when *Billboard* articles were noting the resurgence of ballads, instrumentals, and Latin-flavored rhythms and the decline of the rock 'n' roll beat.

"Heartbeat" itself incorporated a bit of a Latin beat, while retaining as well the steady rhythm guitar sound of "Peggy Sue." The lyrics swing with the melody and allow much play for Holly's vocal slides and hiccups. Like "Love's Made A Fool Of You," "Heartbeat" alternates vocal lines and answering instrumental passages. (The two songs were written about the same time; and although Petty and Bob Montgomery are listed as the writers of "Heartbeat," Holly's parents remember Buddy and Bob working on both "Heartbeat" and "Love's Made A Fool Of You" at the Holleys' home.) Allsup's brief but perfect guitar solo reaches upwards to build the same sort of emotion created by Holly on "Peggy Sue" and "Listen To Me." Something in the tone of the guitar and the sweep of the pretty melody lends the song a "classical" air and provides an illusion of strings. Overall, the song is a fine example of the west Texas rockabilly sound whose roots are difficult to trace, but which has an absolutely distinctive flavor.

The flip side, "Well All Right," has for many years been ranked by Holly's fans as among his best recordings, even though the song has almost never been played on the radio and was for a long time practically unavailable in the United States (the tune was not placed on any of the compilation albums issued between 1960 and 1972). Polls of Buddy Holly Memorial Society members in 1977 and 1978 showed that "Well All Right" was their fourth favorite Holly song, topped only by "That'll Be The Day," "Peggy Sue," and "Rave On."

As with many of Holly's songs, the germ of the tune was just a common saying—here, a simple phrase which the Crickets had picked up from Little Richard and decided to use as the title for a song. So much for their original intentions; by the time they had finished, they had produced one of their most unusual recordings. The song is so unified that just listing some of its distinctive elements hardly does it justice. There is the unusual harmonic pattern with a dominating chord change found nowhere else in Holly's songs: from the tonic major to a major built on the flattened seventh—i.e., if the song is played in C, from C major to B-flat major. The pattern lends the song a modal, folkish air which corresponds to its unelectrified sound and the dominance of the picked-and-strummed country guitar (played by Holly). The song is a polyphony, not of melodies, but of rhythms. The separate rhythms of the guitar and the drums (with cymbals emphasized) contrast dramatically with the vocal, which defies the underlying rhythms and follows its own sense of emphasis and phrasing.

The repressed tension of the instrumental and vocal performances matches the flavor of the lyrics—lyrics which capture so perfectly and poetically the mixture of hope, pride, and uncertainty that is the adolescent experience—if not really the human experience. The lyrics are unified without any air of deliberate construction; they move easily and subtly from the general to the particular, leaving the connection unspoken. Holly sings the words with an unself-conscious sincerity, affirming rather than preaching, and only hinting at the strong emotions veiled by his calm delivery. Rather than addressing a transient concern or narrating just one particular story, the song instead has a timeless quality and carries a general message valid over and over again to those who turn to it:

> **Well all right, so I'm being foolish,**
> **Well all right, let people know,**
> **About the dreams and wishes you wish**
> **In the night when lights are low.**

Well all right, well all right,
We'll live and love, with all our might,
Well all right, well all right,
Our lifetime love will be all right.

Well all right, so I'm going steady,
It's all right when people say
That those foolish kids can't be ready
For the love that comes their way.

Well all right, well all right,
We will live and love, with all our might,
Well all right, well all right,
Our lifetime love will be all right.[2]

In the early fall of 1958, Holly made a decision which he had been contemplating for some time: to end his association with Norman Petty. In the aftermath of Holly's death, the fact that this split did occur was forgotten or ignored or simply covered up; it was never suggested that Holly's and Petty's relations were anything other than amicable. The truth is quite different.

There is no doubt that Norman Petty played a key role in opening up a national audience for the Crickets. One would like to think that, even if he had never met Petty, Holly would have kept knocking on doors until he found a person or a company willing to record him on his own terms; but there is no way to be sure that he would have succeeded. Petty had the stature and the contacts to get the Crickets a record contract and to ensure for them a large degree of control over their recordings. He was the middleman that Holly had lacked during his year on Decca. Holly knew all this when Petty began to work on the Crickets' behalf. At the time, it was literally the only game in town, but even then Buddy viewed his association with Petty as a steppingstone to something else, not as a permanent arrangement. Larry Holley says that Buddy knew he would have to go through Petty to get a contract—but that Buddy intended to go off on his own and be his own boss, once he learned enough about the industry and met enough people so that this would be feasible.

At the start, the Crickets were all young and naive, without experience in handling money or negotiating business arrangements; they were content to let Petty take care of those matters for them. Each member of the group gave Petty power of attorney, and all income from the songs and records was directed to Petty and remained under his control. As mentioned earlier, Petty had assured the Crickets that, regardless of the names on the song contracts, the money would eventually be split up according to who had actually written the songs; he also talked about involving the Crickets in his own

---

[2]"Well All Right," words and music—Buddy Holly, Norman Petty, Jerry Allison, and Joe Mauldin. Copyright © 1958 by MPL Communications, Inc. International Copyright Secured. ALL RIGHTS RESERVED; used by permission.

publishing and recording enterprises. As Joe Mauldin recalls, "Norman kept telling us, 'This is *our* company—we're all in it together, and we're going to all share from it.' Of course, none of us ever saw a nickel of the publishing money. But I saw this beautiful studio and all those nice offices he had, and I was thinking, 'Wow, I own a piece of this—I've got it made.' And I think that's one thing that led us into letting him sign for equal shares on our songs."

In our interview, Mauldin still defended Petty's actions and motives: "Are you going to put this in print, saying Norman Petty is a big so-and-so, and he steals from people and all that? Because I think that would hardly be fair. You know, I have hostilities against Norman—but I think this is only normal with any group that has a manager—at some time in their career, they get crossways. I still do feel that Norman Petty was very instrumental in our career and our success. Number one, if we hadn't met him and gone through him, we might never have gotten a recording contract. And then too, who's to say that the disc jockeys would have played our records if Norman's name hadn't been on them?"

As Holly's insistence on splitting all the income with the Crickets indicates, Buddy was not dominated by a concern for money—but he was unwilling to be taken advantage of and he came to resent the way in which Petty was collecting a share of the songwriting royalties. "I talked to Buddy once early in 1958," says Hipockets Duncan, "and he was steaming mad. He said, 'Hipockets, I wish a thousand times I had talked with you before I got involved with that man.'" Holly didn't believe that Petty would actually carry out his promise and distribute the money according to the way the songs had really been written. In the end, Holly's suspicions were borne out—Petty did keep the share of the royalties granted him in the official song contracts.

Allison still defends Petty's intentions: "I really believe that if we had all stayed together in Clovis, then it would have all been squared away. We would have sat down and said, 'O.K., I wrote half of that and you wrote half of this,' and I think Norman would have probably said, 'Right, we'll split the money that way.' But when it all fell apart, then the way the contracts went—the way Norman had fixed the contracts—that was the way it stayed."

There was, indeed, much more to Norman Petty than just a good business sense. He did make a lot of money from his association with Holly—but Petty had an emotional interest in the Crickets' success as well. Whether or not he thought about it consciously, he in effect tried to act as a father to the boys—he sought to protect them from themselves and others. And that was bound to lead to trouble eventually.

Petty had some reason for setting up financial arrangements as he did—none of the Crickets had had any experience in handling a lot of money, and there were enough sad examples of sports and entertainment figures who had run through vast sums too quickly and been left broke. The Crickets appreciated Petty's concern, but they began to resent his absolute control over even the smallest expenses. They didn't see why they shouldn't be able to make up their own minds on how to spend their money.

Says Allison, "When we needed some tires, we had to go to Norman for the money—and he'd say, 'O.K., you can get a good deal on thin white sidewalls at Ward's, so go to Ward's.' And we'd say, 'We don't want Ward's tires, we want Sears tires.' Or Firestone, or whatever. And he'd say, 'Nope, you don't want to waste your money like that.' He was trying to do the right thing for us, but it just seemed like he had too much control."

Petty's contacts and experience had been crucial when the Crickets were just getting started. However, as the group's first records became hits and they spent almost all their time on the road, Holly himself began to gain the insight and know-how which had been Petty's chief assets as manager. Petty accompanied the group on their first trip to New York and on their foreign tours, but the rest of the time the Crickets were usually on their own, and Buddy was responsible for keeping tabs on the group, its equipment, and the promoters. As a result, he became more sophisticated in handling problems on his own. Allison recalls a "dance party" tour the Crickets made in the early summer of 1958, where they were accompanied only by a dance band headed by Tommy Allsup; the dance would run from eight P.M. to midnight, with the Crickets (including Allsup) performing two forty-five minute sets and Allsup's band playing the rest of the time. At one such show, the local promoter didn't want the dance band to appear on the show, and so the Crickets just did their own sets.

"When it came time to collect the money," says Jerry, "the promoter said, 'O.K., we're only going to pay you half, since the big band didn't play.' Buddy said, 'Man, they were there, out in the audience, playing. Whistling and humming. You didn't want them to play on the stage—but you've still got to pay all of us, the way the contract reads.' And the guy said, 'Well, they didn't play.' And Buddy said, 'O.K., they may not have played, but they're all gonna come over here and beat the hell out of you.' So the guy finally paid up. He was really trying to jive us because he thought we were just a bunch of dumb kids. But Buddy didn't let anything get by him—he'd take care of the business fine." "Taking care of the business" included protecting the money once it was received. Holly began to carry a pistol in 1958, keeping it in a false bottom of his travel bag.

By mid-1958, Holly had reached the point where Petty could not do much more for him than he could do himself. In addition, Holly was displeased with the way his career was actually being handled by Petty. Jerry Allison says, "One of the main reasons that I recall for Buddy splitting was that he wanted more publicity. At the time, people like Fabian and Frankie Avalon were getting all kinds of write-ups in magazines, but Norman didn't believe in that sort of publicity. He told Buddy, 'You don't need that—you'll make it on records, you're making it bigger than all that anyway.' We had a couple of offers for movies, too, and Norman turned them right down—they were just rock 'n' roll movies, and I guess Norman was waiting for a really big one. But that turned us right off, because we wanted to see ourselves in the movies."

Petty replies that the decision to turn down the movie offers was a joint one. "The only time that movies came up," says Petty, "was when they were going to do this Alan Freed quickie." (Probably, *Go Johnny, Go.*) "They called me, and I presented it to the boys. They weren't going to pay them—Jack Hook, who was Freed's personal manager at the time, said, 'The only thing you're going to get out of it is the publicity.' It was Jerry himself who said, 'If they don't want to give us any money, the hell with it—let's don't do it.'" Allison responds with a rhetorical question: "Can you imagine three kids turning down a chance to be in a movie?"

The break would have come sooner or later, once Buddy felt himself fully capable of running his own affairs. But the event which led directly to the split was Buddy's marriage—and Petty's opposition to it.

Allison and Mauldin remember that Petty was against the very idea of any of the Crickets getting married. His reasons appear to have been a mixture of self-interest and paternalism. He feared (correctly) that he would lose dominance over the musicians as they established their own lives and demanded more control over their own affairs. "When you get married," Allison explains, "it's a different thing—because you can't have your wife saying, 'Well, shall I go ask Norman if we can have some money?'" But Allison adds, "I think he thought that we were too young to get married and weren't stable enough—which was probably true. Well, I don't know about for Buddy—but I was definitely too young to know what I was doing." (Allison has since been divorced and has remarried.) Both Holly and Allison were irritated by Petty's objections. "I remember when we were in Hawaii on the way to Australia," says Jerry, "and I had already decided I was going to get married. We were riding along and Norman said, 'Well, Buddy, what are we going to do for another drummer when Jerry gets married?' And Buddy said, 'Well, Jerry, what are we going to do for another manager since Norman's *already* married?' And I was kind of P.O.'d at Norman because of that."

Petty denies that he objected to either of the two marriages. "The only thing I did tell Jerry at the time," says Petty, "was whenever he got married, to make sure, because I felt that marriage was a one-time thing. I don't recall that remark about 'what are we going to do for another drummer.' Jerry was prone to exaggerate. I might have said something that Jerry based it on. But I think if I had made a statement that strong, that I would remember it."

Maria Elena, however, charges that Petty actively tried to dissuade Holly from marrying her. She says, "Norman told Buddy that I was a cheap girl who tried to get picked up by practically every entertainer who walked in the office—that I'd run around with a lot of men. Norman said this certain executive at Peer-Southern Music had told him this. Well, Buddy told me about the stories Norman was spreading. So the next time Norman came into the office I called this executive over and brought him face-to-face with Norman and told him what Norman had been saying and asked him if any of this had come from him. And he said no, he had never told Norman any such thing. They never liked Norman up there very much after that."

Petty denies that this incident at Peer-Southern ever happened. He acknowledges that there was no love lost between himself and Maria, but he rejects the notion that this arose out of any fear on his part that Maria posed a threat to his role. "It was very antagonistic, naturally. But it was a two-way street. There probably was jealousy on both sides. To make it look like I feared Maria Elena's entering the picture is just not so. You never fear something when you do the best you know how to do, and I would certainly not fear anybody that really didn't know anything about the business. If I would be prone to, it would be somebody that was in the management field—a Dick Jacobs, you know—who'd make you feel like your position was jeopardized. But I never felt that Maria Elena jeopardized my position whatsoever." Nevertheless, Petty does trace Buddy's decision to break with him back to Maria Elena's urging: "She told him that he didn't need the Crickets—that he didn't need me."

Whether or not Petty perceived it as such, Maria Elena did in fact represent a threat to his control over Holly. With her personal experience and family ties in music publishing, she had know-how that was to aid Buddy in charting his own career—and also, she was able to make clearer to him just what his association with Petty was costing him. Joe Mauldin notes, "I think Maria Elena, right off the bat, wanted Buddy to move to New York and get away from Norman Petty—because I think she knew what was going on with our money. She probably had access to publishing records that we didn't." Maria was apt to be more businesslike than Buddy. She asked a lot of questions, and she insisted on having everything down in writing—she was less willing than Buddy to settle for vague promises, or to trust in the goodwill of others. But a good business sense wasn't all that Maria Elena Santiago gave to Buddy Holly. She gave him what he most needed just then: more confidence in himself.

"You're the best thing that ever happened to Buddy," Mr. Holley told Maria not long after the marriage. "You've cut his umbilical cords. When he was younger, he was tied to his mother; then he was tied to Norman Petty; but now he's come into his own—he's finally a *man*." It wasn't so much that marriage changed Buddy Holly; rather, it unleashed him, freeing him to put his desires into action—to make realities of his hopes. Holly's personality was always full of contradictions. On stage, he was uninhibited, always trying to reach out and touch an audience and never holding anything back; offstage, he was quiet, shy and cautious towards strangers, sometimes moody and withdrawn even with friends. The tension in his music between the willingness to put absolute faith in high hopes, and the knowledge that fulfillment of those hopes was always uncertain, mirrored a conflict in Holly's own soul. He was outwardly self-confident, often aggressive; but fear of failure, as much as any deep ambition, was what spurred him on. Never quite satisfied with his success, never sure it would last, he sought something permanent—something that would indeed last "through times till all times end." Love gave him that sense of permanence and encouraged him to cut loose from his old moorings and chart his own course with new confidence.

Maria was no silent or passive support. Her spirit had much in common with Buddy's. She was strong-willed and high-tempered, outspoken, and independent. Contrary to what Petty may have thought, she did not make Buddy's decisions for him; but she was a perceptive judge of people and situations, and Buddy put great weight in her judgment. And like Buddy, she looked to the future. She says, "Buddy always seemed to me to be very old for his age—he was more mature than the others around him." (Maria herself was two years older than Buddy.) "He could be happy fooling around for a while—but when he had to be, he was all business. He cared about what happened, he thought about what he was doing. He was always trying to think of ways to improve himself, to improve his performances and his music. Backstage at a show, he'd be thinking all the time about what he was going to do, and whether he should do it differently. Really, everything he did on stage, he had thought it out ahead of time, or planned it out with Jerry and Joe. His mind was constantly working."

(It was a trait Hipockets Duncan noticed too: "When we'd talk, he'd be listening to what I was saying and he'd respond, but you could just feel that his mind was somewhere else at the same time. He was always in a hurry, trying to do so much, and his mind would be working on more than one thing at once.")

The conflict between Petty and Maria Elena flared more intensely after the marriage. "We went to Clovis for a recording session in September," Maria recalls, "and Norman and his wife and his secretary started to make fun of the way I spoke English. Well, I didn't have to take that. I had grown up in New York City—I knew how to eat and dress and act—they thought they were so sophisticated, but I knew more than they ever would. So I said to his wife, 'I want you to talk to me in Spanish.' And of course she couldn't. And I said, 'You see, I can speak your language—but you don't know a word of mine.' But that's how it stood. Norman knew I couldn't stand him—and he knew what he had done, and why he couldn't hold Buddy any longer."

Petty remembers this incident differently. "We had very little contact after the marriage. I don't recall ever having been abusive to Maria Elena. The only thing I can recall is that she said something about the funny way we talk, about our drawl; and if anything was said, Norma Jean [Petty's secretary] or Vi said something, just jokingly, about 'Well, you talk funny, too.' That was the gist of it. But as to making fun of her because she was Puerto Rican, or Spanish, that's just not so."

In October, the Crickets appeared on the Alan Freed television show in New York City and then set out on a seventeen-day GAC package tour with Eddie Cochran, Bobby Darin, Frankie Avalon, Clyde McPhatter, and the Coasters. Buddy and Maria travelled in their Cadillac, while Allison, Mauldin, Allsup, and the Roses (accompanying the Crickets on tour for the first time) rode in a yellow DeSoto station wagon purchased at the time of the summer dance party tour. The tour showed that strains were developing not just between Holly and Petty, but within the group as well.

"On that tour," explains Joe Mauldin, "we weren't as close as we had been before. Of course, now I can understand why—Buddy was a married man and had his wife with him, and he had to devote more time to her than he did to

Jerry and I. But at the time, I felt like Buddy didn't want to be a part of the group anymore, he wanted to be a bigshot star himself. And I was jealous of Maria Elena, because it seemed that she was taking Buddy away from Jerry and I. Buddy had been like a brother for so long, and suddenly Buddy was no longer a brother."

It was probably not wholly coincidental that Allison and Mauldin seemed to show less interest in their work than before. Drinking became an issue between them and Holly—what had only been a sidelight in the past was now starting to affect the trio's performances. Jerry Allison gives his memories of that last tour: "We really didn't see each other that much, except at the shows. And Buddy got kind of put out with us—things got sort of tense. Because we were really shucking it. Sometimes we'd get drunk in the morning and stay drunk all day. And Buddy wasn't out-and-out opposed to drinking, but he didn't like us at it all the time, the way we were doing. Anyway, after that tour was over, he talked to Joe B. and me and said, 'O.K. you guys, I can't take all this—if we're going to do this thing, let's do it right. We're getting older, and we got to take this more seriously. You guys drink too much—it's obnoxious, and I hate it. If you want to stay with me, great—but you've got to be more interested in what you're doing.' So we finally said, 'Yeah, O.K., we understand, we'll tighten up a little bit.' "

Holly's desire to break with Petty was discussed during the tour. Joe Mauldin says, "There were a few conversations where Buddy mentioned, 'Hey, guys, we're gonna have to move to New York, to get away from Petty.' And I was somewhat confused, because I didn't think that was the right thing to do. Norman had hyped us so much on the people in New York, and how we'd never see any of our money. Norman would say, 'Look at all those groups that have had a bunch of hit records, and they've never made a nickel—they're stone broke. They'll take it all away from you, and you'll wind up the same way.' "

Jerry Allison remembers that Holly's decision was definite, and that he and Mauldin agreed at first to follow Holly. "Buddy said, 'I'm going to move to New York, and I'm going to go out from Norman. There's a lot of stuff I want to do.' We agreed that we'd all move to New York and start our own publishing company, and we had it all worked out. We even called Norman and told him that we were hanging it up and moving to New York." Mauldin doesn't remember being very settled about it one way or the other, in his own mind, during the tour.

After the tour itself, the Crickets had two television appearances to make for Dick Clark—one on the Saturday night stage show, on October 25, and the second on the afternoon *American Bandstand*, on Tuesday, October 28. After the last show, Allison and Mauldin flew back to Lubbock, while Buddy and Maria decided to make the long drive back in their car. When Joe B. and Jerry got back, they decided to go over to Clovis to drop in on the Roses and to pick up some personal belongings.

"We went over to Clovis, and Norman talked us out of splitting, that's what happened," says Jerry. "He said, 'You know, you guys better hang down here—when you get to New York, you're gonna see, you'll be cheated out of everything.' All that kind of stuff. So we said, O.K."

Mauldin gives his account of how the conversation went: "The feelings that I had had on the tour could have been one of the reasons that Norman influenced me as much as he did when we got back to Clovis. But it's not that Maria broke the group up—I felt like Petty's the one who broke the group up. Norman said, 'Look, let's stay down here where we have control of everything.' And he had us built up, saying, 'You guys are the Crickets, you will be the Crickets and you'll keep the Crickets name. And we'll get another lead singer and a guitar player'—so forth and so on. He told us that the Crickets were the ones that had had all the hits—Buddy Holly had only had 'Peggy Sue,' and he couldn't make a living on the name Buddy Holly. So if we stayed down in Clovis with Norman, we could keep the name of the Crickets, and Norman had—quote—'all his money in the bank, and we'll starve him to death'—end quote."

Petty objects to this account of what happened. "I didn't talk anybody into anything. I didn't brainchild the whole thing, or engineer it. As for that statement about starving him to death—that's awful strong, for somebody that really thought of all the kids as his sons. I know I never said it."

When Buddy got back to Lubbock, he called Allison's house and discovered that Jerry and Joe had gone ahead to Petty's studio, instead of waiting for Holly to arrive. Still not knowing what had happened in Clovis, Buddy drove up there to make his own settlement with Petty.

"Maria Elena and Buddy were both in the office," says Petty, "but Maria Elena did all the talking. She said, 'Buddy and I have decided that Buddy can do better—that you're not fit for Buddy's manager.' And I said, 'What's this— is it something I've done?' She said, 'It's what you haven't done—you haven't done near enough for him.'"

Maria remembers, "Norman asked Buddy, 'Are you sure that's what you want? You know, I can't give you any money until we get settled who gets what money, and just how much money each of you has coming. I'll need time.' And Buddy said, 'I don't *have* the time. Just give me the money and I'll give it to them—we can split it ourselves.' And that's when Norman told him—he said, 'Uh uh—they're staying with me.'"

Jerry Allison remembers that Buddy was disappointed, but not angry: "We sat in the car and went through it all; and Buddy was agreeable to the whole thing. He said, 'I wish you guys would go with me, you're gonna be sorry you didn't. But I can understand, if you don't want to, you don't want to.' We weren't uptight, or anything like that. And he said, 'O.K., you guys can have the name of the Crickets, and I'll just work as Buddy Holly.'"

In fact, Buddy was hiding his feelings from Mauldin and Allison. He was deeply disappointed, and hurt by what had happened. "He felt sort of betrayed," says Maria. " 'I thought I had treated them fair,' he said, 'I don't see why they should have done that to me.' He felt like they had put a knife in his back; but if that was how they felt, he wasn't going to beg them. But he cried that night." Holly's parents remember him being so discouraged that he talked of quitting; they say Maria Elena talked him out of it. But she doesn't recall him suggesting anything like that: "He was hurt by what had happened, but it didn't change his mind about what he wanted to do—he knew he could still be a star."

The moment of discouragement passed, and Buddy and Maria returned to New York. "There's a lot of stuff I want to do," he had told Allison. New York was the place to start.

Holly in England, March 1958 (Peer-Southern)

7. Plans for the Future

"What would have happened to Buddy Holly if he had not died? What would he be doing today?" Those are common subjects for debate, both among his fans and among those who consider the history of rock music. The intriguing questions can be argued endlessly, since they cannot be answered with any certainty. What Buddy Holly would have done would have depended in part on the state of the industry and the directions of popular taste; but conversely, the industry and popular tastes would have been shaped in part by Holly's music. This much can be said: the scope of Holly's plans in the last months of his life indicates that with his death, rock 'n' roll lost more than a talented performer—more importantly, it lost a creative figure whose innovations could have profoundly affected the development of all American popular music.

Ever since Holly's death, the common assumption has been that his last recordings—the ones with orchestral arrangements—show that he was abandoning rock 'n' roll and turning to pop music, but the songs themselves don't entirely support this contention. It's true that many performers who have begun careers as teen-age stars have later sought to broaden their appeal by moving to a more adult pop sound and into the field of night-club work. Commercially, the adult market is more lucrative and more stable; and such changes are encouraged by the common prejudice that pop music is "better" than rock 'n' roll or any related musical forms—an artist gains in stature by "moving up" into the world of pop music. But not everyone has gone along with the trend; the ones who didn't—artists like Chuck Berry, Gene Vincent, and Bill Haley—sometimes lived through years of obscurity as a result. Buddy Holly wasn't ashamed of his music, either. But his musical horizons were expanding in unexpected and unpublicized directions.

"Buddy was always open to ideas," Maria remembers. "He looked into every type of music. We'd sit at home and listen to records—and he wouldn't just be entertaining himself—he'd be analyzing the sound, noting what he liked, and getting ideas. He'd comment on the records, and talk about how some sound or effect compared with something in a whole different field of music. He'd always listen to suggestions, and be willing to try something out and see if he could do it—see if it sounded good. His attitude was, 'You don't lose anything by trying.' And he wasn't one to just talk and do nothing—when he got something in his head, he wanted to carry it out. There was nothing new he saw that he didn't want to do immediately."

Marriage had brought Holly in contact with Latin American and Spanish music. Spanish guitar styles attracted his attention. Maria recalls, "We went out to eat almost every night, and often we'd go to Spanish restaurants where there were flamenco guitarists performing. Buddy really liked that music. He was attracted by Spanish classical guitar playing, too. He wanted to learn how to play in those styles. So he bought albums by Andres Segovia and by several flamenco guitarists, and he started to take lessons from a neighbor of ours." With Maria's help, Buddy was also learning Latin American songs, with the idea of recording them himself. The first one he wanted to learn was, naturally, "Maria Elena"; others were suggested by Maria's aunt Provi, who hoped that Buddy would record songs from Peer-Southern's large Latin American catalog. "I'd sing songs in Spanish for him to learn," says Maria, "and he'd try to pick up the words that way. We had tapes of us doing this together but somehow they got lost—it's too bad, because it was pretty funny sometimes. But Buddy was really interested—he told me that he wanted to learn how to speak Spanish, so I was going to teach him when he had time."

Others also helped Holly expand his musical interests. Tommy Allsup's wide background included a knowledge of jazz, and he got Holly interested in it; the record collection Holly left behind includes a single by Louis Armstrong and an EP from Miles Davis's "Miles Ahead" album. As shown by the recording of "Jole Blon" made with Waylon Jennings, Holly was also attracted to Cajun music. Holly's brother Larry had a collection of Cajun recordings, and that seems to be how Buddy first heard the style. Tommy Allsup remembers also that Holly liked the records he had heard by the young Cajun-country act, Rusty & Doug (the latter, of course, now performs under his full name, Doug Kershaw). It was just one more interest that Buddy was eager to follow up on—according to Larry Holley, Buddy was planning to spend some time in southern Louisiana, meeting Cajun musicians there and learning their style and techniques.

Rhythm & blues and gospel were streams of music with which Buddy was long familiar, and now he had projects in mind involving those fields, too. Since the early fifties, Holly had been a great fan of Ray Charles. Indeed, while everyone talks of Elvis Presley's influence on Holly, Buddy's rock 'n' roll vocal style owed at least as much to the example of Ray Charles, and the use of vocal background on the Crickets records was likewise related to Charles's gospel-blues recordings. Now, Holly wanted to do an album with the "Ray Charles sound." What he had in mind, says Maria, was an album of Charles's material, with arrangements similar to those Charles used. "When we were in California in the fall," she says, "we managed to find out where Ray Charles lived, and we went over to his house, but he was out on tour. Buddy was hoping to talk with Charles and see if he'd be willing to work with Buddy on this—help with the arrangements, and maybe play on it. Buddy really loved Charles's style, and he wanted to meet him and talk with him about it."

Another album which Buddy was planning to record was an album of gospel music. As the album was meant to be a sort of "gift" for his parents, it would seem that white gospel music would have provided the songs; but Holly liked black gospel singers too, especially Mahalia Jackson, and talked of recording black gospel himself, and so it is likely that some material from that tradition would also have been on the album. Holly's desire to please his parents was, of course, not his only reason for planning such an album; his own religious faith had remained a strong force in his life. In truth, it is by no means stretching matters to see a strong Christian strain in the attitudes of faith and patience that color Holly's songs. Like others in his church, he followed the Biblical practice of tithing and gave ten percent of his earnings to his Baptist congregation. And, as hard as it may be to believe, he sometimes had doubts about the propriety of his vocation. He never expressed his doubts to anyone outside his own family; but to them, and especially to his brother Larry, he talked about these qualms. Music was Buddy's life, and he neither wanted to nor would have been able to break away from it; but he wanted to feel that he was doing "God's work" too, even while remaining a secular entertainer. The planned gospel album would therefore have been an expression of his own conscience.

Holly was becoming involved in other aspects of the music business besides performing. He wanted to make a role for himself on "the other side of the glass," as a producer—he particularly wanted to work with young artists and help them realize their potential. He planned, too, to devote some of his songwriting talents to producing material for these and other artists.

Maria recalls: "Buddy didn't have in mind just writing songs that fit his own style and then finding someone else to record them. Instead, he wanted to try writing songs meant deliberately for somebody else in particular, and meant to suit that singer's style and potential audience. And that's how Buddy was going to record people, too—not just work with rock 'n' roll singers, but also help anyone who had potential at what he was doing. Like with Waylon Jennings—maybe Buddy thought Waylon could become a rock 'n' roll star, I don't know, but he felt sure that Waylon could be popular in country music, so that's the way he meant to record him. 'Let's start with *something*' was his attitude.

"Buddy meant to be really close to the artists he chose to work with. He actually wanted Waylon to come and move in with us—because Buddy felt like that way, he could really come to know Waylon and his feelings, and write songs that matched them. And with other artists too, he wanted to write songs that really expressed how *they* felt."

Besides Jennings, there was one other young artist with whom Holly actually worked during his months in New York. His name was Lou Giordano. In early December, Holly arranged to produce Giordano on a single for Brunswick, and wrote for him "Stay Close To Me," the only one of Holly's compositions which he himself never recorded, not even on a home tape. Holly played rhythm guitar on the record as well. Phil Everly was in on the project, too, and wrote the flip side of the single. The record was released just after Holly's death two months later, and was not a success. Somehow,

Giordano's bland vocal style failed to convey the emotion that Holly was himself capable of expressing in his own songs. Maybe that sort of miscalculation would have troubled Holly's later efforts to move in this direction. "Buddy never realized how much of an impact he had on his audience," says Maria. "He didn't have time. He knew they liked his style, but he didn't know just why." Holly might have been disappointed by what happened when other artists recorded songs he had written. At any rate, it's a pity that Holly never did get the chance to record the pretty and simple tune himself.

Jennings's and Giordano's first singles were Holly's initial efforts as an independent producer; he had made an agreement with Brunswick to produce a certain number of masters for them annually. The first masters were to be made in New York—but Holly intended to build his own fulltime recording studio in Lubbock. Buddy discussed his plans with Tommy Allsup and George Atwood. Holly also thought of asking two others to join him: his old friend Bob Montgomery, and Snuff Garrett. In the sixties, Garrett became one of the most successful producers on the West Coast; but before that, he was active in Texas, and Holly knew of his ability.

Maria explains what lay behind Holly's plans: "The young artists down there had heard what Buddy had gone through with Norman, and they were reluctant to go up to Norman's studio or get involved with him. But there weren't any other really good recording studios nearby, and most of those people were too poor to try studios farther away. So Buddy wanted to build a studio in Lubbock so kids growing up the way he had could have a chance to get started. The studio would have been built as part of the house he was going to build for his parents—the plans were all drawn up. He was going to start his own publishing company, too, to help promote their songs and his own."

But the studio wasn't meant just to help out local talent; it was to serve as a base for recordings by Holly himself. Tommy Allsup remembers that Buddy had in mind assembling a group of Lubbock area country and rockabilly musicians to serve as a studio band. The group would have been used to back up Waylon Jennings; but Holly also meant for them to play on his own recordings. "He wanted to try out fiddles, steel guitars, and all that, on his own releases," says Tommy.

Of course, no one can tell just how all this would have sounded. It seems clear that Holly did not intend just to record country songs in traditional country styles—he was thinking, rather, of adding a novel country flavor to his own brand of rock 'n' roll. One remembers his remark to Larry Welborn: "You have to keep coming up with something new—something they haven't heard before." Fiddles and steel guitars were not new sounds, but they would have been new to the rock 'n' roll audience—rock 'n' roll had been on the scene now for several years, and many fans were too young to remember what had existed before it, or too far removed socially to have ever been familiar with the varied sources of the music. In line with this change in the character of the audience, the trend in rock 'n' roll was to Dick Clark's "Philadelphia sound"; but instead of just following this trend, or even copying the most successful of his own releases, Holly was both moving in new directions and reaching back to his own roots—seeking to create his own trends.

In this and so much else, Holly was at least a decade ahead of his time. He had won a freedom to manage his own career that few artists were to have before the Beatles paved the way. As his varied plans show, he wasn't obsessed by the need for a hit single—they were nice to have, of course, but Holly was already thinking in terms of albums that could stand on their own. And in his specific ideas for integrating rock 'n' roll and country music, Holly was proposing something which was hardly attempted before the "country-rock" movement of the late sixties and seventies.

There is no way to be sure that Holly's efforts would have been commercial successes. The time might not have been right for such a movement. A check of *Billboard* charts shows that although a number of country-flavored records did make the pop charts in 1959, country music as a whole was returning to the isolation from pop music it had had in the pre-rock 'n' roll era. The rock 'n' roll audience might have ignored Buddy Holly, and rock 'n' roll might have suffered through its Fabians and Freddy Cannons just the same. But if Holly had managed to overcome the trends, the subsequent course of American popular music could have been radically altered. When asked once if Holly would have changed back to country music, Waylon Jennings replied, "No—actually, I think country music would have caught up with *him*." At the very least, Holly's studio might have become a recording center with a distinctive regional flavor, as studios in Detroit, Memphis, Muscle Shoals, and elsewhere did in succeeding years. But Buddy Holly did not get the chance; since then, ambitious and talented west Texas musicians have had to travel to Los Angeles or Nashville to get anywhere in the business, with a consequent loss in the regional distinctiveness of the music. Only in the last few years has this trend been reversed; the Austin-Dallas area shows some signs of developing into the musical center Holly envisioned.

The wide-ranging nature of Holly's musical plans and tastes suggests the sense of freedom and opportunity he felt in the last months of 1958. He was occasionally troubled by the failure of his most recent records; but Jerry Allison says that, during the time he and Buddy were together, Holly was never too concerned about it: "He didn't care if he had a number one record, or a record at all, as long as he could play and somebody would like it." Little more than a year before, Holly and his comrades had been poor boys in west Texas with dreams of being rich. Now, Holly no longer felt compelled to make a tour or produce a hit record for the sake of money alone—his circumstances had changed, and so had his attitudes. He wanted to make fewer tours, picking and choosing among them. Jerry says, "It would depend on who was going to be on the tour and if the tour looked like it would be fun to do—if it paid a million dollars and it didn't sound like any fun, he'd pass." Allison remembers one particular discussion with Holly right after the return from their honeymoons in Acapulco: "We got home and we were sitting around, and we had some offers for tours. And I said, 'Man, let's take those tours and make that money. Because one day we may not be able to—it may cool off and we won't be able to make it that way.' And Buddy said, 'Man, what do you want money for? Are you going to buy a Cadillac? If you want one, you go get it, I'll pay for it. Everybody wants to work for work. Why do we want to go out on the road and work all the time? What if you get killed tomorrow? Let's have some fun—let's ride our motorcycles, and just do what we want to do. We've got enough money—let's enjoy it.' And I said, 'O.K., you're right,' and we knocked off for a while after that. Maybe it was a month we goofed off, maybe two weeks; but whatever that time was, it was just what he wanted. Everything that happened afterwards—it really made me think about what he'd said. I was really glad that we had taken that break, and glad that he had had that attitude.''

Holly's recording and producing plans were just that—only plans—when he died; but not all that went on in the last months of his life was so indefinite. It was in this period that Holly wrote some of his finest songs, tunes which show that he was only beginning to develop his potential as a songwriter and as a performer.

In the weeks before his death, Holly recorded six original songs on his tape recorder in his New York apartment: ''That's What They Say,'' ''What To Do,'' ''Peggy Sue Got Married,'' ''That Makes It Tough,'' ''Crying, Waiting, Hoping,'' and ''Learning The Game.'' Holly only taped the songs as a way of taking down the tunes and lyrics and establishing models for eventual studio sessions. Fortunately, his sense of perfection resulted in recordings which were outstanding in their own right. Holly also taped his own versions of several songs written by other artists; he was experimenting, and considering how he might record the songs himself. Although the songs were taped in their final forms in January, Holly had been working on them since he and Maria had returned to New York in November.

Remembering how Buddy went about writing his songs, Maria says: ''He often worked on his songs over at my aunt's apartment, because she had a piano and he liked to work the tunes out on that. I can't say that the words or the music came first. He did them together—he'd get the tune down first, but he'd be writing the words at the same time. Then he'd play the song on his guitar to see how it sounded that way—he'd go back and forth between the piano and his guitar. (He had just gotten a new Guild, custom-made, and that's the one he played when he taped these songs.) But he didn't just write down the words and forget about it. The first set of words would come quickly enough—but then, he'd change it, over and over. Even the way he had it down on the tapes he left behind, I know he wasn't finished with them—he would have changed them some more, or added to them. He really cared about the way the songs sounded and the words he chose—he'd keep asking, 'Do you think this sounds good? It doesn't sound like I want it to.' Or, 'That's not what I want to say—it isn't what I had in mind.' I remember once he was sitting and working on some song, and I did something that was

*Holly rehearsing in London for the British tour, March 1, 1958
(John Beecher)*

distracting—maybe I made some noise. And he suddenly got up and exploded, 'I'll be back directly!' and stomped out, and took a walk to cool off. Then he came back and went to work again.''

Five of these last songs deal with the disappointments of love in striking and sometimes ambivalent fashion. "That's What They Say" is particularly complex. The singer would like to believe the conventional wisdom, but he has not yet found true love himself, and so wonders if what "they" say is true. This doubt is never outrightly expressed, only implied, in the ironic lyrics, the tone of Holly's singing, and the music (the use of minor chords in the refrain). The matter is left unsettled—making the song realistic, since no one in such a position can state the answer.

> **"There comes a time for everybody,**
> **When true love will come your way.**
> **There comes a time for everybody—"**
> **That's what they tell me,**
> **That's what they say.**
>
> > **I didn't hear them say a word**
> > **Of when that time would be;**
> > **I only know that what they say**
> > **Has not come true for me.**
>
> **"You just keep waiting,**
> **And love will come your way—"**
> **That's what they tell me,**
> **That's what they say.** [1]

The other four songs about love deal more specifically with the end of a love affair. They may be, to some extent, autobiographical, drawing on Buddy's high school romance. Holly's experience made it possible for him to express the varied feelings one might have in such a situation. Like a novelist whose fictional characters are based on the reality of human life, even if they are not completely modelled on the lives of specific individuals, so a songwriter or a poet can create a situation which is no less real for being fictional. He can write about such matters in terms based on his own experience, but in such a way that the lyrics have general application. The best of the rock 'n' roll songwriters were able to create this sort of poetic reality in their songs. The devotion of Holly's fans both before and after his death was based in part on the lasting validity of his lyrics and their continued significance to the lives of the listeners.

The title of "What To Do" expresses the singer's dilemma. Although his love no longer wants him, he must admit to himself that he still wants only her; and he cannot escape reminders of the times and places they had shared: the record hops, the soda shops, the walks to school. "That Makes It Tough"

---

has a similar theme. The melody itself and the manner of Holly's performance mark the song as his closest approach during his rock 'n' roll years to the sound of country & western. Holly shows Hank Williams's influence upon his vocal style, while the guitar accompaniment on Holly's original, solo tape—picked bass notes and strummed chords—is reminiscent of Jimmie Rodgers's song style. However, some of Holly's friends say that this was one of the songs he intended to record with a Ray Charles-style blues arrangement. Of course, they may be mistaken; but this shows the impossibility of determining with any precision just what these songs would have sounded like had Buddy lived to record them with a full band or orchestra. Even Maria doesn't know what sort of arrangement Buddy had in mind. In the original undubbed version, "That Makes It Tough" is one of Holly's most compelling performances. There are many who feel that, given the right arrangement, it would have been a sizable hit for Holly in all three record markets.

> ... Memories will follow me forever,
> Though I know our dreams cannot come true,
> All those precious things we shared together—
> Time goes by, I'll still remember you—and

> That makes it tough,
> Oh, so tough,
> When you tell me,
> You don't love me.
> That makes it tough,
> Oh, so tough—
> When you say you don't care for me no more.[2]

"Crying, Waiting, Hoping" expresses the mixture of discouragement and hope that colored some of Holly's earlier songs; in the space of a few lines, the singer first tells himself that his hopes are useless, and then hopes yet again that the past can be restored:

> Crying, waiting, hoping,
> You'll come back,
> I just can't seem
> To get you off my mind.
> Crying, waiting, hoping,
> You'll come back,
> You're the one I love,
> And I think about you all the time.

> Crying,
> My tears keep a-falling,
> All night long.

---

[2]"That Makes It Tough," words and music—Buddy Holly. Copyright © 1959 by Peer International Corporation. Used by permission.

Waiting,
It feels so useless,
I know it's wrong, to keep

Crying, waiting, hoping,
You'll come back,
Maybe some day soon,
Things will change and you'll be mine.[3]

"Learning the Game" does not offer even this limited hope, but it does put the loss in a slightly different light—by treating it as something which is to be accepted as only natural: life and love are games, with victories and defeats—perhaps more of the latter. The song is thus in one sense highly pessimistic; and yet, like "Love's Made A Fool Of You," it offers a sort of consolation by suggesting that the situation is universal.

Hearts that are broken
And love that's untrue,
These go with learning the game.

When you love her
And she doesn't love you,
You're only learning the game.

When she says
That you're the only one she'll ever love,
Then you find
That you are not the one she's thinking of,

Feeling so sad,
And you're all alone and blue,
That's when you're learning the game.[4]

The last of the six songs was the playful "Peggy Sue Got Married." Buddy's father had suggested the title as a possible subject for a sequel to "Peggy Sue"—something along the lines of the thematic sequels of Hank Ballard's "Annie" songs. Like Annie and a few other "names" in rock 'n' roll songs, Peggy Sue had become a figure who could be mentioned in a song to attract the attention of listeners and to gain their identification with the song—rock 'n' roll fans could feel like part of an "in" group by being familiar with the names and tunes referred to in the new song. Thus, Peggy Sue made an appearance at the living room party in "Splish Splash," and was mentioned in Bobby Darin's "Queen of the Hop" and Ritchie Valens's "Ooh My Head."

Peggy Sue had indeed married Jerry Allison, and Holly's song sets out to reveal the event to the uninformed public. Holly ironically places himself in the position of the audience—he cautions the listener that all he's heard is just "a rumor from a friend" which may or may not be true—and only at the end of the lyrics does he reveal his information about "the girl that's been in nearly every song." Although the song's melodic lines follow the AABA pattern Holly used frequently, the structure of the lyrics is without precedent in his songs—rather than making up verses and refrains, the lyrics comprise a continuous whole without breaks or repeats:

> Please don't tell—no, no, no—
> Don't say that I told you so,
> I just heard a rumor from a friend.
>
> I don't say that it's true,
> I'll just leave that up to you,
> If you don't believe, I'll understand.
>
> > You recall a girl that's been
> > In nearly every song,
> > This is what I've heard—of course,
> > The story could be wrong—
>
> She's the one, I've been told,
> Now she's wearing a band of gold,
> Peggy Sue got married not long ago.[5]

The music itself was a bit of a sequel to "Peggy Sue." Holly hints at the chordal pattern of the twelve-bar original in his thirty-two bar sequel, and, in his own rhythm guitar playing, mixes in quotations from the earlier song—for example, the rhythmic I-IV-I-V chord pattern in the opening bars of "Peggy Sue" is repeated on "Peggy Sue Got Married." Unfortunately, the musical joke is totally lost on the released version of the song, where the dubbed vocal and instrumental accompaniment obscures Holly's acoustic guitar. The other five songs discussed above also suffered from the arrangements added to Holly's tapes after his death in hopes of making the songs "commercial." (The circumstances of the posthumous releases are discussed in Chapter 9.) The songs are at their best on the original undubbed tapes; Holly's acoustic guitar style and sense of rhythm and timing are then audible, as they are not in the dubbed versions. Holly's record company, however, has never made the "bare" recordings available.

Holly's last six songs all rank high when compared to his earlier efforts. As in his earlier songs, Holly uses simple melodies which follow patterns long established in American popular and folk music; he apparently felt no cause to lay those traditional forms aside. Although Holly's songs have a distinctive sound, they in fact rarely follow identical chord patterns—each song uses a few chords, but the bar-by-bar chord pattern varies from song to song. In the

---

[5] "Peggy Sue Got Married," words and music—Buddy Holly. Copyright © 1959 by Peer International Corporation. Used by permission.

lyrics to these last songs, Holly demonstrates a growing ability to balance personal directness and laconic generalization. As a result, the songs are notable both for immediacy and timelessness.

When Holly came home to Lubbock for a visit at Christmas, he spent some time with his friends at KLLL, playing some of his new songs for them on guitar and piano. These get-togethers led by chance to the composing and recording of "You're the One." While Holly was visiting one morning, he, Waylon Jennings, and Slim Corbin decided to write a song. In ten or fifteen minutes, it was finished, and someone decided that it should be taped. Holly sang the song and accompanied himself on a borrowed guitar, while Jennings and Corbin tried (sometimes unsuccessfully) to match Holly's driving rhythm with hand clapping.

Fortunately, the tape (less than ninety seconds long) was preserved, and over five years later, was released on an album, just as is. Considering the speed with which the song was composed, it is not really surprising that some of the lines are filled out with pop clichés; and yet, the sum total of the song is something else, going beyond the clichés to create a striking mixture of emotions that is both contradictory and coherent—and quite typical of a Buddy Holly song. Mrs. Holley admits, "I always liked his music; but I couldn't see much sense in his songs then—one line said one thing, and the next said the exact opposite. Like in 'Maybe Baby'—you're the one that makes me glad, and you're the one that makes me sad—that didn't make much sense to me. But now, when I listen to those songs—and think of what the fans have written—I understand the songs better." More than one fan wrote the Holleys to say how directly the lyrics spoke to them; the simple beauty of the lyrics, the melody, and the solo guitar accompaniment made the song a favorite:

> You're the one that's a-causing my blues,
> You're the one I don't wanna lose,
> You're the one that I'd always choose,
> You're the one that's a-meant for me.
>
> You're the one that I'm thinking of,
> You're the one that I'll always love,
> You're the one sent from heaven above,
> You're the one that's a-meant for me.
>
> > Sometimes you make me feel so bad,
> > You make me cry deep in my heart.
> > I feel like an actor in a play,
> > Who doesn't fit the part.
>
> You're the one, and I want you to know,
> You're the one that thrills me so,
> You're the one—I can't let you go,
> You're the one that's meant for me.[6]

---

[6]"You're The One," words and music—Buddy Holly. Copyright © 1961 by Peer International Corporation. Used by permission.

Mr. Holley recalls, "When Buddy came home at Christmas, it seemed like it was one of the happiest times in his life. He was free, and he had it pretty well made—he could do just about what he wanted to do." (It should be mentioned that Buddy didn't have to worry about his career being interrupted by the draft—he had flunked a physical the preceding July because of a stomach ulcer.) Holly could spend his time and energy as he wished. On one occasion, the star who had played the Palladium in London and the Paramount in New York performed live on a KLLL remote broadcast from the Morris Fruit and Vegetable Store. It was Holly's first "appearance" in Lubbock since the Crickets had become national stars. Buddy may have actually avoided opportunities to perform in Lubbock—not out of conceit or arrogance, but from a real timidity. "He said he'd rather make a flop anywhere in the world than in his home town," says Mr. Holley. Now, though, as another indication of his growing ease and confidence, Buddy told Slim Corbin to go ahead and book him for a "homecoming" appearance in Lubbock in the summer of 1959.

On New Year's Eve, Buddy and Maria flew back to New York, where Buddy made arrangements for his first tour since the breakup of the Crickets two months before.

In explaining Holly's continued popularity in the years since his death, it has frequently been said that he died "at his peak," before revealing any decline in the quality of his output. One wonders whether, if the Beatles had died in 1964, the same evaluation would have been made of them? Probably, since what they did thereafter was unforeseeable. There is likewise no way of telling where or how far Buddy Holly's expanding ambitions and interests would have taken him. When he died, Buddy Holly had not yet reached his peak—his career had only just begun.

Advertisement for the last performance in Clear Lake, Iowa,
February 2, 1959 (Mason City Globe-Gazette)

8. The Last Tour

Not all of Holly's activities in the last part of 1958 involved music directly. He and Maria were also deep in the promotional and business aspects of Holly's career which had come under his control following the break with Petty.

As mentioned, publicity had been an issue in the break. Maria says, "Nobody was trying to arrange magazine articles or any other kind of publicity, and nobody was going around to the talent agencies or booking organizations or the disc jockeys to promote Buddy—Norman wasn't doing anything, and neither was the record company. Other artists had fan clubs and newsletters, but nothing like that had been set up for Buddy. And he felt like that was why his records weren't getting played while these artists with Dick Clark were having big hits—Buddy would never criticize other artists or their music, but he knew that publicity was making a big difference.

"So those were the things we started working on. We worked at answering the fan mail and organizing fan clubs—we didn't have any secretaries or anything, we just went ahead and did it ourselves. We started going around to the agencies; and of course they wanted pictures for publicity work, so we went to a studio and had a series of photographs taken." (The photos included the one which appeared on the cover of *The Buddy Holly Story*— the one which, as people say, "makes him look like a concert pianist." It was what the agencies wanted to see—a quiet, thoughtful artist without a hair out of place—the very image of decorum. Later, such shots helped fuel the myth that Holly had ended his rock 'n' roll phase; and it didn't help that his record company never used the few available shots of Holly performing, with his curly hair tumbling over his forehead, and his mouth in a wide, happy grin.)

Buddy and his wife were also spending time just getting settled in New York, and enjoying their new life together. They had rented an apartment, and were in the process of furnishing it—a task in which Buddy took an active role. "Buddy was head-to-toe music," recalls Maria, "and he didn't really have any other interests. But he did like to draw and design. In fact, he said once that if he couldn't be a success in music, he'd like to be an engineer or a draftsman—you know, it wasn't that he was worried about that, it's just something every artist thinks of at some time or another. So Buddy designed all the cabinets for our apartment, and a bar that was going to open up onto the balcony. Did Buddy drink himself? No—he told me he couldn't understand why people had to drink to be happy; he said listening to or playing music was all he needed to feel happy. Anyway, he couldn't drink even if he wanted to, because of the stomach ulcer he had. I remember on the night of my birthday in December I got him to drink a couple of glasses of champagne to celebrate—and he was sick the whole next day. I told him I'd never push him like that again."

"There was one thing we did," continues Maria, "that didn't involve music, but it did have to do with Buddy's career, so I guess it was the same thing. I wanted Buddy to take dance lessons, and go to an acting school, too. He didn't like to dance—said he had two left feet. But I told him he should do this because he could use the training for his work on stage. And acting school was for when Buddy got to make some movies, as he wanted to do. So we started to go to the Lee Strasberg Acting School—that was something we were doing together."

The move to New York was not intended to be permanent—at least, not yet. Buddy and Maria expected to be travelling, going wherever Buddy's plans took him. New York was, of course, the place to be when business and promotion were involved, or when large orchestras (whether of the pop or rhythm & blues variety) were required. But stays in California might have been made for movies or recordings there, and Holly's studio in Lubbock would have required his presence some of the time, so the pair had decided to rent apartments and not buy any home. They had decided for certain not to live in the large house Buddy had planned as a gift for his parents. (After Buddy's death, the Holleys dropped the plans and bought a smaller house instead.)

The racial prejudices in Lubbock were a consideration. Maria explains: "I would never have stayed in Lubbock. The way they felt about blacks and Mexicans—it didn't intimidate me at all, but after growing up in New York City and being with everybody, I couldn't have stood that sort of thinking. Somehow, Buddy had been brought up there, but he didn't have any of those prejudices. I remember that when we were on tour, there was nothing that made him madder than the blacks having to go to one hotel and the whites to another—'We're all part of one show,' he said, 'why shouldn't we be together all the time?' He didn't just 'accept' blacks, that wasn't the way he acted— and the black performers knew that. As for Lubbock, he said to me once, 'This is one of the things I don't like here—but as much as I hate it, that's how these people are.' But he just couldn't see how people who read the Bible could feel like that."

Although he had received offers for new tours, Buddy had been holding off on this. One-nighters were especially unappealing. Being able to travel by car instead of by bus was a little more comfortable, but the schedules were still exhausting. Maria remembers, "I liked show business and I took better to the touring than some others—I wanted to be part of what Buddy did, I wanted to be active, doing things myself. But the tours were no fun. It was all travelling and performing, with no free time. Those kids didn't even have time to do their laundry, so I used to do it for them. Buddy didn't use makeup on stage, but the others did, and it'd be all over the collars; and they'd be wearing these clothes for days because there was never time to get their things cleaned. And everyone thought it was such a glamorous life—if only they could have seen me doing the laundry!

"It's true that we had the Cadillac—but I didn't have a license, so Buddy still had to do all the driving. A couple of times he was just so tired he was falling asleep at the wheel, and so I took over and drove, license or no license. And of course you were trying to go as fast as you could and get to the next city so you could rest up, and a couple of times we got stopped for speeding. Once in New Jersey, Buddy was stopped and he started arguing, so they took him to the station—he had me stay with the car, he thought it'd be safer. When he got to the station and they found out who he was, they said they'd let him go if he'd give them all his autograph! Well, he did, but he told me he was so mad about being held up like that for nothing, that his signature was probably unreadable, the way he dashed it off."

Besides his reluctance to go on a series of one-nighters, Buddy had another reason for delaying new appearances. If he went on tour, he would have to form a new group; and he was still hoping that, given time, the Crickets would change their minds and rejoin him. "He wanted to give them time to think it over," says Maria. "He was hoping the situation would clear up. Buddy was the kind of person who didn't like arguments—they depressed him. He'd stick to what he thought was right, but he worried about hurting others. He felt very bad about what had happened with the Crickets and with Norman Petty. He always wanted everything to come out right for everybody." (Mrs. Holley offers a sidelight to this: "Buddy never really told us why he had broken with Norman. Once when he was home and some of his friends were over, somebody started to make some remark about Norman, and Buddy cut it right off—'I don't want anyone bad-mouthing Norman,' he said, 'I don't want to hear anything about it.'")

Holly preferred to put off touring and instead start carrying out his recording and producing plans. But that required money—and, for reasons which are still subject to angry dispute, the money wasn't there.

The tale of what happened to the money earned by Holly and the Crickets is a tangled one, and the truth is difficult to discern. Maria Elena and all of the Crickets charge that much of the money which was rightfully due to the musicians was instead retained by Norman Petty; Petty denies this and says that all of the money owed to the members of the group was fairly paid out to them. I have talked with each party, but I have not looked at the books; no solution to the question is presented here, but only an outline of the arguments.

The money earned by the Crickets fell into three categories: income from personal appearances; songwriter royalties; and artist royalties on record sales. Each of these three sources was handled differently.

Money from personal appearances and performances was generally paid directly to the Crickets, by the tour promoter (like GAC) or the individual concert promoter (as was the case in the episode recounted on page 157). On the first long tour in 1957, the Crickets were paid $1,000 per week; each of the four kept $100 apiece for expenses, and the remaining $600 was sent back to Petty and placed, Petty says, in a special bank account under the Crickets name. Only Petty had access to this account. He says, "That wasn't at my insistence—it was at theirs. Joe B., in fact, said something about, 'Well, suppose J.I. decides he wants to write himself a check?' So they all agreed that they would not even be co-signers of a check or have access to it. The account wasn't for control of the money; it was for control of paying the bills."

Sometime during 1958, the Crickets began to keep more of this tour income for themselves, rather than sending it home. Petty says, "They got ticked off at me, because they said, 'Well, we're making all this money, why should we just be on salary?' And that's when they stopped sending anything to the Crickets account." Joe Mauldin says, however, that some money was still being sent back to Clovis: "We started taking more for expenses—we were making more, so we felt that it was justifiable to hold back more and spend a little more. But I don't remember any tours where we kept *all* of the money. Like, when we bought those motorcycles, we were still sending money home, because I remember we called Norman and said, 'We want to buy some motorcycles—we're going to go through Dallas and pay for them. So we're not going to send any money home for a few weeks.' And Buddy hung onto the money until we had enough."

Just how much was left over after payment of all expenses for these tours may be hard to figure. Touring was then primarily a vehicle for promoting records, and not always all that financially rewarding in itself. Those musicians who were on salary, like Allsup and (on one tour) the Roses, considered themselves to be well paid. Allsup recalls, "I was paid $250 a week by Holly, plus my expenses, and that was good pay in those days. Before I worked with Holly, I had been getting $80 a week playing in a western swing band."

Songwriter royalties were disbursed by Peer-Southern. The songwriter royalties would have been about one cent per record sold (another cent, the publisher's share, would have been split between Peer-Southern and Nor Va Jak). Also, there would have been payments from BMI of royalties from radio and television stations for airplays of the records. These royalties would have been split according to whose names were on the songs: one-third each for Petty, Holly, and Allison on "That'll Be The Day," for example. Thus, if "That'll Be The Day" had sold five million copies, songwriter royalties should have been $50,000, to be split three ways. According to Petty, the disbursements for songwriter royalties were sent directly to the individual songwriters and did not pass through his hands. Mauldin disagrees with this; he says, "I don't think I ever received any money directly from the music publishers until after we split with Petty, after Buddy's death. All the money, even the BMI checks, went to Petty." Allison agrees with Mauldin that all songwriting royalties were paid to Petty and were not transmitted to the Crickets.

The most significant earnings were those derived from record sales. Niki Sullivan says that the first check received from Coral/Brunswick at the end of 1957, reflecting much of the sales of "That'll Be The Day" and part of the sales of "Peggy Sue," was for $192,000. Ten percent of this income would have gone to Norman Petty as his manager's share; of the rest, the Crickets understood that forty percent would go to their churches and the rest would be divided among them. The contracts with the record company called for the payments to be made to Petty, on the Crickets' behalf, so there is no disputing who first handled this money; but what happened to it thereafter is very much disputed. While Petty will not give any numbers, he maintains that "a great deal" of these record royalties had indeed been paid out to the Crickets by late 1958. He says, "The only thing we were holding up was some of the 'Crickets' money" (the tour income which had been deposited in the special Crickets account), and according to Petty, that was done at the request of Allison and Mauldin. Everyone else, though, tells another story.

Take Niki Sullivan's account. Even before his decision to leave the group, Sullivan and his parents had begun to have questions about what was happening to the money earned by the Crickets. Sullivan says, "My father had been to Clovis quite a few times, just to talk to Norman about seeing the books, and never once did he ever get to see them. They were always at the accountant's or somewhere, being worked on." Though he will not say so outright, Sullivan implies that this inquisitiveness may have been a reason why Petty did not try to keep Sullivan in the group. "It could have been salvaged, with a little effort, but I don't think it wanted to be salvaged, on certain people's parts. That effort never occurred; whether by design or not, that's not for me to question."

After Sullivan had made his exit from the Crickets, something had to be worked out as to what share he would receive of the group's earnings. Since he would no longer be touring and helping to promote the records, it was arguable whether he was entitled to a full share in the royalties, and Sullivan was willing to accept less. He says, "I went back to Norman's when the fellows weren't there. Norman had arranged for me to take ten percent of the income from 'That'll Be The Day,' and I would forfeit everything on anything else that I'd played on. And I said, 'Well, that'll be fine.'"

However, the money was never paid. "To this day," says Sullivan, "I have never gotten any money—not a dime." The only income which Sullivan earned from his association with the Crickets was the $100 a week he retained from the income on the GAC tour, and a thousand-dollar check which the Crickets gave him early in 1958, after their first tour without Sullivan. (Allison explains, "It wasn't part of any settlement, because we didn't know what the deal was that Norman had worked out with him. It was just a gesture, a way of saying, 'Hey, Niki, we don't dislike you.'") Since then, all that Sullivan has received are the songwriting royalties paid to him for his share in "I'm Gonna Love You Too."

Sullivan's church never saw its share of the royalties on "That'll Be The Day," either. In fact, according to Allison, Mauldin, and Mrs. Holley, none of the other churches ever received the funds, either.

When I queried him about Sullivan's story, Petty said, "Niki was to share in everything that he had been on, if I remember right. And then from that day on, anything he wasn't on, he wouldn't share in. To the best of my recollection. But he was paid on whatever he was on, the best I remember. It was reduced to writing, whatever the agreement was. He signed a release." Sullivan denies that he ever signed any agreement on the payments.

What may seem puzzling is why Sullivan never did anything about this. He explains, "I wasn't about to go back to Norman and ask for it. I figured that I had checked out, and that's the way I wanted it. I didn't want the money, it wasn't worth the hassle. Money is just a means to an end—if I've got a lot of it, great, if I don't, what the hell. I still have to watch the sun get up in the morning and go down at night."

Both Allison and Mauldin were unaware, until I told them, that Sullivan had not received the share that was agreed upon. They say they did not fare all that much better: after their own split with Petty following Holly's death,

Niki Sullivan, at home, November 1977 (Bill Griggs)

they settled for what they believed to be a lot less than what was due them, just to put the past behind and to straighten out matters for the future. Mauldin says, "As best I remember, Petty had received all the record and songwriting royalties, and it was all being held—I never saw any royalties until we split with Petty. When we split, Petty said, 'Well, here's all that's in the account, this is all you have coming because you spent the rest of it,' and we didn't agree with him, but there wasn't any way we could prove otherwise. Our lawyer said, 'Take what he gives you and run, and forget it—mark it up as a good lesson learned.' " Allison and Mauldin do now receive songwriting and record royalties directly from the companies involved.

Petty maintains that he dealt fairly with the Crickets and has continued to do the same with all the other artists he has had since. "Any time I have an artist, to this day, they get a Xerox copy of the royalty statements and the check itself. This has been a thing that we established years ago." He also says, "They kept huge sums—it used to worry me, because Buddy would keep six thousand dollars, he had as much as ten thousand dollars in cash. And he would get up in the middle of a bed, he and Jerry would play with it like they were playing Monopoly." His secretary and assistant, Norma Jean Berry, adds, "I think some of the difficulty came after Buddy was dead, when there was so much speculation about how much money had been made, not based on fact. People thought it must be tremendous, and it really wasn't that great, at that point. And the boys themselves forgot how much money they simply wasted. I mean, they'd get several thousand dollars from their engagements, and they didn't remember that they had spent a lot of money. They had wasted a lot of money. And because they didn't have it, they thought, 'Well, Norman's got it.' Except it wasn't true."

Allison and Mauldin also differ with Petty on whose idea it was to hold back whatever money was due to Holly. Mauldin says, "Neither one of us ever insinuated in any way that Petty should hold it. In fact, Jerry and I felt it was unfair that Petty hold it, because Buddy needed it—we knew he needed it." Allison takes a similar line: "I only found out after Buddy's death that Norman had been telling Buddy and Buddy's lawyer that Buddy owed us a bunch of money from tours, and that we'd have to get that all straight before Buddy got his money. I hope to this day that Buddy knew better than that—because we weren't telling Norman to hold the money. Buddy might have owed us money, because when we were touring we used to get the loot in cash and we'd say, 'Look at that!' and Buddy'd say, 'How much you want? Five hundred dollars? A thousand?,' whatever, you know, we kept receipts, but none of us cared. And sure, there might have been some times when we didn't get our part, and some when we might have gotten more than our part. But Joe B. and I didn't ever at one time say, 'O.K., we want to be sure that we get our part of that.' Buddy would never have cheated us out of a thing."

Holly and Maria Elena clearly believed that there was money owing to them, for they undertook legal action in the months after the split with Petty to recover the disputed funds. Despite Petty's position that there was not much money involved, Holly obviously thought otherwise. Tommy Allsup remembers that the day before Holly's death, Holly was infuriated to learn that an audit of one account had found less than $5,000 in it—Holly, according to Allsup, believed that there should have been over $50,000 there. One friend of Holly's says that the total amount in dispute was about $80,000.

There is no doubt that, in the year after the success of "That'll Be The Day," Holly received enough money to pay for some major items, including his Triumph motorcycle, his Cadillac, and the Impala he bought for his parents. On the other hand, Holly had apparently not yet received much of what was due him from all sources. Between his death and the time when his will was probated, some $70,000 was paid to his estate. At the time that he decided to go back on tour in early 1959, Holly was definitely short of cash. Tommy Allsup remembers that Holly had had to borrow money from GAC, drawing an advance on his income from the tour in order to pay for his anticipated expenses.

I am neither an accountant nor a lawyer, and I am not sure that I would be any more able to make sense of all this, even if I were. After talking with each of the Crickets, with Petty, with the Holleys and Maria Elena, and with others who were close to the situation, it is my own judgment that Holly and the Crickets probably never saw much of what was rightfully due to them. Though they may well have been paid all that was *legally* due them—in the entertainment business even more than in other industries, what is fair and what is legal is often worlds apart. This is just my opinion, but others may conclude differently.

The money, and what happened to it, is an issue which is part of Holly's story and can hardly be avoided; but in truth, it is one which none of the parties enjoy discussing. They have willingly laid out their recollections for me, and each wants to give his or her side of it, but it brings them no pleasure to do so. Having to talk about this aspect of the past brings to the surface bitter memories and feelings of antagonism, and these are only aroused further, not eased, by the recollection. For the sake of peace of mind, they wish it could all be put far in the past; no one any longer seeks revenge or recompense. It is, as more than one of them says, "Not worth the hassle."

I have found myself, therefore, regretting that I had to ask the questions I did, wishing not to reopen the wounds, and wanting not to seem so preoccupied with this part of Holly's life. Maybe the best way to react to all this is not to concentrate on how much the conflicts affected the course of Holly's life, but rather on how little they altered Holly's spirit and his music. I find it something to marvel at, that in the midst of all these personality conflicts and financial disputes, and in the face of the enormous emotional and commercial pressures of the pop music business, Holly and the Crickets survived to create and perform music of lasting grace, vitality, and good spirit. The more one learns about the distractions and the obstacles, the more remarkable becomes Holly's legacy, the transcending joy that is released whenever his records are played.

Early in the new year, Holly was asked to head a package tour which GAC was organizing. Influenced by both finances and friendship, Buddy reluctantly agreed. Maria explains: "More than anything, Buddy went on the tour as a favor to GAC. They had put this show together, but they felt that they needed a bigger attraction on the bill than the acts they already had. So they really urged Buddy to help them out. Of course, the money was a reason for going—my aunt had been lending us money to fix up our apartment and all. But I think he went more because he had gone on so many GAC tours before and he had friends there, and he didn't feel like he could turn them down if they said they needed him."

As Jerry Allison said, Buddy didn't want to go on tours if they didn't sound like they would be fun—and a wintertime tour did not sound like fun to a Texas native. Billed as "The Winter Dance Party," this package was booked for a three-week tour through the heart of the Midwest, with most of the appearances scheduled in Minnesota, Wisconsin, and Iowa. The acts on the show were not so numerous or so impressive as on Holly's previous tours. Due to the national economic recession and to changes in rock 'n' roll music itself, the big package shows had declined in size and strength over the previous year, and were becoming much more segregated. The Winter Dance Party had just five acts: Holly, Ritchie Valens, the Big Bopper, Dion and the Belmonts, and Frankie Sardo.

Holly now had to form a new band for the tour. He asked Tommy Allsup to join him again on guitar, and Allsup accepted the invitation. Holly then invited Waylon Jennings to play bass; Waylon jumped at the offer, and KLLL proudly granted him a "leave of absence." (Jennings, who was used to the standard guitar, played electric bass rather than stand-up bass on this tour.) A drummer named Charlie Bunch was hired to complete the group. Holly may also have had in mind asking Niki Sullivan to play with him again; Holly called Sullivan's home, but Sullivan was out for a couple of days, and when Sullivan tried to return the call, he got no answer.

Despite Holly's agreement with Allison and Mauldin giving them title to the Crickets name, Holly's new group was billed as the Crickets. Allison believes that GAC did this without Holly's approval, but it is more probable that Holly, as part of the legal maneuvering over the group's earnings, found it necessary to use the Crickets name as a way of maintaining his claim to the disputed funds. A spectator at Holly's last show remembers that the singer never referred to his band as the Crickets.

Fans wonder how Holly would have responded had the original Crickets asked to rejoin him, now that he had this new band. "Buddy still hoped to patch things up with the Crickets," says Maria. "He tried to call them once, in fact, from New York, but they weren't home, they were over in Clovis. He felt that if he could just talk to them, they could get back together. Of course, Tommy Allsup would have stayed in the band, and Buddy was going to promote Waylon as an individual artist, anyway, so it wasn't a case of having to choose some people over others. When he went on the tour, Buddy really missed the Crickets—he felt like they added something special to his act.

Once when he talked with me on the phone, he said, 'If you get a call from Jerry and Joe B., tell them I'll be back in two weeks, and I want to talk to them—alone.' ''

Buddy and Maria decided that, for reasons of health, Maria should skip this one tour—she was pregnant and had been having spells of nausea, and so it seemed best for her to avoid the rigors of a series of one-nighters. (She suffered a miscarriage a few weeks after Holly's death.) Since he was going to be travelling alone, Buddy decided to leave his Cadillac with Maria in New York and go by bus with the rest of the troupe.

Allsup and Jennings joined Holly in New York, and stayed in his apartment until the group left for the tour. According to Allsup, "Peggy Sue Got Married" and "That Makes It Tough" were taped the evening before their departure, with Tommy backing up Holly's guitar playing on both songs.

At breakfast on their last day in New York, Allsup remembers, Holly told his friends of strange dreams Maria and he had had the night before. Maria tells the details: "I had always had a fear of small planes, and Buddy knew it. But his brother Larry had a plane, and Buddy wanted to fly, too—he was taking lessons behind my back, and when I found out, I got mad. I told him that he shouldn't fly small planes—that it scared me, and that should be reason enough not to do it.

"The night before Buddy left, I had this dream. I dreamed I was with Buddy, and then there was a lot of commotion—people were scared and running every which way, and then I found myself alone in a big, empty prairie or desert. Then I heard shouts and screams, and saw hundreds of people running towards me shouting, 'Look out, it's coming!' They all passed by me and I turned to watch them go; and when I turned back, I saw this big ball of fire coming through the air. It passed by me and fell a few feet from where I was, and made a deep hole in the ground. Then I woke up, and I must have screamed because I woke Buddy up, too. And then he told me about the dream he had been having.

"He had been dreaming that he was in a small plane with Larry and me. Larry didn't want me to be there, but Buddy told him, 'Anywhere I go, Maria comes with me.' They kept arguing about it, and Larry kept landing the plane because he wanted me to get off, and Buddy wouldn't agree, so they'd take off again. Finally, Larry won the argument, and they landed on the roof of a tall building and left me there. And Buddy said, 'Don't worry, just stay put—I'll come back and get you.' And then he flew off. And that was when he woke up. So I guess our dreams meant something, if you put them together. . . ."

The Midwest, for some reason, was prime territory for rock 'n' roll stage shows. There were few real metropolises in the upper Midwest; but even the small cities of 25,000 to 100,000 people had large ballrooms which, for such a touring show as this, were usually filled by crowds wholly out of proportion to the size of the local population.

However, while the shows themselves were enjoyable, the travelling between them was not. It was the worst time of the year for such a tour—the heart of winter, in an area where winter is most severe. Bus travel, never comfortable, was now positively hazardous. Usually travelling in the cold darkness, four, five, six hundred miles sometimes between successive dates, the unheated buses were prone to breakdowns. The troupe had to switch buses several times during the first week of the tour, as mechanical problems sidelined the vehicles. One night, a bus simply died while ascending a hill on a lonely highway. By the time a highway patrol car came along, found the bus, and arranged transportation for the troupe to the nearest town, drummer Charlie Bunch had suffered frostbite on his feet; he had to be left behind in a hospital bed.

Ten miles west of Mason City, a community of thirty thousand people in north-central Iowa, is the small town of Clear Lake. The town is an important resort center thanks to the large lake from which it takes its name; by the shore of the lake lies a large dance hall with the somewhat ludicrous title of the Surf Ballroom. Here, the Winter Dance Party was scheduled to appear on Monday evening, February 2.

In the years since then, the ballroom has expanded in function and has been renamed the Surf Civic and Convention Center. It still retains the raised stage, the beautiful, polished dance floor, and the rows of green leather-covered padded booths lining the side and rear of the dance floor, that were there in 1959.

"The dance business isn't like it used to be," a custodian gazing at the empty floor explains. "Oh, we still have some big names—we had Lawrence Welk in here a couple of weeks ago. But they don't have many teen-age dances now. A few years back, they had nine or ten dances with good crowds; but

The Surf Ballroom, site of Holly's last performance, as it appeared in 1972 (John Goldrosen)

then it started dropping off, and with the price of the bands going so high. . . . That's why they're trying to make this more of a convention center. People don't turn out for dances the way they used to. I don't know—maybe kids just don't like to dance anymore."

On Sunday, February 1, the Dance Party played afternoon and evening shows in Appleton and Green Bay, Wisconsin, and then set out for Clear Lake, about 350 miles away. On the way, they again had trouble with their bus, and it was 6:00 P.M. before the troupe rolled into Clear Lake. The show that night was scheduled to run from eight to midnight; immediately after the dance, the performers would pile back onto the bus and ride all night to Moorhead, Minnesota, where they were booked for two shows the next night. It would be a ride of 430 miles north and west from Clear Lake. In Moorhead, they would hopefully have a few hours to rest in a hotel before the evening shows.

By the time the tour reached Clear Lake, Holly was as tired as the rest of the performers were. He was worried that his weariness might detract from his group's performance. He was also concerned with their stage appearance. The group had been performing every night and then riding in the buses fully-dressed to fight off the subzero weather, and their stage clothes were now pretty well rumpled and soiled—it had been at least several days since the group had been in one town long enough to get their clothes cleaned.

At Clear Lake, Buddy decided to charter a small plane so that he and his sidemen could fly on ahead to Moorhead. That way, the group could get a decent night's sleep and have a chance to do the laundry before the shows the next night. The idea met with the approval of the tour's road manager, Rod Lucier; by going to Moorhead ahead of the troupe, Holly could still take care of needed last-minute arrangements for the shows there, even if the bus were delayed by more mechanical problems.

Buddy explained his plan to Waylon Jennings and Tommy Allsup, and the two agreed to go with Holly and share the cost of renting the plane. Upon arriving at the Surf Ballroom, Holly spoke to the manager of the dance hall, Carroll Anderson, and asked Anderson to try to arrange such a flight. Anderson attempted to reach Jerry Dwyer, owner of Dwyer's Flying Service, the charter company based at the Mason City Airport. Dwyer was at a Junior Chamber of Commerce meeting in Mason City; Anderson next called Roger Peterson, a young pilot who worked for Dwyer, and asked if Peterson could make the flight. Although the next day was supposed to be his day off, the pilot agreed to fly the group to the airport at Fargo, North Dakota, just across the Red River from Moorhead. The flight was scheduled to leave the Mason City Airport about 12:30 A.M.

When the other performers on the tour heard of Buddy's arrangement, Jennings and Allsup got separate requests to give up their seats on the plane. J. P. Richardson, the "Big Bopper," approached Jennings. Richardson pointed out that the long bus rides were particularly rough on large men like himself who could not sleep comfortably on the bus; "Those bus seats bug me," he said. Besides, J. P. had caught a cold, and his condition certainly wasn't going to be improved by a night-long ride on a cold bus. Waylon actually wasn't minding the bus rides as much as the others were—for him, the tour was a novelty, and he was finding it fun to be with the other performers on the tour. Jennings agreed to let Richardson make the flight instead.

When Ritchie Valens heard of the intended flight, he too wanted to be in on it. He tried to convince Allsup to give up his seat, at first without success. But finally, Tommy agreed to flip a coin to decide who would go, provided that he could use the Big Bopper's new sleeping bag on the bus if Valens should win the coin toss. The Big Bopper agreed. Allsup flipped the coin, and Ritchie called "heads." "Heads" it was.

Somewhere between eleven and fifteen hundred teenagers paid the $1.25 admission charge to see the Dance Party that night; Anderson says that it was the best crowd ever for a rock 'n' roll show at the ballroom. A few adults were there, too, since it was Anderson's policy to admit parents free as his "guests."

Bob Hale, a local DJ, was master of ceremonies that night. He agrees with Anderson: "It was the biggest crowd that Carroll Anderson had ever had in the Surf—it was the biggest thing I had ever seen. We had people that had driven in from St. Paul, others that had driven in from Illinois and Minnesota. The place was filled to the rafters."

According to Fred Milano, a member of Dion and the Belmonts, the show was opened by Frankie Sardo, who was followed by Ritchie Valens, the Big Bopper, the Belmonts, and Holly. But both Milano and Bob Hale remember that Holly was on stage earlier in the evening—playing drums! Holly's band had been backing up the other groups on the tour, and with Bunch out with frostbite, Holly filled in on drums. During Holly's own set, the bass singer for the Belmonts, Carlo Mastrangelo, played drums. According to Hale, each act played two sets, and there was also about fifteen minutes of "goofing off," with Holly, Valens, and the Big Bopper singing together as a trio.

The tour had dispelled any fears anyone might have had that Holly's popularity was on the wane. The crowds which turned out for the shows were greeting him as warmly as they had before, and listening to his music and his singing just as closely. At the time, Ritchie Valens had the second best-selling single in the country with his two-sided hit, "Donna"/"La Bamba," while the Big Bopper's "Chantilly Lace" had been on the charts for six months; even so, eyewitness accounts and newspaper reports of the show in Mason City agree that Holly was the best-received act on the bill. Holly and Carroll Anderson chatted backstage in the manager's office before the show; when Anderson asked the singer how far he expected to go in the music business, Holly replied with a grin, "Well, I'm either going to go to the top—or else I'm going to fall. But I think you're going to see me in the bigtime."

Touring as he was with Jennings and Allsup, both of whom were well-acquainted with country music, Holly had occasionally mixed in country songs with his more familiar hits, and the reaction had been good. Waylon Jennings once told an interviewer, "We did country songs on stage—we did 'Salty Dog Blues,' and that's as country as you can get—and the kids really

Waylon Jennings, Tommy Allsup, and Buddy Holly performing in Eau Claire, Wisconsin, January 26, 1959—one week before Holly's death (©1977 Don Larson, Evergreen, CO.)

thought, 'Man, that's it, that's what's happening.'" This night in Clear Lake, Buddy opened his act by coming on stage ahead of his band, strumming his electric guitar and singing a country tune which had crossed over onto the pop charts to become a top ten hit for Billy Grammer:

> **I've laid around, and played around,**
> **This old town too long,**
> **Summer's almost gone,**
> **And winter's coming on.**
> **I've laid around, and played around,**
> **This old town too long,**
> **And I feel like I've gotta travel on....**[1]

Daniel Dougherty, a resident of a small farming village south of Mason City, was at the show. He writes: "The hall was pretty well packed full that

---

[1]"Gotta Travel On," words and music—Paul Clayton. Copyright © 1958 by Sanga Music Inc. ALL RIGHTS RESERVED; used by permission.

night. There wasn't much dancing while Buddy sang—they all wanted to just listen to him sing. He didn't dance around the stage much, but stayed in one place most of the time; he moved his neck a lot when he sang. He wore a suit with a bow tie, and those big black glasses that made him stand out on the stage. After each song he sang, he got right into another one—he never said hardly a word but 'thank you.' "

Holly sang most of his single releases—"Peggy Sue," "That'll Be The Day," "Maybe Baby," "Heartbeat," "Rave On," and "Everyday" were among the tunes he sang that night. "One thing for sure," writes Dougherty, "Buddy never sang 'It Doesn't Matter Anymore' "—even though it was his current release.

Sometime during the evening, Buddy called Maria in New York. She remembers: "He told me what an awful tour it had been. The buses were dirty and cold, and things just weren't as had been promised. He said everybody on the tour was really disgusted with the whole thing. Then he said that the tour was behind schedule, and he had to go on ahead of the others to the next stop to make arrangements for the show. He didn't tell me that he was going to fly. I said, 'Why should *you* go?' And he said, 'There's nobody else to do it.' "

When the Dance Party show was over in Clear Lake, Carroll Anderson drove Holly, Valens, and the Big Bopper to the Mason City Airport. They arrived there about 12:40 A.M., and were met by Roger Peterson and by Jerry Dwyer, who had been informed about the flight during the evening and had come to the airport to help Peterson get the plane ready. Dwyer later expressed his surprise upon meeting the three musicians—"I thought all entertainers got drunk. But they hadn't been drinking; they were just real nice kids."

Peterson had checked the weather forecasts several times during the evening. Conditions were acceptable; all stations en route were reporting visibility of ten miles or greater, although snow showers were forecast for Fargo sometime after midnight. At Mason City itself, the temperature was eighteen degrees, the wind was gusting to thirty-five miles per hour, and light snow was falling by the time the plane was ready to take off—not the best of conditions, but still adequate. The air traffic communicators at the airport did not inform Peterson of two special weather bureau advisories, one predicting lowered visibility in snow and fog over an area including Iowa, and the other reporting a band of snow moving southeastward through Minnesota and North Dakota.

Since he did not see the special advisories, Peterson may not have realized that he might have to fly by instruments. The twenty-one-year-old pilot had been flying for four years, but had not yet been certified for instrument flying. He had failed his first instrument flight check a year before when he had had difficulty holding at the required altitude. That did not mean that he was prohibited from flying by instruments; he had had many lessons on them, and was familiar, though inexperienced, with the equipment involved. However, the Dwyer Flying Service was certificated for visual flights only, and hence its pilots were not supposed to fly under conditions requiring navigation by instruments.

Anderson and the performers went into Dwyer's office, where the three passengers paid their thirty-six-dollar fares individually. They spent a few minutes chatting with Dwyer, who later remembered Holly discussing his own interest in flying small planes. Then, they walked out to the aircraft, a red Beechcraft Bonanza four-seater, and Anderson helped the three load their baggage on the plane. Valens and Richardson climbed into the back seats, while Holly got in front with Peterson. Anderson left for his home, and Dwyer went to the control tower to watch the plane's departure.

It was a little before 1:00 A.M. when the single-engine aircraft moved down the airport's north-south runway and took off. Levelling off south of the field, it made a 180-degree left turn and headed north, and then took up a northwest bearing, in the direction of Fargo.

Now, the lights of Mason City and Clear Lake were left behind. The moon and stars were obscured by the snow and the overcast sky; and the thinly populated countryside below, with its scattered farmhouses and snow-covered cornfields, offered no lights or landmarks or visible horizon to the nighttime travellers. Peterson was immediately forced to depend upon his instruments. The gusty winds caused most of the instruments to fluctuate, making them difficult to interpret. Peterson had to rely on the plane's Sperry attitude gyroscope, which displayed the plane's pitch attitude in exactly the opposite manner from the way it was shown on the conventional artificial horizon gyroscopes Peterson had encountered during his instrument flight training. Under such conditions of stress and inexperience, Peterson probably became confused in reading the unfamiliar gyroscope. He may never have realized that while executing what he thought was a climbing turn, the plane was actually descending.

From the airport tower, Jerry Dwyer watched the plane's white tail light recede in the distance. When the plane was about four miles from the airport, Dwyer saw the plane descend slowly, until it was out of sight. He later stated, "I thought at the time that probably it was an optical illusion due to the plane going away from us at an angle." Dwyer was disturbed, though, by Peterson's failure to file a flight plan immediately after take-off. Attempts were made to contact the plane by radio, but there was no answer.

That same night, Joe Mauldin, Jerry Allison, and Sonny Curtis were at Jerry's house in Lubbock, talking things over. Jerry and Joe felt that they had parted with Buddy as friends; but although they had not seen him or talked to him since the break, they could tell now that some sort of tension had built up, and they did not know quite why. They wondered too why the name of the Crickets was being used for the group touring with Holly. For Mauldin and Allison, the situation had not turned out the way Norman Petty had pictured it—in the three months since Holly's departure from the group, the original Crickets (augmented by Curtis and vocalist Earl Sinks) had gotten no engagements and had cut just one single, "Love's Made A Fool Of You," which had not yet been released. Jerry and Joe decided to call Buddy to talk things out and get matters straight—with the idea that the call might lead to the reunion of the group, perhaps with Sonny Curtis likewise rejoining Holly.

Joe Mauldin explains: "During that tour, Jerry and I broke with Norman. And then we started trying to get in touch with Buddy, because Buddy had said, 'You ever want to get back with me, all you have to do is call.' So we were trying to call Buddy to say, 'We want to put the group back together.'"

They called Maria a couple of hours after her conversation with Buddy; she told the pair where Buddy was playing that night, and where he would be the next day. When Mauldin and Allison called the ballroom in Clear Lake, they found that Holly had already left. Then, says Joe, "We called the next place he was going to play, and left a message, and we were expecting a call that night or the next day when he got there. But we never got to talk to him."

Through the night, Jerry Dwyer checked with the Mason City Airport several times to learn if anything had been heard from Peterson, but there was no news. Airports in Minnesota and the one at Fargo were contacted, and they too had heard nothing from the plane. Shortly before dawn, an alert was issued for the missing aircraft. Dwyer went to the airport in the morning, but found that there was still no news. "I decided I just couldn't sit there," he told Civil Aeronautics Board investigators, "and decided I would go fly and try to follow the same course that I thought Roger would have taken. I was only approximately eight miles northwest of the field when I spotted the wreckage. I believe the time was approximately 9:35 A.M."

Guided by Dwyer's radioed directions, police arrived at the crash site shortly thereafter. The wreckage lay in a cornfield several hundred yards from the nearest farmhouse; no one had seen or heard the crash. The right wing of the plane had struck the ground first and been ripped off as the plane hit the ground, bounced fifty feet on and then plowed five hundred feet through the snow and stubble before piling into a wire fence at the north end of the field. The body of J. P. Richardson had been thrown forty feet beyond the fence, while those of Holly and Valens lay twenty feet south of the wreck; Peterson's body was still in the ball of wreckage which was all that was left of the plane. All had surely died at the moment of impact.

Carroll Anderson was called from Clear Lake to make a positive identification of the bodies; there was some confusion at first, since an extra billfold had been found at the crash site, one belonging to Tommy Allsup. (Allsup recalls that he had given his wallet to Holly, so that Holly could pick up a registered letter waiting for Allsup in Moorhead.) Meanwhile, a radio station in Mason City was listening to the radio conversations between search planes, the airport control tower, and the police. The station soon discovered who had been on the plane, and the story went out over the national newswires, even before the wreckage was discovered and the bodies positively identified.

Later in the morning, the bus carrying the other members of the tour

Site of the plane crash, February 3, 1959 (Elwin Musser, Mason City Globe-Gazette)

reached Moorhead. As Tommy Allsup walked into the hotel lobby, he could see a nearby television. A photograph of the Big Bopper was on the screen, but Allsup could not hear the announcer's words. He walked up to the desk to check in, and it was the desk clerk who told him and the others what had happened.

Maria Elena had been feeling ill, and was still in bed when she got a telephone call from Lou Giordano. "He asked me if I had seen the television or listened to the radio yet," she says, "and when I told him I hadn't, he said, 'Don't turn them on—I'm on my way over.' But I turned on the radio. And my aunt came in just as I heard the news...."

The Holleys learned of the crash in much the same, sudden way. Sometime during the morning, a friend of Mrs. Holley's called her and mentioned that a radio station was playing many of Buddy's songs. "Well, I didn't think much of that," Mrs. Holley says, "they were always doing that. Then the woman asked, 'By the way, how was Buddy travelling?' 'By bus,' I told her. She said, 'Oh,' and said goodbye." Not long afterward, another woman called, and said with little tact, "Have you heard the news? There's some news about Buddy on the radio; turn it on." Mrs. Holley told her husband to do so; the station was indeed playing Buddy's songs, and before long the news story was repeated: "A light plane has crashed in Iowa...." "I don't remember hearing any more," says Mrs. Holley. "I put it all together, and I knew what had happened. And I knew that the plane flight must have been all Buddy's idea."

In Moorhead, the surviving performers at first didn't want to go through with their engagement. Eventually, however, they decided that "the show must go on." The scheduled two shows were combined into one, and an audience of over two thousand tried too to forget their loss with the sound of rock 'n' roll; but when Holly's band appeared on stage, minus its star, and sang his songs, some in the audience could not hold back their tears.

The afternoon of the Moorhead appearance, the show's producers held auditions for local talent to fill out the shortened bill that night. One group which won a spot was a band from Central High School in Fargo. The members of the group bought themselves identical sweaters—as a tribute, perhaps, to Holly, whose new publicity photos showed him wearing a white sweater—and named themselves "The Shadows." Seventeen-year-old Bobby Velline was chosen to be the vocalist, since he knew more lyrics than anyone else in the band. Over the next few years, Bobby Vee used a voice which bore some resemblance to that of Buddy Holly to gain his own degree of success as a recording artist.

The next night, in Sioux City, Iowa, the troupe was joined by Jimmie Clanton and Frankie Avalon, who had dropped other commitments to take the places of the dead stars. In retrospect, there was something symbolic in that. Musicians whose styles had grown out of the very roots of rock 'n' roll were succeeded by a school of performers noted more for their photogenic appeal than for their music. And with the change, rock 'n' roll lost much of the warmth, humor, sincerity, and sheer vitality for which Holly, Richardson, and Valens were remembered.

On Wednesday, the 4th, a plane was sent from Texas to bring Holly's body home; the threatening Midwest storm had finally moved into Iowa, and it was Thursday before the plane could return. The Holleys had already started to receive messages from Buddy's acquaintances and fans around the world; from Germany came a telegram from Elvis Presley, then stationed there with the United States Army. One thousand people, many of them Buddy's young local fans, attended the funeral held Saturday afternoon at the Tabernacle Baptist Church. The pallbearers were the contemporaries with whom Buddy had played and performed since he had picked up a guitar: Bob Montgomery, Jerry Allison, Joe Mauldin, Niki Sullivan, Sonny Curtis, and Phil Everly. Another reminder of Buddy's musical life was included in the service. Someone, remembering Holly's long-time enthusiasm for the Angelic Gospel Singers' "I'll Be All Right," had found a copy of the record, and the black gospel tune was played during the funeral.

DEATH OF SINGERS HERE SHOCKS NATION

Rock 'n Rollers, Pilot Die in Tragic Plane Crash

There was no fearful omen of tragedy Monday night when 1,100 teenagers and their parents packed the Surf Ballroom in Clear Lake for a gala "rock 'n roll" dance. Featured were four nationally-known entertainers: Buddy Holly and the Crickets; the "Big Bopper"; Ritchie Valens; and Dion and the Belmonts.

The entertainers were full of pep, reacting joyously to the big crowd of young people. The "Big Bopper" (J. P. Richardson), who wrote the hit song "Chantilly Lace," and Ritchie Valens, author of several top hits, playfully Indian wrestled backstage between acts.

Two hours after the dance, three of the four singers were dead, along with the pilot who was flying them to Fargo, N.D., for another appear- ance. **Their broken bodies were found in and around the wreckage of the light plane they had chartered after the dance Monday night.**

Dead were the pilot, Roger Peterson, 21, of Clear Lake; Charles (Buddy) Holly, 22, of Lubbock, Texas; Ritchie Valens (Richard Valenzuela), 17, of Los Angeles, Calif.; J. P. (Big Bopper) Richardson, 28, Beaumont, Texas.

Word of their death when the plane was found Tuesday morning in a snow covered field six miles north of the airport focused nationwide attention on Clear Lake. The three singers are considered among the top rock 'n roll artists in the United States and their recordings are currently on the best selling list, some over the million mark.

THE FATAL CRASH occurred on the Albert Juhl farm in a pasture about a half mile west of the farm house. The plane, a Beechcraft Bonanza chartered from the Dwyer Flying service, took off about 1 a.m. from the airport with the three men after they were taken to the air-port by Carroll Anderson, Surf manager, his wife and son, Tommy.

It is believed to have crashed shortly thereafter into the field on the Juhl farm.

WRECKAGE OF THE PLANE was discovered by Jerry Dwyer about 9:30 a.m. Tuesday. He had received no reports from the plane since it departed and he began the search in another plane Tuesday morning.

The craft first scraped the ground at a spot in the middle of the field, breaking off one wing and other parts of the plane.

It then bounced and skidded about 200 yards further to the northwest, scattering wreckage and debris along the way until it piled into a wire fence along the north end of the pasture.

The plane was completely demolished in the crash, but did not burn.

The bodies of the three entertainers were thrown from the plane, two of them lying a short distance to the south of the plane, and the third was thrown over the fence about 20 feet into the next field.

The body of the pilot was entangled amid the wreckage of the main part of the plane. Ambulances took the victims to the Ward and Wilcox Funeral home in Clear Lake.

An investigation was launched by the Civil Aeronautics administration after the crash to determine its cause.

Jerry Dwyer, operator of the flying service, could give no reason, stating that the plane was in good condition and that Mr. Peterson was a competent pilot.

Indications pointed to the fact that the plane touched the ground at a low angle, skidding along the field instead of plunging steeply into the ground. The only mark at the place where it first hit was a furrow scraped out by a wing tip.

CAA INVESTIGATORS arrived in Clear Lake later Tuesday and remained overnight. Guards were posted at the scene throughout the day and through Tuesday night to keep the wreckage intact for the investigation.

The major significance of loss of the three artists to the music world was indicated by the immediate requests of national press associations for full coverage. Requests also have been received from Life magazine for pictures.

Other members of the troupe who appeared at the Surf Monday night were traveling to Fargo by chartered bus.

Ironically, Buddy Holly had told KRIB disc jockey Bob Hale of the Surf that he didn't want to take a chance in the bus since it had broken down while traveling from Green Bay, Wis., to Clear Lake the day before.

The three therefore decided to charter the plane and take care of advance arrangements in Fargo Tuesday.

Valens, who only last year was a high school student at San Fernando, Calif., had just finished his first movie and his song, "Donna" sold more than a million records.

Richardson, known as the "Big Bopper," won nationwide fame for the song, "Chantilly Lace" which he wrote some months ago.

Buddy Holly, singing star of the Crickets, has made eight records, two of which, "Peggy Sue" and "That'll Be the Day," sold over a million and a half copies. His newest record, just released, is "It Doesn't Matter Any More."

* * * * * *

ROGER PETERSON was born May 24, 1937, at Alta, the son of Arthur and Pearl Kramer Peterson. He graduated from Fairview Consolidated school in 1954, attended Rose Aviation school at Tulsa, Okla., and was employed by the Graham Flying service at Sioux City, before coming to Clear Lake about a year ago.

He was a member of the Redeemer Lutheran church at Ventura and of the Clear Lake Junior Chamber of Commerce.

Mr. Peterson and De Ann Lenz were married Sept. 14, 1958, in Alta and had resided in Clear Lake since their marriage in one of the Armsbury cottages on N. Shore dr.

Besides his wife, he is survived by his parents; two brothers, Ronald and Robert; one sister, Janet; his grandmother, Mrs. Elmer A. Peterson of Sioux Rapids.

Funeral services were held at 2 p.m. Thursday (today) at the Redeemer Lutheran church with the Rev. E. H. Widmann officiating. Services also will be held at 2 p.m. Friday at St. Paul's Lutheran church at Alta with burial to be in the Storm Lake Memorial cemetery.

Arrangements in Clear Lake were through the Wilcox Funeral home.

THE BODY OF J. P. RICHARDSON was taken by air Wednesday to Beaumont, Texas, for funeral service. He was born Oct. 24, 1930, and is survived by his wife, Adrian, and a daughter, Deborah, who are in New Orleans. Mrs. Richardson also is expecting another child.

Arrangements here were through the Ward Funeral home.

THE BODY OF RITCHIE VALENS was scheduled to be taken by rail Wednesday to San Fernando, Calif., for funeral services.

Richard Valenzuela was born May 13, 1941, to Mr. and Mrs. Joseph Valenzuela. He is survived by his mother, Conception Reyes of Pacoima, Calif. Arrangements for Mr. Valens were completed through the Ward Funeral home.

THE BODY OF CHARLES (BUDDY) HOLLY, who was born Sept. 7, 1936, was taken by plane Wednesday afternoon to Lubbock, Texas, for funeral services. Arrangements here were completed through the Wilcox Funeral home.

Latest in Home Improvement . . . .

Home Show Feb. 19-22

Clear Lake's third annual Home Show, Feb. 19 through 22 will introduce the most modern and latest in equipment and materials for making home improvements and changes, announced Roscoe Miller, president of the local home show association.

According to Miller, the 1959 home show will be even better and larger since all the space of the All Vets Social Center, where the show again is being held, will be used for displays and exhibits.

The show should captivate the interest of all householders, home builders, and the do-it-yourself fans, since dozens of practical ideas, suggests as well as the latest merchandise will be on display, Miller stated.

Prizes valued at several hundred dollars will be given away during the show, including at least two valuable prizes each night, according to Bill Eaton and John Perkins, who are in charge of prizes. The grand award will be a stereophonic hi-fi player system.

The charge for admissions will remain the same, 10 cents, and the proceeds will go to the Junior Chamber of Commerce. The Jaycees will handle the admissions, and the registrations. A lunch and coffee bar, and a rest lounge, will be available for the con- venience of all. The Music Mothers will handle the preparations, and even serve complete meals.

One of the features of the show will be a display of small model homes, designed and built to scale by the high school industrial arts class under the direction of James Killam, instructor. The model homes will be judged by a panel of professional home builders for prizes, Miller stated.

Last year, over 3,000 people paid to view the home show, and they represented 80 Iowa communities.

Twp. Trustees Express Approval Of Expanded Fire Protection Plan

Trustees of six rural townships indicated their approval of the formation of a fire protection district centering in Clear Lake at a meeting with the Clear Lake city council Monday evening.

The meeting was called by the city council to present a proposed agreement to the township representatives, to provide vastly improved fire protection service to the rural areas surrounding the city.

In exchange for payment to the city of tax funds levied by the respective townships, the city council has agreed to:

(1) Provide a tanker truck capable of carrying not less than 1,200 gallons of water to farm fires.

(2) Provide a rural pumper truck.

(3) Maintain the equipment and man it with members of the Clear Lake fire department.

(4) Equip the trucks with hoses, nozzles, extinguishers, portable lights and other items needed to fight fires.

(5) The equipment would include two-way radio communications connecting with Nichols Turkey farm. Taken to Mercy hospital by Ward ambulance were Gary Manson, Clear Lake; Merlin Baker, Mason City, the driver, and Marlene Abernoth.

The two men received facial cuts and Miss Abernoth a back injury.

3 Hospitalized in Rural Crash Tuesday Morning

Three persons were injured in a one-car crash Tuesday morning when it struck a culvert ½ mile north of the

Two Violations In Same Auto Cost Pair $50

Two Minnesota men, arrested by city police for traffic violations in the same car, were fined $25 each by Justice of the Peace C. E. Ashland last weekend.

Robert D. LaTaurell, driver of the car when first stopped, was fined $25 and costs for careless driving.

Later in the evening, the same car was stopped and police arrested his companion, Arlen B. Ladwig, then driving the car, for speeding. He was fined $25 and costs.

Others fined in Ashland's court during the week were:

Richard E. Lampman, Clear Lake, $10 for careless driving; Robert L. Hayungs, Waterloo, $15 for speeding and $5 for stop sign violation; J. A. Gullickson, Northwood, $10 for speeding.

Edward R. Boyle, special attorney for the city who drew up the proposed agreement, explained its provisions to the group and reviewed changes in state law which gave the townships power to provide fire protection and levy a tax.

He noted that such a system was by far the most fair and equitable to rural residents. There are persons who actually are paying three different fire protection bills, he said. These who pay the Ventura Fire association

Reviews Law Change

(Continued on Page 7)

PTA Children's Movie Series Starts Saturday, Feb. 14, for Seven Shows

The Parent-Teacher association's Children's Movie series at the Lake Theatre will start Saturday, Feb. 14, and continue on Saturdays weekly through March 28.

The PTA will sponsor the series of seven approved children's shows, which will start each Saturday at 2 p.m. Doors will be open at 1:30 p.m.

Tickets will be sold at the schools on Tuesday, Feb. 10, at 8:15 a.m. and 12:30 p.m. Only those pupils buying season tickets will be able to get seats. Cost of the season tickets is $1.

The following pictures have been selected by the PTA for the series:

Saturday, Feb. 14 — "The Yearling" plus color cartoon.

Saturday, Feb. 21 — "Francis in the Navy" plus three cartoons and "Little Rascals."

Saturday, Feb. 28—"Heidi" plus three cartoons.

Saturday, March 7 — "Kettles on Old MacDonald's Farm" with two cartoons and the Three Stooges.

Saturday, March 14 — "Adventures of Robinson Crusoe" plus four cartoons.

Saturday, March 21 — "My Pal Gus" plus three cartoons and the "Three Stooges."

Saturday, March 28 — "Painted Hills" with Lassie.

MRS RATH DIES SUDDENLY

Mrs. Richard Rath, 27, died suddenly in the Iowa Falls hospital Wednesday. She resided in Clear Lake about a year ago when her husband was employed by Landis Building. Funeral services will be at 2 p.m. Saturday at the Cedar Falls St. Paul's Evangelical Lutheran church.

BODY OF CRASH VICTIM, one of four killed Monday night north of Clear Lake, lies in front of wreckage of light plane. Accident took the lives of three nationally famous rock 'n roll entertainers and the pilot, Roger Peterson. (Mirror-Reporter Photo)

BODIES OF THREE plane crash victims were thrown from the craft in crash north of Clear Lake. Shown as they were found by authorities Tuesday morning were Ritchie Valens, lower center; Buddy Holly, far left; and J. P. Richardson, across fence and to the center left in background. Body of pilot remained in the wreckage, right. (Mirror-Reporter Photo)

Front page from the Clear Lake Mirror-Reporter, *February 5, 1959 (From the Buddy Holly Memorial Society Collection)*

The body was buried in the Lubbock City Cemetery, on the eastern edge of town, where the land is as flat and open as on almost all of the bare but imposing west Texas plains. The grave lies one hundred yards up the road which leads north from the office at the cemetery entrance. The site is but a few feet from the road, as if to be all the more accessible to the many fans who have come there from up to ten thousand miles away in the years since Buddy Holly's death. The inscription on the headstone reads simply, "In Loving Memory of Our Own Buddy Holley—September 7, 1936–February 3, 1959." On the stone, to the right of the inscription, is one last gesture of silent affirmation to a city which hardly accepted his music in his lifetime, and has only grudgingly acknowledged him since his death: a raised carving of Buddy's electric guitar.

Holly's grave, Lubbock, Texas (John Goldrosen)

Holly in London, before the appearance on the Off The Record *television show, March 1958 (From the Buddy Holly Memorial Society Collection)*

9. The Making of a Legend (1959-1972)

One day soon the reservoir of Holly's songs will be drained. I give the cult five years.
— Adrian Mitchell, London *Daily Mail,* July 13, 1962

"The day the music died"—so Don McLean termed that cold February day in his number one song "American Pie" almost thirteen years later. He was not the first to see Holly's death as a decisive event in the history of rock 'n' roll. At the time, no one could sense fully just what the fatal accident meant for the development of the music; and yet, on three continents, the news brought an indescribable feeling of something lost—something which could never be regained. Holly was memorialized in song and honored by imitation; these sorts of tribute, as well as Holly's long-term influence on rock music, will be covered in the second part of this chapter. First, the several albums which have been issued since Holly's death will be discussed.

Within weeks of Holly's death, "It Doesn't Matter Anymore" climbed to number thirteen on the Hot 100 ("Raining In My Heart" also made the list). Coral then issued a new album, *The Buddy Holly Story,* which included hits from the two earlier albums as well as some singles not previously available on an LP. This release climbed high on the album chart and was in and out of *Billboard*'s list of top one hundred albums for some three-and-a-half years, eventually earning a gold record. These successes led Coral to look for other recordings by Holly which could be issued to meet the continued demand.

Few studio masters still remained unissued; and so, almost immediately, Coral turned to unmastered material which might somehow be made to sound "commercial." A pattern was set which was followed on almost all future Holly releases: Holly's demos and tapes were not released "as is," but were instead given a bigger or fuller sound through overdubbing. The results have rarely been satisfactory—at least, not to the ears of Holly's fans.

The first songs subjected to this "sweetening" were the six original songs which Holly had written just before his death. Coral obtained the tapes of these from Maria Elena, and put them in the hands of in-house producer Jack

Hansen. "Peggy Sue Got Married" and "Crying, Waiting, Hoping" were issued on a single in July 1959; all of the songs were released on *The Buddy Holly Story, Volume 2* (April 1960), along with the unreleased masters "True Love Ways" and "Moondreams"; "Little Baby," from Holly's first album; and three songs which had been flip sides on singles: "Well All Right," "Now We're One," and "Take Your Time."

Though it could not be known how Buddy himself would have arranged the material, there was a general feeling that the Coral recordings were not even close to Buddy's intentions. Vocal backgrounds were added to all the songs, probably with the thought of matching the vocal and instrumental blend of the Crickets recordings; however, at times Holly's own vocal is barely audible through the "background" instrumentation. All of the songs were "stretched" to some extent by repeating the instrumental break or the closing verses. All this made it necessary to obscure Holly's own guitar playing. Even so, the accompanists sometimes fail audibly in trying to follow Holly's shifting, accented rhythm.

Of the six songs, "Crying, Waiting, Hoping" suffered the least, "That Makes It Tough" and "That's What They Say" suffered the most, and "What To Do," "Learning the Game," and "Peggy Sue Got Married" fell somewhere in between. Overall, the songs came out sounding more "pop" than anything Holly had done to that point; and ironically enough, with the passage of years and the ignorance among newer fans about the posthumous nature of these arrangements, the songs strengthened the impression that Holly had been turning decisively away from rock 'n' roll or rockabilly and toward pop music.

The new album's sales were nowhere near those of *The Buddy Holly Story*, but there was still a clear demand for more Holly recordings. At first, Holly's family was reluctant to allow new releases. Neither Maria nor the Holleys wanted Buddy's name exploited, and they felt it would be wrong to allow Coral to issue material which would have been below Holly's own professional standards. However, the flood of letters from Holly's fans asking that all such material be issued convinced his widow and parents to allow the release of these additional recordings. The continued flow of new albums during the sixties reflected the fans' willingness to accept the technical limitations of the previously unissued material.

Legal complications prevented any new releases for a couple of years. At the time of Buddy's death, his recordings were scattered along the course of his musical career. Demos made in the days of the Buddy and Bob Show were in the hands of the Holleys, Bob Montgomery, Hipockets Duncan, and others in Lubbock; sides cut during the period of Holly's Decca contract were in Decca's Nashville office or in the possession of Jim Denny's Cedarwood Publishing firm; Norman Petty had masters Holly had recorded before the break between them; and Coral had a claim to anything Holly had recorded during his period on the label. (Maria had turned all her tapes over to the Holleys shortly after Buddy's death, feeling that the tapes could have only sentimental value. She had also, it should be added, assigned half of Holly's estate to his parents, even though his death without a will had left her sole heir.) The legal tangle involved in determining rights to these recordings is obvious enough on the surface, and would be beyond a layman's powers of explanation even if all the facts in the matter were readily available.

As part of the settlement finally reached in 1962, Norman Petty regained control of Holly's recordings. Petty's leverage in the negotiations had been that he still possessed some of Holly's material and was not obligated to give it up or allow it to be issued; but Mrs. Holley denies that this was a factor in Petty's return to authority. The main reason, she says, was simply that Norman was the person who could do the best job of producing the remaining material, since he presumably had the most familiarity with Holly's style and taste in arrangements. Also, the Holleys knew they would need someone to handle the complicated business arrangements involved, and so they turned to Norman for that aid. Under the agreement worked out, Coral remained Holly's label (and took over as well the recordings he had made on Brunswick with the Crickets), and Maria Elena, the Holleys, and Petty split Holly's future royalties.

Jerry Allison comments: "I think Buddy would have been terrifically unhappy with the fact that his folks went back to Norman. I can understand why they did it—when you're in Lubbock, Texas, you don't have much choice. They didn't have any choice if they wanted to keep Buddy's name alive, and keep records coming out for the fans. They couldn't go flying to New York to keep it going—if they had, they would have just gotten mixed up with some straight biz cat who just wanted to put more records out. Like, what those people had done with Buddy's last songs—that was awful, Buddy would have hated that stuff. But Norman kept it straight for the Holleys, as good as possible, and he was more into Buddy's style than those biz cats in New York. Plus the fact that he had all the tapes. So Norman got back in charge. But I think that's the last thing Buddy would have wanted."

Petty's studio band was the Fireballs, a Texas–New Mexico group most famous for their hit recordings of "Sugar Shack" and "Bottle of Wine." They were undoubtedly more capable of providing suitable backgrounds for Holly's recordings than were the musicians associated with the Decca complex in New York. Still, there were instances where there was really no reason to use any overdubbing at all.

The first album released under the new contract was *Reminiscing*, issued in early 1963 (a single of the title song had been released the previous summer). Besides the title song, the album included two songs recorded by Holly on his own tape recorder in the months before his death: "Slippin' and Slidin' " and "Wait Till the Sun Shines, Nellie," and eight others recorded in 1956 before the formation of the Crickets: "Baby, Won't You Come Out Tonight," "Because I Love You," "I'm Gonna Set My Foot Down," "Rock-A-Bye Rock," and "I'm Changing All Those Changes," all written by Holly; "It's Not My Fault," written by Ben Hall and fellow country musician Weldon Myrick; and the rock 'n' roll classics "Bo Diddley" and "Brown Eyed Handsome Man."

On this set of recordings, the Fireballs contributed the most to Holly's rendition of "Slippin' and Slidin'," a recording which leaves few Holly fans indifferent—they either admire his interpretation of it, or they wish it had never been released. The song had been recorded originally by Little Richard in his usual wild and swinging fashion. By contrast, Holly's version is slow, quiet, and rather eery, but still faithful to the lyrics and spirit of the song. Although Buddy performs the song at a slow pace, there is nothing loose or mild to the performance; his manner of phrasing and vocalizing builds tremendous tension and the sort of finely-wrought inner excitement found in a slow blues or spiritual.

Overdubbing was less restrained on "Wait Till The Sun Shines, Nellie," an old favorite of Mrs. Holley's which Buddy had promised to record for her. Holly's practice tape, just seventy seconds long, was subjected to splicing and rearranging; the added instruments and vocals which hide these alterations obscure Holly's own performance. The whole feel of the recording is too heavy for the low-keyed and reflective mood of Holly's rendition.

"Bo Diddley" and "Brown Eyed Handsome Man" were two demos which Holly had cut in Clovis sometime during 1956 at the suggestion of his brother Larry. Though the tunes had been recorded with a full band, the Fireballs were still used when the cuts were prepared for the *Reminiscing* album. Most of the lead guitar playing on the released version of "Bo Diddley" was, in fact, not on the original demo. All Buddy had played on his recording was a lower-pitched tremolo effect similar to Diddley's own playing on the hit version of the song; but on the overdubbed release, a whole new guitar part was added, and the other instruments on Holly's original recording were also "reinforced." The changes made on Holly's recording of Chuck Berry's "Brown Eyed Handsome Man" were less significant; the lead guitar work is entirely Holly's.

The six remaining recordings on the *Reminiscing* ablum illustrate the variety of Holly's style at the time of his first Decca contract. The version of "I'm Changing All Those Changes" included here is simply a shorter, alternate take of the song previously released on the Decca album of Holly's Nashville recordings. The other five, it is believed, were recorded as demo tapes for Jim Denny's Cedarwood Publishing; they were not published then, and were filed and forgotten until a search was made for unissued Holly material in the early sixties. "It's Not My Fault" is a tune closer to country music than "Blue Days, Black Nights," Ben Hall's other effort for Holly, but the lilting beat and accented vocal effects produced by Holly give a different flavor to the country melody. "Because I Love You," a slow, emotional ballad, is one of the first songs which Holly wrote himself, and he gives it a beautiful and moving performance.

By sharp contrast, the three remaining tunes on the album are driving rock 'n' roll dance numbers. "Rock-A-Bye Rock," "I'm Gonna Set My Foot Down," and "Baby, Won't You Come Out Tonight" demonstrate vividly Decca's failure to appreciate the talent it had on hand. These recordings *are* Buddy Holly in 1956, not as he sounded in a recording studio under the direction of older country musicians, but as he sounded with Allison, Curtis, and Don Guess on the bandstand at a teen-age rock 'n' roll dance. The numbers are as furious and exciting as any contemporaneous rockabilly, and lack only the polish and finesse of such later recordings as "Rave On" and "Oh Boy!".

Since the five recordings just discussed were not cut as masters, the sound quality is low; still, these are complete performances with a full band, and so it is hard to understand why extra background was added to these records. The additions only annoy the fan who is intent on listening closely to the original performances by Holly and his group. Allison is still irked by this procedure: "The Fireballs were good boys and I really like them, and the way they played is fine for the Fireballs—but not for Buddy Holly records. I really hated that things got all mixed up—because if somebody was gonna play some drums on those things, I would have liked to play on them. I mean, I was back in Texas and back in Clovis, and Norman could have called me and said, 'Hey, you want to overdub some stuff?' And I would have loved it. But he had all these hang-ups. The Fireballs were his boys at the time. He had them play on some stuff that didn't even need it, like 'Brown Eyed Handsome Man' and 'Bo Diddley'; and when he did it, it was like a slam at Joe B. and me, if nothing else—like 'O.K., we'll put the Fireballs in and cover them up.' Even now, it kind of bugs me to pull all those records out and listen to them and hear all that bad overdubbing."

The next album of previously unissued material was *Showcase*, released in early 1964. On this album, more of the original recordings were left intact. Two of the cuts, "Rock Around With Ollie Vee" and "Girl On My Mind," were from the recordings Holly had made with Decca in 1956; the others (including "Come Back Baby," "Love's Made A Fool Of You," and "You're The One," already discussed) appeared publicly for the first time on this album.

"I Guess I Was Just A Fool" was recorded as a demo for Decca in 1956. The song, written by Holly, is closely modelled on Elvis Presley's Sun recording of "I Forgot To Remember To Forget," which was a special favorite of Holly's. (Buddy in fact once made a demo of the Presley tune for KDAV, but the demo was destroyed when it seemed that playing it might violate Holly's Decca contract.) Holly's vocal owes something to both Presley and Hank Williams. The lead guitar on the recording was probably played by Sonny Curtis. Holly's one-minute recording of "Gone" apparently dates from about the same time—Allison guesses that it was made at KDAV sometime in 1956. This would have been, then, a couple of years before Ferlin Husky recorded the hit version of the song; the tune had in fact been written in 1954.

Four cuts on the album were versions of the early rock 'n' roll hits "Shake, Rattle and Roll," "Blue Suede Shoes," "Rip It Up," and "Honky Tonk." All of the tunes appear to have been Holly-Allison duets, recorded in late 1956, when the two were playing without a bass player or second guitarist; the original performances are, once again, obscured by overdubbing. The tapes were made on a friend's primitive tape recorder, but regardless of the technical limitations, the recordings offer good performances. Particularly interesting is Holly's guitar playing, both on the three vocal cuts where he must accompany himself, and also on the instrumental "Honky Tonk." The original recording of that tune by Bill Doggett and his combo was in two parts, issued on both sides of a 45 r.p.m. single record; Holly used figures from both parts of the Doggett original and adapted the tenor sax and guitar solos on that recording to his own style of guitar playing. On the other three cuts, Holly is clearly aware of preceding recordings of the tunes, but his guitar solos follow his own ideas on how the songs should sound.

One revealing feature of Holly's version of "Shake, Rattle and Roll" is the set of lyrics he uses. Holly was aware of three recordings of the song: the original version by Joe Turner; the cover of that by Bill Haley; and a version by Elvis which was first released in 1956 on an RCA single. In making his cover version, Haley changed or omitted some of Turner's original lyrics, believing them to be too suggestive for airing on pop stations, however normal they might be as rhythm & blues lyrics went. As was mentioned earlier, the national pattern did not hold in Lubbock—white teenagers there listened to the original Turner recording as much as they did to Haley's cover version. Presley and Holly each use just one of Haley's verses, choosing to follow the rougher Turner wording most of the way. Their choices reflect the tastes of their peers and audiences, and reveal the general familiarity with Turner's recording in that part of the country.

The remaining cut on the *Showcase* album was drawn from the solo tapes Buddy had made on his own tape recorder shortly before his death. "Ummm, Oh Yeah"—or "Dearest," as it was correctly called on a later album—had been recorded by Mickey and Sylvia, the duo whose "Love Is Strange" had been such a favorite of Holly's. Buddy apparently intended to record both Mickey and Sylvia tunes himself, giving them a quiet, folkish flavor. The overdubbing obscures Holly's rhythm guitar playing, but the soft, restrained mood of Holly's vocal comes through clearly enough.

The following album, released in early 1965, offered a valuable glimpse at the origins of Holly's music, and certainly surprised many of his fans unfamiliar with the roots of his career. *Holly In The Hills* (a catchy and suggestive title, to be sure, though obviously coined without much regard for the topography of the Lubbock area!) reached farther back into the past than previous albums had done, back to recordings made by Holly and Bob Montgomery in country & western and rockabilly styles. Eight of these early sides were included. The album was filled out with "Lonesome Tears" and "Fool's Paradise," the only two Crickets recordings which had not previously appeared on albums; "Wishing," one of the songs Buddy had hoped to have the Everly Brothers record; and a new version of "What To Do," substituting a more adequate backing by the Fireballs for the unsatisfactory New York arrangement.

Exact information is lacking as to where and when the early demos were made, and who played on them. Apparently, most of them were made at the Nesman Studios in Wichita Falls, while others were recorded at a small studio in Dallas and at KDAV's studios; the demos seem to date from 1954 to 1955, although it is possible that some were made even earlier than that. Most of the vocals on the country tunes are duets, with Montgomery handling solo choruses and Holly providing instrumental breaks—along with Sonny Curtis, who plays the fiddle on some of these recordings. Holly's guitar playing is most notable on "Gotta Get You Near Me Blues," an example of his picking ability which shows why Lubbock area musicians and disc jockeys remember Buddy today as much for his fine country guitar playing as for his singing style. The two rock 'n' roll-oriented cuts, "I Wanna Play House With You" (called "Baby, Let's Play House" when Presley recorded it for Sun) and "Down The Line," demonstrate how quickly and surely Holly and his friends had moved into rockabilly in the wake of Presley's original recordings. Whatever their inexperience and amateur status, the entire group performs with a drive and energy that could make later rock 'n' roll groups envious.

Regrettably, the *Holly In The Hills* cuts are not totally accurate presentations of what Holly and his fellow musicians were playing in those years, since, as on the earlier albums, overdubbing distorts the original sound. Most significant is the addition of drums, which were not present originally on the six country-style recordings—made at a time when drums were rarely used in small country groups. Jerry Allison probably did play on "I Wanna Play House With You" and "Down The Line," even though most of the drumming heard on the finished release was provided by the Fireballs—as was some of the guitar playing.

After several years delay (caused in part by the new popularity of older Holly records in the mid-sixties), the last collection of Holly's home-type recordings was released in 1969, under the title *Giant*. The advent of multi-track recording equipment enabled Norman Petty to experiment more freely with the recordings; several include unusual orchestral effects, and those with backings by studio musicians have a brighter sound in which the dubbing is a bit less obvious. As with the earlier posthumous releases, though, opinions differ as to the propriety of the backings.

On "Love Is Strange," "You're The One," and "Dearest," Petty added a string effect, actually played on an organ, to give the songs a lush, full sound more in line with "the sound of the times." Of the three, "Love Is Strange" has perhaps the most successful arrangement; at least, it is not out of line with Holly's rendition. Still, one wonders if Holly ever would have chosen to record the piece that way. Holly gives the 1957 "chalypso"-flavored hit a surprisingly quiet, reflective treatment—the mood presented is quite different from that found in Mickey and Sylvia's original version. As for "You're The One" and "Dearest"—the original, simpler versions released on the *Showcase* album five years before were, to many fans, preferable to the new dubbed versions.

Three songs on *Giant* were early rock 'n' roll hits recorded in late 1956 under the same circumstances as the similar cuts on the *Showcase* album. They are Fats Domino's "Blue Monday," Clarence "Frogman" Henry's

"Ain't Got No Home," and "Good Rockin' Tonight," which dates back to Roy Brown's 1948 rhythm & blues recording of it—Holly may have heard that at some time, but he was undoubtedly thinking of Elvis Presley's Sun version when he made his own recording. As on the *Showcase* tunes, Holly and Allison were probably the sole performers on the original tapes.

Holly recorded "Smokey Joe's Cafe" and "Slippin' and Slidin'" in late 1958 or early 1959 on the tape recorder in his apartment, accompanying himself on electric guitar (the strange guitar break after each verse on "Smokey Joe's Cafe" is Holly's own). The dubbed backing on these matches the style of Holly more closely than had the backings on earlier albums. Although this fast version of "Slippin' and Slidin'" shows Holly's appreciation for Little Richard's vocal style, the slower recording of the song on the *Reminiscing* album has more interest as a unique recording in itself.

"Have You Ever Been Lonely" was recorded at Buddy's home one day in 1956 when he and his band were practicing there. As the album liner notes explain, Holly recorded it for his mother, who liked the song. Left on the tape is Holly's call, "Mother!" at the song's conclusion. It is really quite fitting that the recording was left as is, for the tone of his voice, and the fact that he made such recordings, is simple testimony to the close family ties Holly had and to the encouragement he received from his kin in pursuing his ambitions.

The last cut on the album was an instrumental, "Holly Hop," a brief introduction to Holly's individual guitar style and some of the figures he commonly used. The acclaim for Holly's singing should not cause anyone to overlook his instrumental talent, though it is less often heard and more difficult to appreciate immediately or fully.

In coming down as harshly as I have on the use of overdubbing on Holly's posthumous albums, I have not meant to imply that the job could have been done any better. The sound on the tapes and demos was of poor quality to begin with, so that the clearer, "live" sound of the overdubbing was likely to obscure the original performance, no matter what. The question which remains is, how much dubbing was really necessary? What was the intention in providing such backings—and what *should* have been the intention?

A clue to the attitude is to be found in one remark in the liner notes written by Norman Petty for *Giant*. In speaking of guitarist George Tomsco's added accompaniment to Holly's performance on "Holly Hop," Petty writes: "What a combination Buddy and George, together, would have been for the music fans!" Maybe so—but should these releases have been used to make that point? Originally, the creators of the posthumous albums wanted to ensure that the record buyer did not feel cheated by being presented with home-type recordings of limited instrumentation and/or fidelity. As a solution, the records were overdubbed, with the hope of making them sound like studio recordings—thus bringing them up to contemporary standards, one might say. (Not that there was any attempt at deception—except for *The Buddy Holly Story, Volume 2,* each album's liner notes made clear the limitations of the recordings and the use of dubbing.) But too often, the original Holly recordings wound up being used as a base for something else—"Play Along With Buddy Holly" became the appearance, if not the intent, of such releases.

In attempting to create "contemporary" albums, the producers of the posthumous releases both failed to reach their own objective and lost sight of the original purpose of the series. Primarily, these albums served fans already acquainted with the recordings released during Holly's lifetime. The fans wanted the recordings never intended for release made available, regardless of the technical limitations—for they knew that Holly was an artist even when recording under casual conditions with limited intentions. Such buyers never expected the new releases to have the full sound of "That'll Be The Day" or "It Doesn't Matter Anymore"; it was enough that Buddy's performances not be discarded simply because they had not been recorded in a modern studio. Overdubbing just obscured Buddy's vocal or (especially) instrumental performance without adding much to the total recording, since the final product always *sounded* dubbed.

The object of the releases should have been to present the recordings in their original form, doing all possible to eliminate technical flaws (such as scratches on demos) without harming the sound. Where the original pieces were unfinished, they should have been left that way. As a parallel, consider the various modern LP releases of early jazz and blues recordings dating from the twenties. Though the fidelity on these is poor by modern standards, no one suggests that new trumpet parts should be added to Louis Armstrong's recordings, or that a vocal chorus should be assigned to sing along with Bessie Smith. The buyers of these albums know what they are getting, but want the original material anyway. It is my guess that Holly's fans would have reacted in a similar fashion.

"Are there any more recordings still unreleased?" is a question frequently posed to the Holleys or Norman Petty. The answer is a conditional "no"; at least, the Holleys have released all that they have, with the exception of a couple of badly-scratched early Buddy and Bob demos and alternate versions of "Love Me," "Down The Line," "Don't Come Back Knocking," and "You And I Are Through." One of the more persistent rumors about unreleased songs concerns a tune called "I Tried To Forget;" a notation in the record company files indicates that this was just an alternate title for "I Guess I Was Just A Fool." Several cuts have been released on albums in England, but never on Holly's American albums; these include "That's My Desire" (the rejected master from the session which produced "Rave On"); the original version of "Maybe Baby"; "Memories," "Queen of the Ballroom," and "Baby, It's Love," all Buddy and Bob recordings; and the versions of "Peggy Sue Got Married," "That Makes It Tough," "Crying, Waiting, Hoping," "That's What They Say," and "Learning The Game" which have overdubbing by the Fireballs, rather than by the Jack Hansen combo. It is always possible that new material will be discovered unexpectedly in the attics or record collections of Holly's friends—for instance, several releases of Holly's early recordings came from demos discovered by Hipockets Duncan when he happened to go through his collection sometime after Holly's death. Such a possibility is, of course, much more remote now.

After the initial nationally-carried newspaper reports on the fatal plane crash, the deaths of Holly, Richardson, and Valens went largely unnoticed in the adult media; it was, appropriately, through popular music that they were eulogized, and then honored by imitation.

Tommy Dee was a disc jockey on KFXM in San Bernardino, California. He was on the air on February 3 when the story of the plane crash came in over the wire services. "I read it on the air," he remembers, "and so many people called up—kids calling, girls crying, everyone upset. It made such an impression on me that when I got off the air, I wrote a song about it, as I was driving home in my car."

The song was "Three Stars," a slow narrative ballad in which the narrator in turn described the "three new stars" in the heavens and expressed the most striking traits of each singer. The physical description of Holly—hair out of place, a shy grin on his face—was followed by an acknowledgment that Holly had been a complicated and distant figure. "Not many people actually knew you, or understood how you felt," said the song, though they all could respond to the warmth of Holly's songs. Dee recalls, "A lot of people thought I had a feel for Buddy Holly in the record, which was strange, because I had never met him. I felt, just from looking at his picture, that he was a shy and bashful type of guy. It seems that I hit the nail on the head."

The next day, Dee brought a tape of the song to a music publisher (American Music), and the following Monday, he recorded the song for Crest, backed on the vocals by Carol Kay and the Teenairs. Dee's record eventually reached number eleven on the *Billboard* Hot 100, despite competition from a cover version on King by Ruby Wright.

"Three Stars" has been criticized for being maudlin or corny. In response to the criticism, it should be pointed out that in its topicality, eulogistic tone, and acceptance of the afterlife, the song followed older traditions of folk, gospel, and country music; the religious view expressed was one shared, after all, by Holly and his family. The honest emotions in the song were best expressed in the recording of it by Holly's friend and fellow rock 'n' roll star Eddie Cochran. According to Tommy Dee, the idea of having Cochran record the song came up the day Dee brought it to American Music. Cochran came to the office to hear the song, and recorded it himself that night. Overcome by his own sense of loss, Cochran's choked voice broke, as he sang and spoke the lyrics about Holly. (Cochran had originally been scheduled to go on the Winter Dance Party tour himself.) Cochran's recording of "Three Stars" was not released until several years later. He had wanted to donate the royalties on it to the families of the dead singers, but problems arose in working out the details with his record company, and the proposed single was never issued. Just fourteen months after Holly's death, Cochran was himself killed, in an automobile accident in England.

"Three Stars" was by no means the only tribute song: over the years, there have been about a dozen tunes written about Holly (or about the three singers collectively), and another dozen more which mention Holly in the longer roster of now-dead rock 'n' roll stars. Waylon Jennings has recorded two: "The Stage" and (more recently) "Old Friend." The best-known tribute song from England is "Tribute to Buddy Holly," by Mike Berry. Several of the other tribute records are in the country-music tradition of ballads written to commemorate tragic events; examples of these include "Gold Records in the Snow" by Bennie Barnes and "The Great Tragedy" by Hershel Almond.

Imitation of Holly's vocal style and melodic patterns began during his own lifetime—Robin Luke's "Susie Darling" (1958) being a notable example. In the years after Holly's death, several new figures built careers around their ability to copy his performances. (The popular image of the Holly hiccup may owe more to its use by his imitators than to his own use of the device, which wasn't nearly so frequent.) Bobby Vee's voice and style resembled Holly's so closely that many people are still under the delusion that "Rubber Ball" was recorded by Holly, not by Vee. Vee did have a sincere respect for Holly's talent, and never disguised the origin of his style; he recorded one album with the revived Crickets and toured with them for a time, and also made an album of Holly's songs titled *I Remember Buddy Holly*. The overall sound of Holly's records also became a subject for imitation. The best-remembered attempt to duplicate the instrumental feel of Holly's recordings was Tommy Roe's "Sheila," which copied the rolling drumbeat and background guitar arrangement of "Peggy Sue."

The Crickets—or at least one set of them—attempted to carry on after Holly's death and enjoyed some success, especially in England. However, personal plans and military obligations prevented the group from establishing a stable lineup—and anyway, without the drive Holly had lent the group, the Crickets were never quite the same. They were always willing to play rock 'n' roll as long as anyone wanted to hear them—but they knew themselves why the band had been a success in the first place. Jerry Allison says with a smile, "We've pretty well proved in the years since 1958 that the Crickets without Buddy Holly aren't too hot an item." Only Allison remained a constant member of the group; others at times included Joe Mauldin, Sonny Curtis, and several other west Texas natives—Glen Hardin, Earl Sinks, and Jerry Naylor—who had never actually played with Holly. (One vocalist, David Box, was with the group just a short time before he was himself killed in a plane crash in Texas.) Neither Tommy Allsup nor Waylon Jennings ever belonged to the re-created Crickets; Allsup went to the West Coast and worked on country and pop recordings for Liberty Records, while Jennings quit performing for several years before resuming a career that has now placed him among the top stars in the country field.

In England, Holly's popularity actually increased in the decade after his death. Recordings which had not been released prior to Holly's death or had been available only on albums were issued as singles in a steady stream through the early sixties, and continued to rise high in the charts. "It Doesn't

Matter Anymore'' was number one for three weeks in 1959, "Midnight Shift" was a hit later the same year, "True Love Ways" was a success in 1960, and in 1963, Holly's recording of "Bo Diddley" reached the top five of the British singles chart, while *The Buddy Holly Story* was still among the top twenty LP's. Even as late as 1967, Holly came in seventeenth in a British music weekly's popularity poll—rather remarkable when one considers how many of the paper's readers were too young to have heard Holly's music before his death.

The early recordings of Holly and the Crickets had made a profound impact upon young British rock 'n' roll musicians. The Crickets were the first group to establish the concept of a self-contained, guitar-oriented rock 'n' roll band, writing its own material and sharing the spotlight—obviously, Holly was the leader, but Allison and Mauldin got attention from the British press and fans as well during the 1958 English tour. The Crickets' lineup of drums, bass, and lead and rhythm guitars was a starting point for many of the early British groups. At least two English groups chose names which paid tribute to Holly and the Crickets: the Hollies and, less obviously, the Beatles—whose name was coined by John Lennon in 1959 when the example of the Crickets brought other insect names to mind. (This is the explanation which appears in Hunter Davies's *The Beatles: The Authorized Biography*.)

The specific musical influence of Holly and the Crickets varied from group to group. Though they admired the recordings of the Crickets, the Beatles owed their own style more to the hard rock 'n' roll sound of Larry

Allison, Mauldin, and Holly in England, March 1958 (Peer-Southern)

Williams, Chuck Berry, and Little Richard, the choral effects of female groups like the Shirelles and the Crystals, and the duet style of the Everly Brothers. The Beatles were indeed influenced, though, by the unique vocal texture of the best Crickets recordings—the careful but unobtrusive arrangement of background and lead voices—and by the melodies of Holly's songs. The latter influence is most noticeable in songs the Beatles wrote for other artists: "Nobody I Know" and "World Without Love," Peter and Gordon's earliest hits, and "Bad To Me" and "From A Window," recorded by Billy J. Kramer and the Dakotas. Among the Beatles' own songs, "Every Little Thing" (on the *Beatles VI* album) was very reminiscent of Holly's material, as was, strangely enough, one of their last recordings: "Here Comes The Sun"—which in rhythm and melody was not far removed from "What To Do," "That's What They Say," "Words of Love," or similar Holly songs.

For other English groups, the clear tenor vocals and quick driving beat of Holly's recordings were also important influences. Peter and Gordon owed their early style to the duet example of the Everly Brothers and the less nasal, lower-pitched sound of Holly's singing—a combination which Holly had himself produced five years before by double-tracking his own voice on "Wishing." The Searchers, one of the finest early English groups, recorded Holly's "Listen To Me" and "Learning The Game" (which they sang as "Led In The Game") on an early "live" album, and showed his influence on such songs as "Don't Throw Your Love Away" and "Whenever You Walk In The Room." Freddie and the Dreamers, a curious short-lived phenomenon, featured a lead singer who not only sounded somewhat like Holly and sang some of his songs, but who even *looked* like him. The list could be carried much further. But this is not to claim that Buddy Holly was the father of all English rock 'n' roll—those who make such generalizations are going a bit overboard. It could be said, though, that English fans and performers had the good fortune, or good taste, to be influenced by the best of the early rock 'n' roll performers, with Holly, Chuck Berry, Little Richard, Eddie Cochran, and Elvis Presley as the most influential.

The rock 'n' roll renaissance brought to the United States by the English groups in 1964 sparked new interest in the recordings of rock 'n' roll pioneers—especially when the new groups not only imitated the sound, but also recorded songs made famous by the preceding generation of performers. Many younger fans learned for the first time who Chuck Berry was after hearing the Beatles sing "Roll Over Beethoven" and "Rock and Roll Music"; Buddy Holly also benefited from this sort of recognition. In 1964, "Not Fade Away" was the Rolling Stones' first American release, while Peter and Gordon recorded "Tell Me How." In 1965, "Words of Love" appeared on the *Beatles VI* album, "It Doesn't Matter Anymore" was recorded by Freddie and the Dreamers, "Heartbeat" was sung by Herman's Hermits, and, most notably, "True Love Ways" became a top-ten hit for Peter and Gordon.

The Beatles' recording of "Words of Love" was particularly important in making Holly's name familiar again. Their version was a fairly close imitation of Holly's original recording, and it was released at a time when every song on a new Beatles album attracted close and constant attention and tremendous airplay. The Beatles' frequent mention of Holly as one of their early favorites likewise brought new attention to Holly's recordings. When "True Love Ways" became a hit later in the year, some disc jockeys presented special features on Holly's recordings, or periodically juxtaposed the original and new versions of the revived Holly songs.

In the United States, the influence of Holly's work in the mid- and late sixties was reflected most genuinely in occasional outbreaks of individual performers and groups whose debt to Holly sometimes went unrecognized. The career of one such group, the Bobby Fuller Four, involved close personal and stylistic ties to early rock 'n' roll. Bobby Fuller was from El Paso and grew up listening to, and admiring, the recordings of Buddy Holly. Fuller corresponded with Holly's parents and, after making some local recordings on minor labels, got a contract in Los Angeles with Bob Keene, who had been Ritchie Valens's manager.

In early 1966, the Bobby Fuller Four had one of the best-selling records of the year with "I Fought The Law"—a song which had been written by Sonny Curtis and recorded by the Crickets not long after Holly's death. The song had the "Buddy Holly sound"—the rhythm, the pounding drumbeat, the tenor vocal, the chordal guitar solo, the shifting chords and triadic effects of the melody. Still, it was not an "imitation" of Holly's style—the song came from a major songwriter who composed what came naturally to him, and was played by artists as was natural for them. Though the term "Tex-Mex sound" was really a promotional creation, there was still a Texas brand of rock 'n' roll, though not even the performers themselves could explain just what it was or where it came from.

Fuller's first album was one of the most danceable rock 'n' roll albums in some time. Most of the album cuts were written by Fuller, and were obviously modelled on Holly and Cochran tunes. And yet, something was lacking—the songs had the drive and feel of Holly's recordings, but lacked the lyrical content and emotional depth of those songs. Maybe Fuller would have developed as a songwriter later; but in the summer of 1966, he was found dead of asphyxiation in his car. (His death was officially ruled a suicide, despite strong evidence that he was murdered.)

The limited artistic success of the Bobby Fuller Four brings up a quite troubling and controversial element in the inheritance left by Buddy Holly to later popular performers. A line of influence can be traced from the music of Buddy Holly through that of Bobby Fuller to the much shallower sounds of Gary Lewis and the Playboys, and on to the simplistic "Bubblegum" sound of the late sixties, as typified by the Archies' "Sugar, Sugar." Some critics have therefore suggested that Holly was somewhat responsible for the deterioration of rock music in the decade after his death. (For an extreme and rather grotesque statement of this argument, see Nik Cohn's *Rock From the Beginning*.)

Blaming a man for the mediocrity of his imitators or the extreme applications of his tendencies is unfair and dishonest. Great art occurs at a moment of intangible and unconscious unity of style and substance—an equilibrium at which emotion and form co-exist, and the art achieves a height of perfection. When the unity breaks down and the opposite elements of freedom and formalism are separated, the art degenerates as it moves to one extreme or the other, or tries too consciously to achieve the old balance. The artist at the moment of balance cannot be blamed for the mediocrity or banality of those who later imitate just one element of his work, while losing the balance that is essential. Such is the case with Holly; his art was a fusion of surface simplicity and actual complexity, both in musical forms and emotion. Those who could not grasp the complexity strove for the apparent simplicity—but where the whole is all that is important, a part of the whole is worth nothing at all. Buddy Holly can no more be blamed for "Sugar Sugar" than Woody Guthrie could be blamed for the awful pretentiousness of "Eve of Destruction."

Here and there in the late sixties, a few American performers began to acknowledge the true value of Holly's music (and that of other early rock 'n' roll performers). Tom Rush's album *Take A Little Walk With Me* included his quite individualistic interpretations of several rock 'n' roll songs, including Holly's "Love's Made A Fool Of You"—which Rush also made a standard in his concert performances. Rush's quiet and reflective rendition of the song fully captured the spirit of the lyrics, and his instrumental accompaniment was at one and the same time quite distinct from that of the original Holly version, and yet totally appropriate to the song. Hundreds of artists have recorded Holly's songs at one time or another, but few have been as successful as Rush in producing a recording which, while the artist's own creation, fully captures the spirit of Buddy Holly's music.

In the years that followed, several other rock and folk performers acknowledged their debt to Holly or showed his influence in their songs. Bob Dylan grew up on rock 'n' roll, and has stated that Holly was an influence upon his style. In 1974, a *Newsweek* feature article on Dylan's national concert tour contained the following:

> *Musically, he says, he doesn't consider his taste a part of the nostalgia so fashionable today in pop. 'I just carry that other time around with me,' he says. 'The music of the late fifties and early sixties when music was at that root level—that for me is meaningful music. The singers and musicians I grew up with transcend nostalgia—Buddy Holly and Johnny Ace are just as valid to me today as then.'*

Bob Dylan wasn't the only singer to antagonize his folk-music following by revealing his rock 'n' roll roots. In 1970, Phil Ochs stepped out on the stage of Carnegie Hall, wearing an Elvis-style gold-lamé suit and carrying an electric guitar, and played medleys of songs by Presley and Holly, to a mixture of boos and cheers. (A live album of the concert was later released under the title *Gunfight At Carnegie Hall*.) In introducing his favorite Holly tunes, Ochs tried to offer an explanation to those who had come to hear him play the protest songs for which he was best known:

> *I'd like to sing some songs that are just as much Phil Ochs as anything else. These songs were first recorded by somebody I hold very dear to my heart, from the 1950's*—[boos and groans]—*Could this be a generation gap?...He formed that part of my musical mind which wrote anything like "I Ain't Marching Anymore," "Changes"—that thought process came from certain people, and this is one of them: Buddy Holly.* [applause and jeers] *These are a collection of his songs I memorized as a kid....*

Another performer with roots in Holly's music was John Denver (a graduate of Texas Tech, for whatever significance that might have). Denver recorded "Everyday" and released it on a single in 1972; some of his most successful compositions, like "Leaving on a Jet Plane" and "Country Roads," bear the mark of Holly's influence. The Nitty Gritty Dirt Band paid their respects to Holly with a recording of "Rave On." When they appeared in Lubbock in late 1971, they were amazed to find that most of their young audience didn't know who Buddy Holly was, and so they tried to enlighten the crowd by playing a medley of Holly's songs.

Critics, too, began to praise Holly and the brand of rock 'n' roll he had fashioned. Holly was the subject of articles in *Rolling Stone;* and in *Rock Encyclopedia,* Lillian Roxon had this to say about Holly:

> *He was one of the giants of early rock, a figure so important in the history of popular music that it is impossible to hear a song on the charts today that does not owe something to the tall, slim, bespectacled boy from Lubbock, Texas....More than any other singer of that era, he brings back a time when music was fun....Adults put him down with the rest of the Presley era as shock rock. Kids just remembered it was impossible not to dance, not to groove, while he sang. Most of the giants of ten years later, of the booming rock scene of the late sixties, were teenagers when Holly was king and their music reflects it. Looking back from the twin peaks of psychedelia and electronic gadgetry, he comes through fresher than ever.*

No tribute to the legacy of Buddy Holly had more impact than Don McLean's "American Pie," which won gold records and spent weeks in the number one positions on the *Billboard* pop singles and LP charts in late 1971 and early 1972. Some of the symbolic lyrics could be given many (or no) explanations, and, although the album was openly dedicated to Holly, the song never mentioned him by name. However, anyone familiar with the story of Buddy Holly had little trouble understanding the first verse:

A long, long time ago,
I can still remember, how that music used
    to make me smile.
And I knew if I had the chance,
That I could make those people dance,
And maybe they'd be happy for a while.
But February made me shiver,
With every paper I'd deliver,
Bad news on the doorstep—
I couldn't take one more step.
And I can't remember if I cried,
When I read about his widowed bride,
But something touched me deep inside,
The day the music died.[1]

In a matter of weeks, Holly received more publicity and recognition than he had ever gotten in his own lifetime. And by 1973, McLean's view of rock history had been expressed so widely and become so standard that it rated inclusion in the much-acclaimed movie, *American Graffiti*. "I can't stand that surfing shit," says hot-rodder John Milner as he turns the radio off in disgust—"rock 'n' roll's been going downhill ever since Buddy Holly died."

The resurgence of interest created by McLean's song led after some delay to Decca's release of a new collection of Holly's recordings. (By 1972, the separate Coral label had been dropped and its roster absorbed by Decca.) The new double album showed all the flaws in thinking which had affected the presentation of the posthumous releases and the selection of cuts on two previous "greatest hits" albums. What is most regrettable is that an opportunity to do better was lost. Decca originally had an independent producer, John Boylan, working on the project; plans were for a low-priced three-album boxed set containing a booklet with photographs, biographical information, and a discography. All songs were to be presented in their original, undubbed forms, and the choice of songs reflected the consensus of most fans as to the best of Holly's recordings.

Then, Decca got cold feet. The plans were scrapped, and a two-album set which had been released in Germany a year before was issued instead, under the title *Buddy Holly: A Rock 'n' Roll Collection*. There were no liner notes of any sort—this at a time when other companies, notably United Artists and Atlantic, were re-releasing recordings by their own rock 'n' roll artists in attractive packages with informative commentaries. The choice of selections was irrational—among the cuts not included in the new album were "Everyday," "Early In The Morning," "Think It Over," "True Love Ways," "I'm Gonna Love You Too," and "It's So Easy." The original tapes of the posthumous releases were once more passed over in favor of the dubbed versions made with the Jack Hansen combo and the Fireballs. And, as the

---

[1]From the song "American Pie," written by Don McLean. Published by Mayday Music, Inc. and Yahweh Tunes, Inc. © 1971.

most astonishing boner of all, the recording of "Love's Made A Fool Of You" included on the new set was not Buddy Holly's own recording of it, but instead the recording cut by the Crickets shortly after Holly's departure from the group. A lot of strange things had been done to Holly's recordings over the previous thirteen years, but never before had a Buddy Holly album included a cut that Holly himself did not play on.

The new seed of interest in Holly which was planted in the early seventies took several years to come to fruition. When the rock 'n' roll nostalgia craze had come and gone, musicians, fans, and critics began to look more closely at those few artists whose impact had been truly lasting. It was Buddy Holly as much as anyone who benefited from that attention. The late seventies were to demonstrate the breadth of the new interest in and respect for Holly.

10."Buddy Holly Lives" –The Holly Renaissance

As the second decade after Holly's death came to a close, interest in his music surged upwards, and a whole new musical generation was introduced to him. Many people played their role in this "Holly Renaissance": musicians, filmmakers, and Holly's own fans helped to bring Buddy Holly back into the spotlight.

The level of general public interest in Holly has varied through the 1970's, but his strong influence on knowledgeable musicians has been continuous. The range of Holly's material has been a key to his continued popularity: he has provided inspiration for performers whose styles cover a broad spectrum. Such disparate recording artists as the late Phil Ochs, John Denver, Waylon Jennings, Linda Ronstadt, Elvis Costello, and Bruce Springsteen have recorded Holly's songs, performed those songs in their own concerts, or pointed to Holly as an influence. In a period when it has been hard to discern any decisive trends in pop music, Buddy Holly's sound has remained a common reference point for musicians of all kinds.

Of all the performers who have recorded Holly's songs in the two decades since his death, Linda Ronstadt has scored the biggest commercial successes, with her recordings of "That'll Be The Day" (1976) and "It's So Easy" (1977). These were the first Holly compositions to make the top ten on pop charts since Peter and Gordon's version of "True Love Ways" in 1965 (fittingly enough, the man who produced the two Ronstadt records was Peter Asher, late of Peter and Gordon). Ronstadt's versions were embued with the spirit of Holly's original recordings, but were anything but slavish imitations, and were all the better for the difference. Once more, Holly's name was before the public, and the timing could hardly have been better. Ronstadt's hits served to prime interest in the film biography of Holly which, coincidentally, was about to begin production.

Proposals for films on Holly's life first arose in the early 1960's, but it was 1973 before studios began to show serious interest in the idea. In 1973, the

Gary Busey as Buddy Holly in The Buddy Holly Story *(© Columbia Pictures. Used by permission)*

American Broadcasting Corporation (ABC) gave Universal Studios the go-ahead to make a television *Movie-Of-The-Week* dramatization of Holly's life. A preliminary script was prepared, but the project was shelved in 1974 when the studio was unable to obtain authorizations from all of the people (including Allison, Mauldin, Petty, Maria Elena, and the Holleys) who were to be portrayed in the television film. It seemed to be impossible to arrive at a financial agreement (and, perhaps, a script) that satisfied all parties.

It was not long before two other proposals surfaced for films on Holly. Both were intended to be for general theatrical release, in contrast to the ABC-TV project.

One of the proposals was initiated by a small Philadelphia-based firm called Innovisions, whose principals—Steve Rash and Freddy Bauer—had experience in producing TV rock concert productions, but had never made a full-length motion picture. Working with the pair was Ed Cohen, who specialized in packaging TV and movie production proposals and seeking independent investors as backers. In late 1974, Rash and Bauer travelled to Florida to meet Maria Elena and present their proposal for a movie biography of Holly. In 1975, Maria Elena and the Holleys signed contracts with Innovisions granting the rights for a Holly movie, in return for a percentage of the profits (an arrangement ABC-TV and Universal Studios had been unwilling to offer on the *Movie-of-the-Week* proposal). Also, Innovisions signed an agreement for the right to base the movie on the original edition of this book.

In the same time period, Jerry Allison was working on a different project. Allison's idea was for a Holly movie that would be a fictionalized account of the Crickets' first tour in 1957, when they played on shows where they were the only (or one of just a few) white performers. Such a movie would not be a complete biography of Holly but would instead take the approach of showing his character by focusing on just a month in his life. The movie would have a broader purpose, too: to comment on race relations in early rock 'n' roll and the music's role in breaking down racial barriers.

Allison worked on this idea with a screenwriter named Tom Drake, and the pair sold the rights to the film (eventually titled *Not Fade Away*) to Twentieth Century-Fox. The limited scope of the film seemed to simplify the problem of securing permissions: with only Allison, Mauldin, and Holly portrayed in the movie, any need to obtain portrayal rights from Petty, the Holleys, or Maria Elena appeared to have been eliminated. The Holleys and Maria Elena were in fact contacted about becoming involved in the film, but they did not endorse it. The Holleys were unhappy with the subject matter of the script and its frequent use of vulgar language. Maria Elena also insisted, as she had in the case of the proposed ABC-TV movie, that she and the Holleys were entitled to more than the small portrayal fee that Twentieth Century-Fox was offering.

The filming of *Not Fade Away* began in Mississippi in September, 1975. Steve Davies was cast as Holly, Gary Busey as Jerry Allison, and Bruce Kirby as Joe B. Mauldin. Allison himself was cast in a bit role as the owner of a music store, and Bob Montgomery was cast in a major role as the white promoter of the all-black tour. MCA agreed to allow the use of Holly's original recordings in the film.

Three weeks after filming began, when the movie was one-third complete, Twentieth Century-Fox halted the shooting and announced that the film had been cancelled. The stated reason was "differences in artistic interpretation" between the studio and the director, Jerry Friedman. It was the view of the studio that the film was dwelling too heavily on the fictionalized conflicts between the Crickets and the black acts on the tour and was too serious in tone; although the language had been toned down from early versions of the script to ensure a PG rating, the film still had a roughness that the studio feared would make it commercially unacceptable. Friedman was told to lighten up the story and make it more comic—like the highly successful *American Graffiti*—but Friedman resisted. It appears that an expensive game of "chicken" was played. Friedman, knowing the amount of money already spent on the project, thought he could successfully insist on doing the film his own way, and Twentieth Century-Fox, with its bluff called, felt compelled to show who was in charge. In the end, nobody won; another Holly film was shelved, and Twentieth Century-Fox, it can be estimated, lost a million dollars by shutting down the half-completed film.

Some attempts were made by the film's production team to interest another studio in the project, but Twentieth Century-Fox put a high price on the rights to the story and the completed footage (perhaps to prevent anyone from testing its judgment about the film). Any lingering hopes for the project were probably finished off when Innovisions, having signed its agreements with the Holleys and Maria Elena, placed a full-page ad in *Variety* on October 28, 1975. The ad announced that the exclusive rights to Holly's life story had been granted by his estate to Freddy Bauer and Steve Rash, and warned that "No other person or entity may use the name, represent the person, or interpret the life of Buddy Holly in film, TV, or any other performance media." The threat of legal action was enough to ward off any lingering interest in *Not Fade Away*. (Actually, the claim of exclusive rights over dramatic portrayal of a deceased person's life was of dubious legal validity; Innovisions itself ultimately portrayed deceased performers Sam Cooke, Eddie Cochran, Ritchie Valens, the Big Bopper, and King Curtis in its film, without obtaining releases from the survivors of those individuals. In any event, no one tested the Innovisions claim.)

Two years passed before Innovisions could begin to film *The Buddy Holly Story*. The trio of Bauer, Rash, and Cohen sought independent financing rather than involvement with a major studio, and it took time to find interested investors. After the financing was obtained, the decision was reached to make the film in the Los Angeles area, beginning in late 1977.

Innovisions never did secure portrayal permissions from any of the Crickets or from Norman Petty. Bauer did speak to Allison in early 1975, before the filming of *Not Fade Away* began, but Allison (and Mauldin) were already committed to that project. According to Allison, he was never contacted again, even after the demise of *Not Fade Away*. "I just kept waiting for Innovisions to contact me," he says, "because I just assumed that they couldn't make a movie portraying me without talking to me first." Mauldin was never contacted at all. In the end, Innovisions decided to portray Allison and Mauldin in the film, but altered their names to "Jesse" and "Ray Bob": no knowledgeable Holly fan who saw the film, however, had any doubts that the two film characters represented Allison and Mauldin.

Niki Sullivan and Norman Petty never made it into the film at all, even under fictional names. Sullivan had not been included either in the scripts to the aborted ABC *Movie-of-the-Week* and *Not Fade Away*. One reason for this exclusion was that Sullivan's time with Holly had been shorter and his role less publicized than that of Allison and Mauldin, who had continued to perform as the Crickets after Holly's death. Scriptwriters seeking to condense Holly's story found it too easy to omit Sullivan for the sake of simplicity. (Similarly, the musicians that Holly played with before the formation of the Crickets, including Bob Montgomery and Sonny Curtis, were not included in the scripts.) Also, unlike Allison and Mauldin, Sullivan was not living in Los Angeles, where the scripts for the two ill-fated projects were written, and that, too, made it easy to overlook him. Therefore, Sullivan's absence as well from the Innovisions script was not surprising, although regrettable.

The situation with Petty was more complicated, and the reasons for his absence are unclear. After the release of the movie in 1978, Innovisions stated that Petty had not been portrayed because he had sought control over the script as a condition for granting the portrayal release. Petty says that he merely asked to *see* the script—and that not until late 1977, just a few months before filming began, when Innovisions last contacted him. In truth, Innovisions does not seem to have cared one way or the other whether Petty was involved in the movie. Disagreements over money or script content might ultimately have blocked Petty's participation, but it does not appear that any negotiation ever took place on these issues.

One of the most crucial choices faced by Innovisions concerned the music for the film. One option was to have the actors lip-sync to Holly's original recordings; a second was to have a new vocalist and band re-record the songs (as was done, for example, in *Lady Sings The Blues*, where Diana Ross sang the Billie Holiday numbers herself). An argument in favor of using the original recordings was that Holly's own music was what people would most want to hear; but on the other side of the coin, it was argued that lip-syncing usually looks as unnatural as it truly is, so that re-recording the songs would make the film more believable. Also, scenes showing songs being composed or practiced were only possible if the songs were to be re-recorded.

After considering these arguments, Innovisions decided to re-record the songs, and to have the actual actors in the film make the new recordings. Innovisions gambled that the right actors would make the movie believable, and that the music could be made close enough to the spirit of Holly's original recordings to win acceptance, or at least avoid strong criticism. It was a decision which was to prove to be a correct one.

The actor chosen to play Holly was Gary Busey, who was to have played Jerry Allison in the defunct *Not Fade Away*. Busey, who was born in Texas and grew up in Oklahoma, had several years of experience as a rock drummer under the name Teddy Jack Eddy, and had performed regularly with Leon Russell; he also knew how to play the guitar. Busey's acting credits included the role of Jeff Bridges's brother in *The Last American Hero* and Kris Kristofferson's road manager in *A Star Is Born*. The other lead roles went to Don Stroud, cast as the drummer "Jesse," and Charles Martin-Smith, chosen as the bass player "Ray Bob." Stroud's most recent film appearance had been in *The Choirboys;* unlike Busey, he did not have a professional musical background. Smith is best remembered for his performance as "Terry the Toad" in *American Graffiti.* Though he had not played string bass before, he had played piano and guitar, and had performed in a rock band in high school.

The filming of *The Buddy Holly Story* began in November 1977 and was completed in January 1978. Shortly thereafter, Columbia Pictures purchased the distribution rights to the movie from Innovisions. (Like Holly's records, then, the movie was produced independently and then distributed by a major company.) At first, the premiere was scheduled for Lubbock; however, it was later decided to open the movie on the same night in several Texas and

Billboard for the world premiere of The Buddy Holly Story, *near Lubbock, May 1978 (John Goldrosen)*

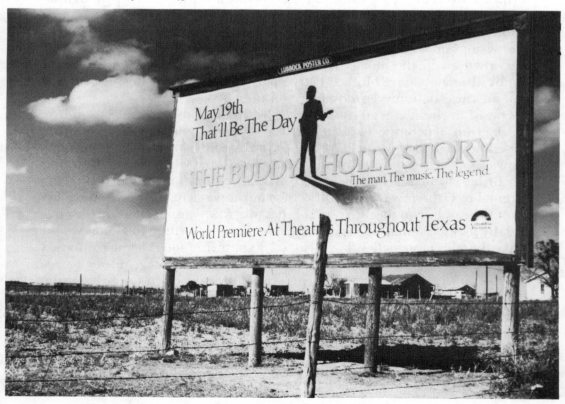

Oklahoma cities, including Lubbock, and to hold the major festivities in Dallas, where Maria Elena now lives.

On May 18, 1978, the world premier was held at Dallas's Medallion Theater, and was followed by a private party at the Longhorn Ballroom, a famous country music showplace originally opened by Bob Wills in the early 1950's. Busey, Stroud, and Smith were at the premiere, as were Niki Sullivan, Jerry Allison, Joe Mauldin, and Sonny Curtis, who had been invited by Columbia at the suggestion of Steve Bonner, a Dallas resident and longtime Holly fan. Sullivan had not seen the other original Crickets in over a decade, and none of them had seen Maria Elena since shortly after Holly's death.

The early reviews of the movie in the Dallas newspapers and in *Variety* were highly favorable, and the stream of good notices continued as the movie opened on the West Coast in mid-June, in New York a month later, and in New England late in August. The film was on *Variety*'s list of the fifty top-grossing films for fifteen weeks, reaching as high as number ten.

It was a summer when a wave of movies featuring rock music swamped American theaters. Rather than suffering from the competition offered by other rock movies (*Thank God It's Friday, FM, American Hot Wax, Grease, Sergeant Pepper,* and so on), *The Buddy Holly Story* benefited by the comparison. The Holly movie was one of the few which was more than a mere device for publicizing a soundtrack album or furthering the careers of leading rock musicians, and it was praised for the difference.

In almost every review, Gary Busey's performance was singled out for special praise, as the major factor contributing to the movie's success.[1] Since film clips of Holly are rare and relatively few people can remember seeing him perform live, Busey did not have to match any widely-held preconceived image of how Holly looked when performing. Instead, Busey was free to play the role as he felt it—and he did exactly that, becoming so caught up in the spirit of the music that he became, indeed, a rock 'n' roll performer himself, and not just an actor playing one. The movie's music was, in most spots, acceptable rock 'n' roll, and a reasonable attempt was made to match the essence of Holly's style; only the movie's closing medley, in which Busey was backed by a large orchestra, strayed far from the Holly sound. The vibrancy of Busey's visual performance obscured his vocal limitations, which were more obvious if one played the soundtrack album separately. (The music was performed and recorded live, without overdubbing; some of the more difficult lead guitar parts were played not by Busey, but by an off-camera guitarist.)

Although most Holly fans and the public at large found the movie enjoyable, there was some adverse reaction to the liberties taken with the facts of Holly's career. The basic features of Holly's character did shine through in Busey's performance, but the storyline itself contained many inaccuracies, some of which seriously distorted the nature of Holly's relationships with his family and fellow musicians, as well as the direction in which his career was

---

[1] Busey's performance in *The Buddy Holly Story* gained him an Academy Award ("Oscar") nomination for Best Actor.

headed. To cite just a few of the most obvious and most important changes:

—Holly's parents never tried to dissuade him from a musical career, as the movie indicates; rather, they wholeheartedly supported him.

—Holly's pastor, portrayed in the movie as a bigoted antagonist of rock 'n' roll, was in fact a close friend who welcomed Holly's success and whose only comment on Holly from the pulpit was in praise of him.

—Holly's first hits were recorded in Clovis at Norman Petty's studio, not in New York City. Though Holly did have the most say as to how the music was to be arranged and performed, it was Petty who produced the records and provided the careful technical expertise that made Holly's recordings sound so bright and unaffected.

—Dick Jacobs, not Holly, arranged and produced the string session. Holly did not read music.

Gary Busey as Buddy Holly in The Buddy Holly Story *(© Columbia Pictures. Used by permission)*

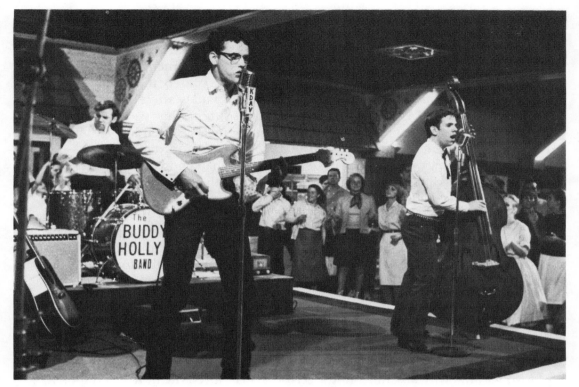

Gary Busey as Buddy Holly in The Buddy Holly Story, *accompanied by Don Stroud as drummer "Jesse" and Charles Martin-Smith as bass player "Ray Bob" (© Columbia Pictures. Used by permission)*

—Holly went on his last tour for financial reasons and as a favor to GAC, not to boost sagging record sales.

—Holly had neither turned his back on Lubbock nor made a decisive move in the direction of pop orchestral music, as the movie implies. At the time of his death, he was planning to establish his own recording studio in Lubbock and experiment on his own recordings with everything from country fiddles to big-band jazz musicians.

The inaccuracies in the movie reflected Innovision's desire to film what it considered to be the "legend" of Buddy Holly. "We're not out to make a true-to-life movie," Bauer had told me at one point, "we're out to make a movie that's *bigger* than life." Facts were consequently adapted, altered, overlooked, and re-arranged, as suited the production team's idea of what would be most "commercial." The movie was about a man who broke new ground and trusted his own instincts rather than the existing formulas for pop music stardom; and yet, the movie itself clung to clichés about rock 'n' roll history and followed standard Hollywood plot formulas.

I was not directly involved in the film's production. I did not see a preliminary script until a few months before filming began; my reaction at that time was that the truth of Holly's life would make for a more interesting and more successful movie than the version presented in the script. When I saw the completed movie, I enjoyed it and was able to applaud it for what it was, but I felt twinges of regret, as well, for what it could have been and was not. The movie certainly did publicize Holly and lead to increased sales of his records, but it missed an opportunity to depict accurately the early years of rock 'n' roll. I worried how the movie would ultimately affect our memories of Holly. History is not what really happened, but what we *think* really happened, and a movie which does not distinguish between fact and fancy threatens to create more confusion than comprehension.

The film drew mixed reactions from those who had known Holly best. The person who displayed the most enthusiasm for the film was Maria Elena. Although she had had her own objections to some items in the script (particularly the fictional scene in which Maria's aunt is portrayed as an antique Spanish *señora* whose permission Holly must win before he can court Maria), she was emotionally overwhelmed by the completed film upon seeing it for the first time at its Dallas premiere, and was unable to sit through to its completion. "Gary Busey came through so vividly," she said later. "It seemed like Buddy was inside him. All of Buddy's characteristics, his forcefulness and determination, came through."

Although he was left out of the movie, Niki Sullivan was nevertheless happy with it. "That was just the way Buddy was," Sullivan said. "Busey picked up a lot of Buddy's mannerisms—how, I don't know." Dick Jacobs, who was likewise absent from the script, also enjoyed the movie and took a relaxed attitude to the movie's liberties with the truth, including the scenes in which Holly is shown creating his own string arrangements. Jacobs says, "People ask me if it bothers me that I don't get mentioned, and I say, 'No, why should it? It's just a movie."

Others, however, were unhappy with the movie. Norman Petty was angered by his absence from the film. "I felt like a nonentity," he told Chet Flippo of *Rolling Stone*, "like some very important years of my life had just been wiped out." Jerry Allison said something similar to me not long before the movie was released: "The years I spent with Holly are really precious to me, and it's like they are trying to steal those times away." Allison was particularly angered by the racist remark ("you can get all the dark meat you want") attributed to him in the film. He and Mauldin were bitter that they were portrayed without their permission and that the name Crickets (which they long ago trademarked) was used in the movie and on the soundtrack album. They were also irked that the movie's script, in places, borrowed from the story line for *Not Fade Away*, and also from chats Allison had had with Gary Busey on the set of that ill-fated film.

The Holley family was upset with several aspects of the film, especially its skimpy treatment of Holly's youth. "We were disappointed that they didn't have more about the Holley family and about Buddy's life in and around Lubbock," Mrs. Holley told me. "We felt like we played a big part in his career, but there isn't very much about that in the film." Larry Holley said, "I didn't feel like I was watching my brother on the screen." Mrs. Holley was

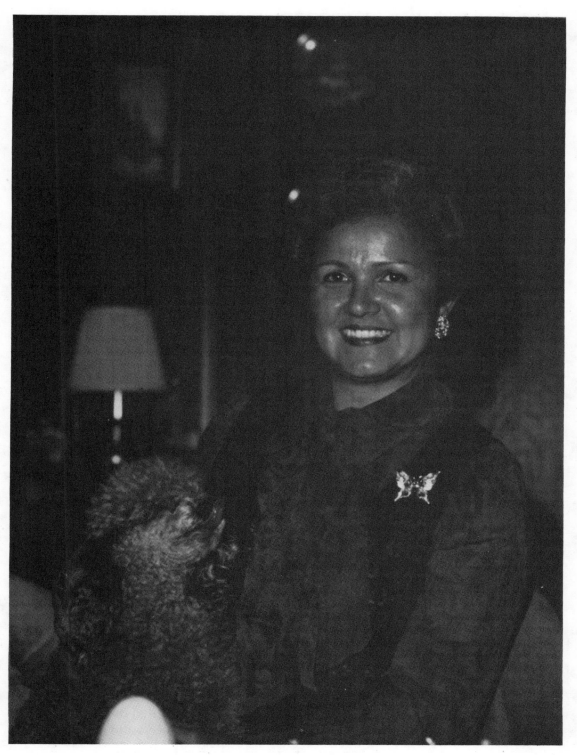

Maria Elena, at home, November 1977 (Bill Griggs)

also bothered by the occasional swear words (which, to be sure, were few and mild compared to most contemporary movies), and by the fictional church scene. Innovisions had not involved the Holleys at all in the film's production. "We never did see a script," Mrs. Holley told a reporter after the premier. "We just took their word for it that we were going to like it. I guess we were kind of stupid, huh?" When asked how much of the movie differed from the truth, Mrs. Holley answered, "Almost all of it."[2]

Some months after the film, Mrs. Holley reflected further on it: "Now that we have had time to think about it, we realize that the movie did show some of Buddy's ways and his characteristics; and Gary Busey did portray Buddy real well. We do hope the movie does well, so people will be more interested in Buddy. We're not mad, then—just disappointed." But both she and Larry Holley express the wish that there could be another movie about the Buddy Holly *they* knew.

Like Holly's fans and rock music critics, the family recognized the dilemma. The movie gave a tremendous boost to Holly's popularity, but it also threatened to misguide forever the public's perception of Holly. The September 21, 1978 issue of *Rolling Stone* highlighted the growing controversy with two articles, printed side-by-side: "The Gary Busey Story" and "The Buddy Holly Story." The latter article, written by Chet Flippo, was subtitled "Friends Say Movie's Not Cricket." It explored the film's dramatic liberties and Innovisions's excuses for the deliberate inaccuracies. "There's no way to refute the reality that is invented by a movie," wrote Flippo. "*The Buddy Holly Story* now stands as the official version of his life, but the movie does not seem to be about the real Buddy Holly."

The very appearance of the *Rolling Stone* article itself highlighted the dilemma: if the film had not been made, would Buddy Holly ever have become the subject of a three-page, profusely illustrated article in *Rolling Stone*? Though the film may not have given a satisfactory or truthful answer to the question, "Who was Buddy Holly?", it at least provoked a lot of people into asking the question for the first time.

For those who wanted to learn more about Holly by acquiring his records, in 1978 as in years past, it was better to be in Britain. British releases of Holly records continued to outdistance by far the quality and scope of MCA's American efforts. (MCA, the parent company of Decca, Coral, and Brunswick, eliminated the old label names in 1972.)

Beginning in 1974, the British branch of MCA began a series of Holly reissues and packages, with the assistance of John Beecher, president of Britain's huge Buddy Holly Appreciation Society through the 1960's. First came *Legend,* a well-compiled and sensibly-ordered two-album set of Holly's best-known recordings. Later, there were reissues of the original *Buddy Holly* and *Chirping Crickets* albums, with the original front covers and new liner

[2]William D. Kerns, "Holly Hoopla Missing in Lubbock," *Southwest Airlines Magazine,* August 1978, pp. 20-21.

notes; an album entitled *The Nashville Sessions*, containing most of the 1956 Decca recordings; and one called *Western and Bop*, containing material from the *Holly In The Hills* and *Reminiscing* albums. The albums were all marked by accurate liner notes, complete discographical information, and careful production. Another package of outstanding technical quality and physical attractiveness was prepared by Malcolm Jones, who produced a five-record box set titled *The Buddy Holly Story* for World Records, under a license from MCA. The World Records set, which was sold only by mail, included nearly all Holly material except for the Buddy and Bob recordings. At this writing, Beecher and Jones are collaborating on a definitive multi-record set for the English division of MCA; the package is expected to be available by early 1979. This set will supplant a nine-record package issued in Germany several years ago.

The almost inexhaustible market for Holly records overseas was shown most recently by the unprecedented success of an album titled *Twenty Golden Greats*, issued by the English branch of MCA in the spring of 1978. The album contained the songs which had been hit singles for Holly in England, and featured a graffiti-styled front cover with the slogan "Buddy Holly Lives." Well-promoted on British radio and TV, the record soared to the top of the British charts, establishing itself as the best-selling album in Britain for some five weeks, and earning gold and platinum records. A similar package (with a different selection of cuts) also went to the top of record charts in Germany and Switzerland. Nineteen years after his death, Holly had his first number-one album, and his first overseas gold record.

Sullivan, Allison, Curtis, and Mauldin performing at the Buddy Holly Convention, August 1978 (John Goldrosen)

Some of these British albums could be found in the import sections of large American record shops. Most American record buyers, though, had to settle for *A Rock and Roll Collection,* the 1972 two-record album. MCA continued to maintain that the *Collection* package was sufficient to meet the demand for Holly records in the United States.

Only with the success of Ronstadt's cover versions of "That'll Be The Day" and "It's So Easy" did MCA begin to consider any new Holly releases. Company executives authorized the planning of a two-record set which would include most of Holly's hits plus some of the original undubbed tapes never released before, and would be accompanied by adequate liner notes. Then, as had happened six years before, an ambitious and innovative project was shelved in favor of the tried and true. Noting the success of the British *Twenty Golden Greats* album, MCA issued the same record in America to coincide with the release of the film, and postponed indefinitely any plans for new albums. MCA did not bother to change the wording on the back of the *Twenty Golden Greats* album which read, "In just eighteen months, Buddy Holly recorded 9 Top Ten smash hits"—a statement which was true for Great Britain, but not for the United States. Nor did MCA alter the selection of songs, which had been chosen according to their success as singles in Britain, not their popularity in the United States. More importantly, the sound quality of the American pressing was simply atrocious: the brilliant ring of the guitar solo in "Peggy Sue" on the original *Buddy Holly* album of twenty years before became a muffled tinkling on the brand-new *Twenty Golden Greats.* MCA attributed this loss in fidelity to the number of cuts—ten—on each side of the album, and yet the sound of the identical English album was far superior.

It was, all the same, a compact collection of Holly's best-known songs, and the album soon rose into the Top 100 on the *Billboard* charts; it was the first Holly album to reach that high since *The Buddy Holly Story* in 1959. The album did make Holly's music more widely available, and it received some favorable reviews. *Time* advised its readers, "You will not hear better rock 'n' roll this summer." But knowledgeable rock critics, like Ken Emerson writing for *High Fidelity,* laced into MCA:

> *MCA has done it again. The company cannot have spent more than $100 of its money and ten minutes of its time packaging "20 Golden Greats". . . . there are no liner notes, no indication that at least three of the tracks were overdubbed after the artist's death, and within twenty-seven words, the blurb on the jacket's back makes two factual errors. . . . In short, MCA has accorded one of rock 'n' roll's most brilliant artists less respect than it does the least talented of the many mediocre contemporary artists on its roster.*

In truth, the American division of MCA has not released any Holly album of its own creation since *Giant* in 1969, and has not produced its own greatest-hits package since *The Best of Buddy Holly* in 1966. Since that time, the only two packages issued (excepting Vocalion budget-line assortments) have been

A Rock And Roll Collection, originally assembled by a German subsidiary, and the English-derived *Twenty Golden Greats.* As the executor and trustee, figuratively, of Buddy Holly's musical estate, MCA has been a disaster.

In the absence of much support from Holly's American record company, the "Holly Renaissance" of the mid- and late-1970's was spurred on by others. In Britain, the fortieth anniversary of Holly's birth became the occasion for a "Buddy Holly Week" celebration in September 1976. The promotion was the brainchild of Paul McCartney, whose company, MPL Communications, had purchased from Norman Petty the Nor Va Jak publishing rights to Holly's songs. For this first Buddy Holly Week, Petty was invited to Britain to be the guest of honor at a luncheon attended by leading rock stars. Later in the week, a rock 'n' roll dance attended by thousands was held in a London theater. When Buddy Holly Week was repeated in September 1977, the main event was a concert by Jerry Allison, Joe Mauldin, and Sonny Curtis at the Gaumont Theater in London's Kilburn section, where Holly and the Crickets had played in 1958. For 1978, Buddy Holly Week began with a special midnight showing of *The Buddy Holly Story,* which had not yet been released in Britian. In originating the annual celebrations, McCartney was acting both as a fan and as a smart businessman, since it was to MPL's interest to promote the songs it owned. The publicity given to Holly through these promotional efforts certainly helped lay the basis for the enormous success of the *Twenty Golden Greats* album in 1978.

The same month that the first Buddy Holly Week was held in Great Britain, a new organization of Holly fans came into existence. Bill Griggs, a Holly fan and record collector from Wethersfield, Connecticut, was bothered that Holly fans lacked any way to communicate with each other, buy and sell records, exchange photos and new information, and work cooperatively to promote Holly. (The British-based Buddy Holly Appreciation Society had been inactive for a number of years.) At his own initiative and expense, Griggs began the Buddy Holly Memorial Society (BHMS), and issued its first newsletter in September 1976. The BHMS soon attracted thousands of members from nearly every state in the Union and over a dozen foreign countries. The organization kept fans up-to-date on new releases and the progress of the forthcoming movie, provided definitive lists of recordings associated with Holly (including cover records and tribute songs), and provided access to photos and otherwise-unavailable records, including imports.

While the respect for Holly's work increased around the world in these years, his home town of Lubbock continued to pay him little heed or honor. When advance men for the Columbia Pictures publicity department arrived in Lubbock in the spring of 1978 to begin planning the premiere of *The Buddy Holly Story,* they were surprised to find nothing in the city memorializing Holly. There were no markers or statues, no parks or schools or streets or public buildings named after him, and no brochures available publicizing his connection with the city.

With some embarrassment, the city scrambled for a way to honor Holly and commemorate the opening of the film Lubbock. It was decided to name a new park on the city's northern outskirts after Holly. The site, which had once been the location of the city landfill, was still a barren spot, but Lubbock had made plans to develop the site over a period of several years into a well-landscaped park with special facilities for physically and mentally handicapped children. On the morning before the movie's premiere, with city officials, Holly's family, and Gary Busey in attendance, a marker was unveiled identifying the site as the "Buddy Holly Recreation Area."

Several days after the park dedication, Bill Griggs, John Beecher, and I drove to Lubbock from Dallas, where we had attended the premiere of *The Buddy Holly Story*. I had not been to Holly's home town for several years, and I wondered if the advent of the movie had altered the community's previous attitude of indifference towards its native rock 'n' roller. Not much had changed. When we tried to find out the location of the Holly Recreation Area, the information office at Lubbock City Hall, the reception desk at the Chamber of Commerce, and even the city parks department itself were unable to give us exact directions to the site. Neither the city government nor the Chamber of Commerce had any special leaflets available on Holly, and Holly went unmentioned in their historical and promotional brochures.

When we drove down Sixth Street, we received a shock: the site where Holly's birthplace had once stood was now an empty lot. A check with city

John Goldrosen, Bill Griggs, Niki Sullivan, and John Beecher, in Lubbock, May 1978 (Mary Griggs)

building department officials showed that the property had been inspected the previous fall, found to be in unsuitable condition for human habitation, and condemned to be demolished—with the demolition date set, ironically enough, for February 3, 1978, the anniversary of Holly's death. Before the city-ordered destruction could be carried out, a man had bought the house, moved it outside the city limits (and thus beyond the jurisdiction of the city's building code), and begun to fix it up for his family's use. The city officials who had condemned the house for demolition were unaware that the house was Holly's birthplace, as was the man who had, providentially, bought it and saved it for his private use. A city report inventorying all historically significant sites and buildings in Lubbock, including those connected with the lives of famous persons, did not list Holly's birthplace or any other site associated with him.

In the town of Tupelo, Mississippi, a city park has been established at the birthplace of Elvis Presley. In the tiny community of Turkey, Texas, the residents have erected a $15,000 monument to honor the memory of Bob Wills, who grew up there. But in the city of Lubbock, the achievements of Buddy Holly and other west Texas musicians have been given scant recognition. In the wake of the movie, the city has begun to develop a brochure for visitors, identifying places associated with Holly's life. Perhaps this will be the start of a change in attitude, and a recognition that Buddy Holly has made the name of Lubbock, Texas famous around the world.

In the 1978 movie *American Hot Wax,* a fictionalized account of Alan Freed's last days as a rock 'n' roll disc jockey in New York, one of the leading characters is a young teenager, identified as the head of a 5,000-member Buddy Holly Fan Club. A huge yellow button reading "Buddy Holly Lives" decorates the fan's sports jacket. When a slick promo man who is pushing an unknown but sure-to-be-big pop singer (undoubtedly from Philadelphia) tries to switch the youth's allegiance by questioning the logic of promoting a dead singer, the fan replies, "Well . . . sure, he's dead—but his music isn't." He tears up the agent's business card; "Buddy Holly lives, man!" he says defiantly, as he flings the pieces down and walks away.

The thoughts expressed by the character are commonplace today, but hardly anyone would have been able to put it that way in 1959. There was at that time no Buddy Holly Fan Club and no "Buddy Holly Lives!" buttons; while many mourned Holly, few could appreciate fully the loss that Holly's death represented, or the strength of the dedication to his music. In fact, to be a Buddy Holly fan in America was, for many years, an isolated act. When I began wearing *my* custom-made "Buddy Holly Lives!" button in 1967, strangers would occasionally stop me and ask me for one, but for the most part I (like most other Holly fans in the United States) wondered if I was the only one in the world who felt so strongly about Holly and his music. It took "American Pie," *The Buddy Holly Story,* and the Buddy Holly Memorial Society to bring the "Buddy Holly Underground" to the surface and to reveal its extent.

After the years of privacy, the fans wanted a chance to meet each other in person. In August 1978, the BHMS held its first Buddy Holly Convention at the Ramada Inn in Wethersfield, Connecticut. The fans came from as far away as England, Canada, California, and Florida. Some had been Holly fans since 1957 and were now in their thirties or forties; others had not even been born when "That'll Be The Day" became a hit, and had not discovered Holly until the 1970's. Some were full-fledged record collectors who owned thousands of singles and LP's; others owned but one or two Holly albums of recent vintage. There were high school graduates and Ph.D's, truckdrivers, clerks, teachers, and engineers.

When asked why they had come, they gave a variety of reasons. Some came simply to learn more about Holly by talking with the other fans, watching rare film clips and listening to tapes, and asking questions of the speakers. "I want to learn all I can about him," was their explanation. Others came as a way to pay tribute to Holly. "I felt I owed it to Buddy to be here," said one fan; another said, "The trip was a pilgrimage—it was the least I could do." Another reason offered by some was to pick up tips on what could be done to publicize Holly and get his records played and displayed more widely—they saw the BHMS as a movement, and wanted to become more involved in an active way. And finally, they came just to prove to themselves that it was not so eccentric or unusual, after all, to believe so strongly in the music and message of a long-dead pop singer. "Until this weekend," said one, "I thought I was all alone. Now, I know I'm not." Holly's own song furnished a theme: "Well, all right, so I'm being foolish—well, all right, let people know...."

As I talked with them and saw their enthusiasm, I wondered how it would be for these people when Holly did gain the recognition they desired for him. What is it like when a private religion becomes a public fad, and a minority opinion becomes a cliché? It is not outlandish to compare the Holly phenomenon to a religious or political movement: how will the true believers, the veterans of the Long March, feel if Holly's music becomes blurred or commercialized? What will it be like, for instance, to hear "That'll Be The Day" played over a supermarket Muzak system? In an age of superlanguage and superstars, of hype and effect, will Holly be falsely elevated to a pedestal, when his appeal has in fact been based on his very simplicity and ordinariness? Like Holly's other fans, I rejoice in his new-found popularity, but I wonder at the same time if, for any of us, it will ever be quite the same.

For all those who came, the highlight of the Convention was the surprise on-stage reunion of the Crickets. For the first time in twenty years, Jerry Allison, Joe Mauldin, and Niki Sullivan played together, joined and led by Sonny Curtis, who has been lead guitarist and vocalist for the Crickets over most of the period since Holly's death. Sullivan had been planning for some time to attend the Convention, but Mauldin, Allison, and Curtis decided to come only at the last moment. The day before the Convention, Allison telephoned Bill Griggs to ask a question: "Bill," said Allison, "do you need a band?"

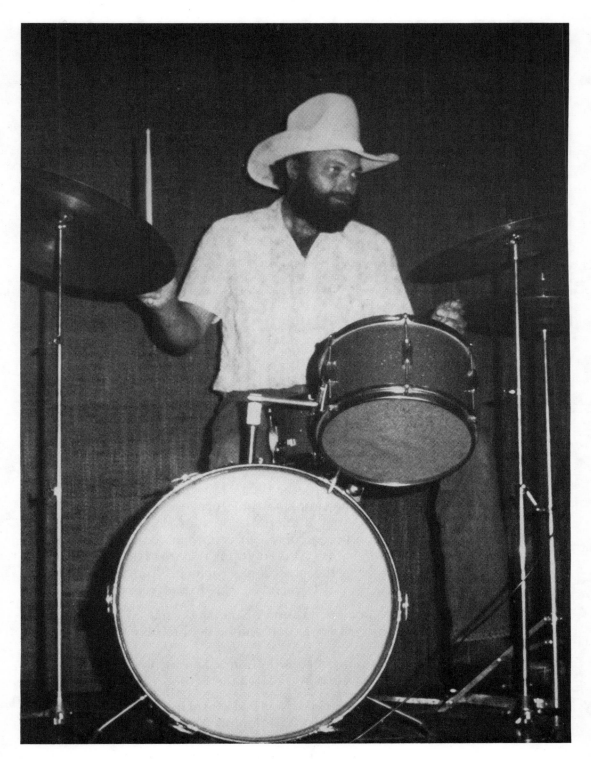

*Jerry Allison, performing at the Buddy Holly Convention, August 1978
(Bill Griggs)*

*Allison and Mauldin at the Buddy Holly Convention, August 1978
(John Goldrosen)*

The Crickets' presence and performance turned the Convention into an emotional event which those who were present would never forget, and those who could not attend would long regret having missed. They played the old Holly hits—"Oh Boy!", "Peggy Sue," "That'll Be The Day," and others— plus the post-Holly Crickets hit "I Fought The Law," showing all of the drive and exuberance identified with the West Texas rockabilly sound. But the audience's longest and loudest applause came for a new song—one which Sonny Curtis had finished writing just hours before the Crickets got on stage at the end of the Convention's second day. Curtis introduced the song as his reaction to *The Buddy Holly Story.* "I didn't think that they had all of their facts quite straight when I saw the movie," he explained, "so I thought I'd just write my own version, the way I remembered it." In part, it went like this:

> **. . . We had a good country band, and I played the fiddle,
> Buddy played the guitar, and he used to play the
> banjo some,
> We harmonized like Bill Monroe and the Bluegrass Boys,
> Bob wore my hat and played the flat-top with his thumb.**
>
> **We picked them joints and had a lot of fun with the women,
> Swigged on bootleg beer and played licks in the sun,
> We got our picture in the paper with our eyes
> covered up,
> They said our music made the kids do sinful stuff,
> We were crazy back then, but we sure had lots of fun.**

Then Elvis came along and old Bud' just loved him,
But I couldn't tell where rock 'n' roll was coming from,
But I stuck around, 'cause someone had to pick like Scotty,
Joe B. played the bass, and J.I. played the drums.

Then I grew up and had to go out and make a living,
I played a Slim Whitman tour, and I wound up on the
    road,
And them good ol' boys begin to make some noise
    around Texas,
And they got hot as a pistol, picking that rock 'n' roll.

But "That'll Be The Day" came much too soon for Buddy,
He was a good ol' boy, and he had a good Christian soul,
    He never knocked nobody down in his life—
    He loved us all, and he treated us right.
And you know, the music didn't die—
And the levee ain't dry—
'Cause Buddy Holly lives, every time we play rock 'n' roll.[3]

When the Crickets left the stage the cheering and applause made it evident that everyone hoped this would not be a one-time affair. If Don McLean's "American Pie" had expressed what was lost "the day the music died," the Crickets' performance reminded us of how much has lasted and will never be lost. The music is still there, for all with ears to hear, echoing through the years in a sound that does not fade away.

---

[3]"The Buddy Holly Story," words and music by Sonny Curtis. Copyright © 1979 by Skol Music. Used by permission. All rights reserved.

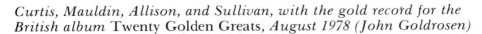

Curtis, Mauldin, Allison, and Sullivan, with the gold record for the British album Twenty Golden Greats, *August 1978 (John Goldrosen)*

Holly in London, March 1, 1958 (Flair Photography, London)

Cadence

The best rock 'n' roll musicians, though openly attentive to commercial considerations, still created music which honestly reflected their own personalities and the problems and assumptions of their audience. Their songs chronicled the concerns of a musical generation. Whether or not such musicians can be properly labelled "folk artists," it is at least certain that no country but America could have produced them or their music.

Rock 'n' roll was both revolutionary and conservative. For the first time ever, teenagers had their own culture. But for all their proclaimed independence of the standards of their elders, teenagers could still hunger for fast and fancy cars and sharp clothes, boast of steady girl friends or boy friends or else long for the security of one true love, and worry about their esteem (and "reputation") among their peers. Although rock 'n' roll provided a new sound, it was also a reaction against the artificiality and sterility of pop music, and a return to music that was more basic and sincere—music that had an emotion and spontaneity that modern adult life seemed to lack. Teenagers were tugged between old and new customs, and rock 'n' roll had the fortune to thrive at that moment of tension.

Buddy Holly was labelled a "giant" on one album, but that was really a bit of a misnomer. He may indeed have been a giant in terms of business and advertising clichés. But giants are curiosities, abnormal, removed from the race of men. Buddy Holly was anything but that; his hold on his fans is to be explained by his very humanity. He did not inspire the awe or ecstatic adoration that Elvis Presley did; nor was he able, like Chuck Berry, to stand above the fray and comment upon it. Holly was always in the struggle himself. And like the others of his generation, he was fresh and new, but still lived by old rules of ambition and achievement, and longed for the accepted standards of success.

Buddy Holly was not a giant, or a god—but he was a sort of hero. Though a star, he still sounded and looked like a friend. He was one with his listeners, with one important difference: he could successfully express through his music the feelings that those listeners could not express for themselves. And since he was unusual only in his ambition, perseverance, and musical talents, his concerns were shared by his audience. When he sang his song, his audience could claim it for their song, too.

Buddy Holly's life was an enactment of the American dream, and his music mirrored its spirit. What we long for, we never quite obtain, and yet we keep reaching; and if we have no reason to be sure of the outcome, we cling to our faith that the effort will not go unrewarded. In Holly's music, there is this knowing trust in the very process of life—a willingness to hope for the best, even when it is unrealistic to expect it. The promise may have failed in the past, but there is still hope that this time, or next time, the promise will be fulfilled; and so we all think we see a light, though it be but dim and distant. As we listen to Buddy Holly's songs, they bring us closer to the glow, and the light burns brighter.

Down the Line: Biographical Notes

Ella and Lawrence Holley, now in their seventies, still live in Lubbock in the house they bought shortly after Buddy Holly's death. The Holleys' children, Pat, Larry, and Travis, also live in Lubbock.

Maria Elena now lives in Irving, Texas, just outside Dallas. She has remarried and has three children, Carlos (named after Buddy), Miguel, and Elena.

Niki Sullivan, who managed a stereo equipment store in Lubbock for several years, has recently moved to the Kansas City area to take a new position as a regional sales manager. He and his wife, Fran, have twin sons, Eryn and Marty.

Jerry Allison, Joe Mauldin, and Sonny Curtis, who for many years lived near each other in Los Angeles, have all recently moved to the Nashville area. Mauldin and Bobby Russell (composer of "Honey" and "The Night The Lights Went Out in Georgia") have opened a new recording studio, Malrus Studios, on Music Row in Nashville. Mauldin and his wife, Jane, have a daughter, Jennifer. Jerry and Joanie Allison and Sonny and Louise Curtis have settled about seven miles from each other in the farm country west of Nashville, and both couples raise beef cattle and chickens on their farms. The Curtises have a daughter, Sarah.

Other persons who were associated with Holly's career are also active in the Nashville music business. Bob Montgomery is head of House of Gold, a music publishing firm. Ben Hall designs recording facilities and works as a studio engineer. Owen Bradley has retired from Decca but remains active as an independent producer. Tommy Allsup is a session musician. Waylon Jennings has become one of country music's biggest stars. Recently, he released an album containing a Holly medley and has on occasion asked Allison, Mauldin, and Curtis to join him on tour.

Norman Petty is still active as a producer in Clovis. Dick Jacobs, Murray Deutch, and Bob Thiele still work in the music business in New York City. "Hipockets" Duncan operates KRAN in Morton, Texas, about sixty miles west of Lubbock.

Paul Cohen, Jim Denny, and Eddie Crandall are deceased.

Discography

(Compiled with assistance from Bill Griggs of the Buddy Holly Memorial Society)

Part I: American Releases (D—Decca, Br—Brunswick, C—Coral)

A. Singles, 1956–59

Record No.	Title	Date Released
Decca		
D 29854	"Blue Days, Black Nights"/ "Love Me"	4/16/56
D 30166	"Modern Don Juan"/ "You Are My One Desire"	12/24/56
D 30434	"Rock Around With Ollie Vee"/ "That'll Be The Day"	9/2/57
D 30543	"Love Me"/ "You Are My One Desire"	1/6/58
D 30650	"Girl On My Mind"/ "Ting-A-Ling"	6/23/58
Coral/Brunswick		
Br 55009	"That'll Be The Day"/ "I'm Looking for Someone to Love"	5/27/57
C 61852	"Words of Love"/ "Mailman, Bring Me No More Blues"	6/20/57
C 61885	"Peggy Sue"/ "Everyday"	9/20/57
Br 55035	"Oh Boy!"/ "Not Fade Away"	10/27/57
C 61947	"I'm Gonna Love You Too"/ "Listen To Me"	2/5/58
Br 55053	"Maybe Baby"/ "Tell Me How"	2/12/58
C 61985	"Rave On"/ "Take Your Time"	4/20/58
Br 55072	"Think It Over"/ "Fool's Paradise"	5/27/58
C 62006	"Early In The Morning"/ "Now We're One"	7/5/58
Br 55094	"It's So Easy"/ "Lonesome Tears"	9/12/58
C 62051	"Heartbeat"/ "Well All Right"	11/5/58
C 62074	"It Doesn't Matter Anymore"/ "Raining In My Heart"	1/5/59

(1)	(2)	(3)	(4)	(5)	NME
4/21/56					
12/29/56					
6/10/57	8/12	3–9/23, 9/30	23	2	1
6/24/57					
9/30/57	11/11	3–12/30	22	3	6
11/4/57	11/25	10–1/20/58	20	15	3
2/3/58					16
2/3/58	3/3	18–3/31	14	8	4
4/21/58	5/26	39–6/16	7		5
6/2/58	7/21	27–8/4	9		11
	8/4	58–8/4	1		
6/30/58	8/4	31–8/25	7		17
9/22/58					
10/27/58	12/29	82–1/19/59	4		30
1/19/59	2/3	13–3/30	14		1
	3/30	88–4/6	2		

Explanation of column headings:
(1)—Date on which the single was rated in *Billboard*'s reviews of new records.
(2)—Date on which the song entered *Billboard*'s Top 100 (after July 1958, the Hot 100),
    the list of the top hundred sides (both sides of a single could appear on the list).
(3)—Highest position reached on the Top 100, and date.
(4)—Number of weeks in the Top 100.
(5)—Highest position reached on *Billboard*'s list of the top twenty best-selling singles in R & B markets.
NME—Highest position reached on the *New Musical Express*'s list of the top thirty best-selling singles in Britain.

B. Singles Released since Holly's Death

C 62134	"Peggy Sue Got Married"/ "Crying, Waiting, Hoping"	7/20/59
C 62210	"True Love Ways"/ "That Makes It Tough"	6/29/60
C 62329	"Reminiscing"/ "Wait Till The Sun Shines, Nellie"	8/20/62
C 62352	"Bo Diddley"/ "True Love Ways"	4/1/63
C 62369	"Brown Eyed Handsome Man"/ "Wishing"	7/29/63
C 62390	"Rock Around With Ollie Vee"/ "I'm Gonna Love You Too"	1/6/64
C 62448	"What To Do"/ "Slippin' and Slidin'"	3/15/65
C 62554	"Rave On"/ "Early In The Morning"	7/22/68
C 62558	"Love Is Strange"/ "You're The One"	3/17/69
C 65618	"That'll Be The Day"/ "I'm Looking for Someone to Love"	(Not Available)
MCA 60000	"That'll Be The Day/ "I'm Looking for Someone to Love"	1973
MCA 60004	"Peggy Sue"/ "Everyday"	1973
MCA 40905	"Peggy Sue"/ "It Doesn't Matter Anymore"	1978

C. Extended-Play Singles (EP's)

Br 71036	*The Chirping Crickets* "I'm Looking for Someone to Love"/ "That'll Be The Day"/ "Not Fade Away"/"Oh Boy!"	11/27/57
Br 71038	*The Sound of the Crickets* "Maybe Baby"/"Rock Me My Baby"/ "Send Me Some Lovin'"/"Tell Me How"	1/12/58
C 81169	*Listen To Me* "Listen To Me"/"Everyday"/ "I'm Gonna Love You Too"/ "Peggy Sue"	2/20/58
D 2575	*That'll Be The Day* "That'll Be The Day"/ "Blue Days, Black Nights"/ "Ting-A-Ling"/ "You Are My One Desire"	4/14/58
C 81182	*The Buddy Holly Story* "Early In The Morning"/"Heartbeat"/ "It Doesn't Matter Anymore"/ "Raining In My Heart"	2/20/59
C 81191	*Peggy Sue Got Married* "Peggy Sue Got Married"/ "Crying, Waiting, Hoping"/ "Learning The Game"/ "That Makes It Tough"	6/25/62
C 81193	*Brown Eyed Handsome Man* "Brown Eyed Handsome Man"/"Bo Diddley"/ "True Love Ways"/"Wishing"	7/23/63

Note: C 81192, *The Crickets*, includes one song by Holly and the Crickets ("It's Too Late") and three by the Crickets without Holly ("Don't 'Cha Know," "Great Balls of Fire," and "Baby My Heart").

D. Albums (Stereo indicated by "7" as initial digit)

Br 54038	*The Chirping Crickets* (Re-released in 1962 as *Buddy Holly and the Crickets*, C 57405/757405)	November 1957

"Oh Boy!"/"Not Fade Away"/"You've Got Love"/"Maybe Baby"/"It's Too Late"/"Tell Me How"/"That'll Be The Day"/"I'm Looking for Someone to Love"/"An Empty Cup"/"Send Me Some Lovin'"/"Last Night"/"Rock Me My Baby"

C 57210   *Buddy Holly*   March 1958
"I'm Gonna Love You Too"/"Peggy Sue"/"Look At Me"/"Listen To Me"/"Valley of Tears"/"Ready Teddy"/"Everyday"/"Mailman, Bring Me No More Blues"/"Words of Love"/"You're So Square"/"Rave On"/"Little Baby"

D 8707   *That'll Be The Day*   April 1958
(Re-released in 1967 as *The Great Buddy Holly*, Vocalion 73811 [later renumbered as MCA 20101], with all of the cuts listed below included, except for "Ting-A-Ling")
"You Are My One Desire"/"Blue Days, Black Nights"/"Modern Don Juan"/"Rock Around With Ollie Vee"/"Ting-A-Ling"/"Girl On My Mind"/"That'll Be The Day"/"Love Me"/"I'm Changing All Those Changes"/"Don't Come Back Knocking"/"Midnight Shift"

C 57279/757279   *The Buddy Holly Story*   March 1959
"Raining In My Heart"/"Early In The Morning"/"Peggy Sue"/"Maybe Baby"/"Everyday"/"Rave On"/"That'll Be The Day"/"Heartbeat"/"Think It Over"/"Oh Boy!"/"It's So Easy"/"It Doesn't Matter Anymore"

C 57326   *The Buddy Holly Story, Volume 2*   March 1960
"Peggy Sue Got Married"/"Well All Right"/"What To Do"/"That Makes It Tough"/"Now We're One"/"Take Your Time"/"Crying, Waiting, Hoping"/"True Love Ways"/"Learning The Game"/"Little Baby"/"Moondreams"/"That's What They Say"

C 57426/757426   *Reminiscing*   February 1963
"Reminiscing"/"Slippin' and Slidin'"/"Bo Diddley"/"Wait Till The Sun Shines, Nellie"/"Baby, Won't You Come Out Tonight"/"Brown Eyed Handsome Man"/"Because I Love You"/"It's Not My Fault"/"I'm Gonna Set My Foot Down"/"I'm Changing All Those Changes"/"Rock-A-Bye Rock"

C 57450/757450   *Showcase*   May 1964
"Shake, Rattle and Roll"/"Rock Around With Ollie Vee"/"Honky Tonk"/"I Guess I Was Just A Fool"/"Ummm, Oh Yeah (Dearest)"/"You're The One"/"Blue Suede Shoes"/"Come Back Baby"/"Rip It Up"/"Love's Made A Fool Of You"/"Gone"/"Girl On My Mind"

C 57463/757463   *Holly In The Hills*   January 1965
"I Wanna Play House With You"/"Door To My Heart"/"Fools Paradise"/"I Gambled My Heart"/"What To Do"/"Wishing"/"Down The Line"/"Soft Place In My Heart"/"Lonesome Tears"/"Gotta Get You Near Me Blues"/"Flower Of My Heart"/"You And I Are Through"

C CXB-8/7CXSB-8   *The Best of Buddy Holly*   April 1966
"Peggy Sue"/"Blue Suede Shoes"/"Learning The Game"/"Brown Eyed Handsome Man"/"Everyday"/"Maybe Baby"/"Early In The Morning"/"Ready Teddy"/"It's Too Late"/"What To Do"/"Rave On"/"True Love Ways"/"It Doesn't Matter Anymore"/"Crying, Waiting, Hoping"/"Moondreams"/"Rock Around With Ollie Vee"/"Raining In My Heart"/"Bo Diddley"/"That'll Be The Day"/"I'm Gonna Love You Too"/"Peggy Sue Got Married"/"Shake, Rattle and Roll"/"That Makes It Tough"/"Wishing"

C 757492   *Buddy Holly's Greatest Hits*   March 1967
"Peggy Sue"/"True Love Ways"/"Bo Diddley"/"What To Do"/"Learning The Game"/"It Doesn't Matter Anymore"/"That'll Be The Day"/"Oh Boy!"/"Early In The Morning"/"Brown Eyed Handsome Man"/"Everyday"/"Maybe Baby"

C 757504   *Giant*   January 1969
"Love Is Strange"/"Good Rockin' Tonight"/"Blue Monday"/"Have You Ever Been Lonely"/"Slippin' and Slidin'"/"You're The One"/"Dearest"/"Smokey Joe's Cafe"/"Ain't Got No Home"/"Holly Hop"

Vocalion VL 73923   *Good Rockin'*   1971
"I Wanna Play House With You"/"(You're So Square) Baby, I Don't Care"/"Little Baby"/"Ting-A-Ling"/"Take Your Time"/"Down The Line"/"Now We're One"/"Words of Love"/"That's What They Say"/"You And I Are Through"

D DXSE7-207   *Buddy Holly: A Rock & Roll Collection*   August 1972
(Later renumbered as MCA 2-4009)
"Rave On"/"Tell Me How"/"Peggy Sue Got Married"/"Slippin' and Slidin'"/"Oh Boy!"/"Not Fade Away"/"Bo Diddley"/"What To Do"/"Heartbeat"/"Well All Right"/"Words of Love"/"Love's Made A Fool Of You"/"Reminiscing"/"Lonesome Tears"/"Listen To Me"/"Maybe Baby"/"Down The Line"/"That'll Be The Day"/"Peggy Sue"/"Brown Eyed Handsome Man"/"You're So Square"/"Crying, Waiting, Hoping"/"Ready Teddy"/"It Doesn't Matter Anymore"

MCA 3040   *Buddy Holly/The Crickets: 20 Golden Greats*   May 1978
"That'll Be The Day"/"Peggy Sue"/"Words of Love"/"Everyday"/"Not Fade Away"/"Oh Boy!"/"Maybe Baby"/"Listen To Me"/"Heartbeat"/"Think It Over"/"It Doesn't Matter Anymore"/"It's So Easy"/"Well All Right"/"Rave On"/"Raining In My Heart"/"True Love Ways"/"Peggy Sue Got Married"/"Bo Diddley"/"Brown Eyed Handsome Man"/"Wishing"

Part II: List of Recording Dates and Personnel

A. Studio Masters

1. Produced by Owen Bradley in Nashville

1/26/56: "Love Me"/"Don't Come Back Knocking"/"Midnight Shift"/"Blue Days, Black Nights"—Holly, vocal; Sonny Curtis, lead guitar; Grady Martin, rhythm guitar; Don Guess, bass; Faris Coursey, drums.

7/22/56: "Rock Around With Ollie Vee"/"I'm Changing All Those Changes" (two versions)/"That'll Be The Day"*/"Girl On My Mind"/"Ting-A-Ling"*—Holly, vocal and guitar (lead on starred tunes); Curtis, lead and rhythm guitar; Don Guess, bass; Jerry Allison, drums.

11/15/56: "Rock Around With Ollie Vee" (remake)/"Modern Don Juan"/"You Are My One Desire"—Holly, vocal; Grady Martin, lead guitar; Boots Randolph, saxophone; unknown bass, drums, piano.
    Note: The November version of "Ollie Vee" was used on Decca single 30434; the July master has been used on all other single and album releases in the United States.

2. Produced by Norman Petty in Clovis, New Mexico

Note: Dates and locations listed are for recordings by Holly and his sidemen; vocal backings by the Picks and the Roses were usually added in Clovis at a later time.

2/25/57: "That'll Be The Day"/"I'm Looking for Someone To Love"—Holly, vocal and guitar; Larry Welborn, bass; Jerry Allison, drums; Niki Sullivan, rhythm guitar; Sullivan, June Clark, Gary and Ramona Tollett, vocals.

3/12/57: "Last Night"[6]/"Maybe Baby" (alternate version)

4/17/57: "Words of Love"/"Mailman, Bring Me No More Blues"[2]

5/29/57: "Everyday"[4]/"Not Fade Away"[1]

6/30/57-7/2/57: "Peggy Sue"/"Oh Boy!"[6]/"Listen To Me"/"I'm Gonna Love You Too"

7/20/57: "It's Too Late"[6]/"Send Me Some Lovin' "[6]

April-July, 1957: "Look At Me"[2]/"Ready Teddy"/"Valley of Tears"[5]/"Little Baby"[3]/"Tell Me How"[6]—Holly, vocal, lead, and rhythm guitars; Sullivan, rhythm guitar and [1]vocal; Joe Mauldin, bass; Allison, drums; Vi Petty, [2]piano; C. W. Kendall, Jr., [3]piano; Norman Petty, [4]celesta and [5]organ; the Picks (Bill Pickering, John Pickering, and Bob Latham), [6]vocals.

September 1957 (recorded at Tinker Air Force Base, Oklahoma City): "Maybe Baby"/"You've Got Love"/"An Empty Cup"/"Rock Me My Baby"—Holly, vocal and lead guitar; Sullivan, rhythm guitar; Mauldin, bass; Allison, drums; the Picks, vocals.

December 1957: "You're So Square"—Holly, vocal and guitar; Mauldin, bass; Allison, drums.

February 1958: "Think It Over"[1,3]/"Fool's Paradise"[1,3]/"Well All Right"/"Take Your Time"[2]—Holly, vocal and guitar; Norman Petty, [1]piano and [2]organ; Mauldin, bass; Allison, drums; the Roses (Bob Linville, Ray Rush, and David Bigham), [3]vocals.

"Real Wild Child"/"Oh, You Beautiful Doll"—Allison, vocal; Holly, lead guitar; Mauldin, bass; Bo Clarke, drums; the Roses, vocals. (Released on C 62017 in September 1957 under the name "Ivan.")

June-August 1958: "It's So Easy"[1]/"Lonesome Tears"[1]/"Heartbeat"[2]—Holly, vocal and guitar; Tommy Allsup, lead guitar; Mauldin, [1]bass; George Atwood, [2]bass; Allison, drums; the Roses, [1]vocals.

"Love's Made a Fool Of You"/"Wishing"—Holly, vocal and guitar; Allsup, lead guitar; Atwood, bass; Bo Clarke, drums.

September 1958: "Reminiscing"/"Come Back Baby"—Holly, vocal and guitar; King Curtis, saxophone; Mauldin, bass; Allison, drums.

3. Produced by Bob Thiele and Norman Petty in New York City

January 1958: "Rave On"/"That's My Desire"—Holly, vocal and guitar; Petty, piano; Mauldin, bass; Allison, drums; unknown vocals.

4. Produced by Dick Jacobs in New York City

June 1958: "Early In The Morning"/"Now We're One"—Holly, vocal; Sam "The Man" Taylor, saxophone; Panama Francis, drums; Helen Way Singers, vocals; other personnel unknown.

October 21, 1958: "True Love Ways"/"It Doesn't Matter Anymore"/"Raining In My Heart"/"Moondreams"—Holly, vocal; Boomie Richmond, saxophone; Dick Jacobs's Orchestra.

5. Produced by Buddy Holly for other performers

September 1958: "Jole Blon"/"When Sin Stops"—Waylon Jennings, vocal; Holly, rhythm guitar; Curtis, saxophone; Atwood, bass; Clarke, drums. (Released under Jennings's name on Br 55130)

December 1958: "Stay Close To Me"/"Dontcha Know"—Lou Giordano, vocal; Holly, rhythm guitar; others unknown. (Released under Giordano's name on Br 55115)

B. Demos and Home Tapes

1. 1954-55—recorded in Wichita Falls, Lubbock, and Clovis

"I Wanna Play House With You"[1]/"Down The Line"[1]/"Door To My Heart"/"I Gambled My Heart"/"Soft Place In My Heart"/"Gotta Get You Near Me Blues"/"Flower of My Heart"/"You And I Are Through"/"Memories-"/"Queen of the Ballroom"/"Baby, It's Love"—Holly and Bob Montgomery, vocals and guitars; Sonny Curtis, guitar and fiddle; Larry Welborn and Don Guess, bass; Jerry Allison, [1]drums.

2. 1956—recorded in Lubbock and Clovis

"Have You Ever Been Lonely"/"Gone"—Holly, vocal and guitar; others unknown.

"It's Not My Fault"/"I Guess I Was Just A Fool"/"I'm Gonna Set My Foot Down"[1]/"Rock-A-Bye Rock"[1]/"Baby, Won't You Come Out Tonight"[1]—Holly, vocal and guitar ([1]lead); Sonny Curtis, lead and rhythm guitar; Don Guess, bass; Jerry Allison, drums.

"Brown Eyed Handsome Man"/"Bo Diddley"/"Because I Love You"—Holly, vocal and guitar; Allison, drums; others unknown.

"Blue Monday"/"Good Rockin' Tonight"/"Ain't Got No Home"/"Honky Tonk"/"Blue Suede Shoes"/"Shake, Rattle and Roll"/"Holly Hop"/"Rip It Up"—Holly, vocal and guitar; Allison drums.

3. December 1958—recorded at KLLL, Lubbock

"You're The One"—Holly, vocal and guitar; Slim Corbin and Waylon Jennings, hand clapping.

4. January 1959—recorded in Holly's apartment in New York City

"Slippin' and Slidin' " (slow and fast versions)/"Smokey Joe's Cafe"/"Wait Till The Sun Shines, Nellie"/"Love Is Strange"/"Dearest"—Holly, vocal and guitar.

On most of the demos and home tapes listed above, vocal and instrumental backings were added later by the Fireballs: George Tomsco and Jimmy Gilmer, guitars; Stan Lark, bass; and Doug Roberts, drums, and by Norman Petty, organ.

"Crying, Waiting, Hoping"/"Learning The Game"/"That's What They Say"/"What To Do"/"That Makes It Tough"[1]/"Peggy Sue Got Married"[1]—Holly, vocal and guitar; Allsup, [1]guitar.

Overdubbed recordings of these last six songs were made on two occasions. The first set was recorded in New York in 1959 with instrumental and vocal backing added by Jack Hansen and his combo. The second set was produced in Clovis some time later by Petty, with backing added by the Fireballs. Petty's versions of "What To Do" and "Peggy Sue Got Married" appeared on the *Holly In The Hills* and *Buddy Holly: A Rock & Roll Collection* albums, respectively. On all other releases of the songs in the United States, the Jack Hansen versions have been used.

Part III: Tribute Records

The following is a selected list of songs recorded about Holly or about Holly, Valens, and the Big Bopper collectively. (There are other songs which mention Holly within a list of rock 'n' roll stars.) For each song, the artist, label and record number, and year of release is given:

"Three Stars"—Tommy Dee, Crest 1057 (1959); Ruby Wright, King 5192 (1959); Eddie Cochran, United Artists 9959 (LP, 1971).

"The Great Tragedy"—Hershel Almond, Ace 558 (1959).

"The Ballad of Donna and Peggy Sue"—Ray Campi, D 1047 (1959).

"Gold Records In The Snow"—Bennie Barnes, D 1052 (1959).

"Three Young Men"—Lee Davis, Cub 9026 (1959).

"Buddy, Big Bopper, and Ritchie"—Loretta Thompson, Skoop 1050.

"Tribute To Buddy Holly"—Mike Berry, Coral 62341 (1963).

"American Pie"—Don McLean, United Artists 5535 (LP, 1971).

"Old Friend"—Waylon Jennings, RCA 1816 (LP, 1976).

"Oh, Buddy (The Music Will Never Die)"—Matlock, Le Cam 213 (1978).

Part IV; Cover Versions of Holly Songs

The following is a selected list of other artists' recordings of Holly's songs (that is, songs either written by Holly or known for his version of them). To list all the cover versions would require many pages: such recordings number in the hundreds. This, then, is just a sampling.

A. Albums and Medleys

Several artists have recorded entire albums of Holly songs. These include:

Bobby Vee—*I Remember Buddy Holly*, Liberty 3336 (1963).

Jimmy Gilmer—*Buddy's Buddy*, Dot 3577 (1964).

Tommy Allsup—*Buddy Holly Songbook* (instrumentals), Reprise 6182 (1965).

Skeeter Davis—*Skeeter Davis Sings Buddy Holly*, RCA 3790 (1967).

The Crickets—*Rocking 50's Rock 'N' Roll*, Barnaby 30268.

Raw—*Raw Holly*, Coral 757515 (1970).

Denny Laine—*Holly Days*, Capitol 11588 (1977).

Matlock—*A Salute to Buddy*, Le Cam 711 (1978).

Gary Busey—*The Buddy Holly Story* (soundtrack), Epic 35412 (1978).

Two examples of medleys of Holly songs are the following:

Phil Ochs—On *Gunfight At Carnegie Hall*, A&M 9010 (1974).

Waylon Jennings (with the Crickets)—On *I've Always Been Crazy*, RCA AFL1-2979 (1978).

B. Individual Songs

(*Note:* Cover versions contained in the albums listed above are not repeated in the following listing.)

"Crying, Waiting, Hoping"—Beatles, Together 102-205 (bootleg LP)

"Everyday"—John Denver, RCA 4607 (LP) and 0647 (45); Don McLean, United Artists LA161 (LP) and 35519 (45).

"Fool's Paradise"—Don McLean, United Artists LA161 (LP) and 363 (45); Tommy Roe, ABC 432 (LP).

"Heartbeat"—Herman's Hermits, MGM E4295 (LP).

"I'm Gonna Love You Too"—Hullaballoos, Roulette R-4587 (45); Terry Jacks, London 188 (45) and Bell 1307 (LP); Thirteenth Floor Elevators, International Artists 126 (45); Blondie, Chrysalis-2251 (45) and 1192 (LP).

"I'm Gonna Set My Foot Down"—Carl Perkins, Columbia 9931 (LP).

"I'm Looking For Someone To Love"—Jackie DeShannon, Liberty 55678 (45).

"It Doesn't Matter Anymore"—Freddie and the Dreamers, Mercury 61017 (LP); Wanda Jackson, Capitol 1511 (LP); Linda Ronstadt, Capitol 4050 (45) and 11358 (LP); Don McLean, Arista 0379 (45).

"It's So Easy"—Hot Tuna, Grunt 10776 (45); Trashmen, Garrett 200 (LP); Linda Ronstadt, Asylum 45438 (45) and 6E-104 (LP).

"Last Night"—Jimmy Bowen, Roulette 25004 (LP).

"Learning The Game"—Hullaballoos, Roulette 25310 (LP) and 4612 (45); Searchers, Mercury MG 20914 (LP) (listed as "Led In The Game"); Andrew Gold, Asylum 53052 (LP).

"Listen To Me"—Searchers, Mercury MG 20914 (LP).

"Lonesome Tears"—Carolyn Hester, Dot 3604 (LP).

"Look At Me"—Tommy Roe, ABC 432 (LP).

"Love's Made A Fool Of You"—Crickets, Brunswick 55124 (45); Bobby Fuller, Mustang 3016 (45); Tom Rush, Elektra 308 (45) and 74062 (LP).

"Maybe Baby"—Chanteys, Dot 3771 (LP); Outsiders, Capitol 2501 (LP); Susie Allanson, Warner Bros. 3217 (LP) and 8534 (45).

"Midnight Shift"—Commander Cody and the Lost Planet Airmen, Paramount 0130 (45) and 6017 (LP).

"Not Fade Away"—Dick and DeeDee, Warner Bros. 5426 (45) and 1586 (LP); Rolling Stones, London 9657 (45) and 375 (LP) (also, other LP's); Everly Brothers, RCA 2286 (45) and 4781 (LP); Grateful Dead, Warner Bros. 1935 (LP); Bo Diddley, RCA 10618 (45); Black Oak, Capricorn 0284 (45); Stephen Stills, Columbia 35380 (LP); Tanya Tucker, MCA 3066 (LP) and 40976 (45).

"Oh Boy!"—Jackie DeShannon, Liberty 55678 (45) and 3390 (LP); Everly Brothers, Warner Bros. 6074 (45) and 1676 (LP); Rivieras, USA 102 (LP); Nitty Gritty Dirt Band, United Artists LA184 (LP).

"Peggy Sue"—Sandy Nelson, Imperial 12400 (LP); Billy Crash Craddock, ABC 788 (LP); Bobby Vinton, Columbia 3780 (LP) (instrumental); Tremeloes, CBS 26388 (LP); John Lennon, Apple SK3419 (LP); Mike Berry, Polydor 2383-392 (LP); Beach Boys, Reprise RPS 1394 (45).

"Raining In My Heart"—Dave Clark Five, MFP 50197 (U.K. LP); Leo Sayer, Warner Bros. 8682 (45).

"Rave On"—Waylon Jennings, A&M 722 (45); Hullaballoos, Roulette 25310 (LP); Nitty Gritty Dirt Band, United Artists 7642 (LP) and Liberty 56159 (45); Commander Cody, Paramount PAS6054 (LP); Steeleye Span, B&C 164 (45); Jesse Colin Young, Elektra 45530 (45).

"Reminiscing"—Beatles, Bellaphone 5560 (LP); Flaming Groovies, Sire 6059 (LP).

"Take Your Time"—Hollies, Imperial 9312 (LP).

"Tell Me How"—Peter and Gordon, Capitol 2115 (LP).

"That'll Be The Day"—Ravens, Argo 5276 (45); Foghat, Bearsville 0019 (45) and 6950 (LP); Pat Boone, Dot 3346 (LP); Crossfires (the Turtles), Lucky Token 112 (45); J. Frank Wilson, Jubilee 4006 (LP); Hullaballoos, Roulette 25310 (LP); Everly Brothers, Warner Bros. 5611 (45) and 1676 (LP); Francoise Hardy, Reprise 6318 (LP); Cliff Richard, U.K. Epic 510178 (45) and U.K. Columbia 1147 (LP); Tommy Roe, ABC 467 (LP); Kenny Vernon, Capitol 3331 (45) and 11227 (LP); Linda Ronstadt, Asylum 45340 (45) and 7E-1072 (LP); Pure Prairie League, RCA 10679 (45).

"True Love Ways"—Frank Ifield, Capitol 5275 (45); Peter and Gordon, Capitol 5406 (45) and 2368 (LP).

"Well All Right"—Blind Faith, Atco 33-304 (LP); Santana, Columbia 10839 (45).

"Words of Love"—Diamonds, Mercury 71128 (45); Beatles, Capitol 2358 (LP).

"You're The One"—Billy Swan, Monument 8706 (45).

Sources

This book is based principally on information gathered through my interviews and correspondence with the persons whose help is acknowledged in my Introduction. I have also drawn on interviews first published in *Reminiscing,* the newsletter of the Buddy Holly Memorial Society, or supplied to me by Holly collectors. Other sources included tapes of various radio programs on Holly and his music, most notably the memorial shows broadcast on Lubbock's KLLL each year on the anniversary of Holly's death: the KLLL shows often included interviews with Holly's friends, family members, or fellow performers. Other bits of information were derived from occasional newspaper and magazine articles, record company files, newsletters of the English Buddy Holly Appreciation Society, concert programs, and the like.

All of the following books, periodicals, and articles either provided information used in the book, or presented arguments which influenced my more general thoughts on the development of American music and Holly's place in it:

Belz, Carl. *The Story of Rock.* New York: Oxford University Press, 1969.

The *Billboard.* New York.

Civil Aeronautics Board. "Aircraft Accident Report: Beech Bonanza, N 3794N...." Washington, D.C.: September 23, 1959.

Dachs, David. *Anything Goes: The World of Popular Music.* Indianapolis: Bobbs-Merrill, 1964.

Davies, Hunter. *The Beatles: The Authorized Biography.* New York: McGraw-Hill, 1968.

Eisen, Jonathan, ed. *The Age of Rock: Sounds of the American Cultural Revolution.* New York: Random House, 1969.

Finnis, Rob. "Rock's First Singer-Songwriter?" *Let It Rock,* London, February 1973.

Ford, Larry. "Geographic Factors in the Origin, Evolution, and Diffusion of Rock and Roll Music." *The Journal of Geography,* Volume LXX, No. 8 (November 1971).

Gentry, Linnell, ed. *A History and Encyclopedia of Country, Western, and Gospel Music.* 2nd ed. Nashville: Clairmont Corp., 1969.

Gillett, Charlie. *The Sound of the City: The Rise of Rock and Roll.* New York: Outerbridge & Dienstfrey, 1970.

Graves, Lawrence J., ed. *A History of Lubbock.* Lubbock: West Texas Museum Association, 1963.

Grissim, John. *Country Music: White Man's Blues.* Paperback Library. New York: Coronet Communications, 1970.

Hemphill, Paul. *The Nashville Sound: Bright Lights and Country Music.* New York: Simon and Schuster, 1970.

Buddy Holly Memorial Society. *Reminiscing* (quarterly, 1976–). Wethersfield, Conn.

Hopkins, Jerry. *Elvis: A Biography.* New York: Simon and Schuster, 1971.

Jones, Leroi. *Blues People: Negro Music in White America.* New York: William Morrow, 1963.

Kiel, Charles. *Urban Blues.* Chicago: University of Chicago Press, 1966.

Lubbock *Avalanche-Journal.*

Lydon, Michael. *Rock Folk: Portraits from the Rock 'n' Roll Pantheon.* New York: Dial Press, 1971.

Malone, Bill C. *Country Music U.S.A.* Austin: University of Texas Press, 1968.

Mark, Norman. "The Life and Legend of 'This Unforgettable Texan.'" Chicago *Daily News* "Panorama," April 15, 1967.

Mason City (Iowa) *Globe-Gazette.*

The *New Musical Express.* London.

The New York Times.

Nite, Norm N. *Rock On: The Illustrated Encyclopedia of Rock 'N' Roll.* New York: Thomas Y. Crowell Co., 1974.

Peer, Ralph and Elizabeth. *Buddy Holly...a biography in words, photographs, and music.* New York: Peer International, 1972.

Roxon, Lillian, ed. *Rock Encyclopedia.* New York: Grosset and Dunlap, 1969.

Shaw, Arnold. *The Rock Revolution.* New York: Crowell-Collier Press, 1969.

———— *The World of Soul: Black America's Contribution to the Pop Music Scene.* New York: Cowles Book Co., 1970.

Shelton, Robert, and Burt Goldblatt. *The Country Music Story: A Picture History of Country and Western Music.* New Rochelle, N.Y.: Arlington House, 1966.

Shemel, Sidney, and M. William Krasilovsky. *This Business of Music.* Paul Ackerman, ed. New York: Billboard Publishing Co., 1964.

Stambler, Irwin. *Encyclopedia of Popular Music.* New York: St. Martin's Press, 1965.

Stambler, Irwin, and Grelun Landon. *Encyclopedia of Folk, Country, and Western Music.* New York: St. Martin's Press, 1969.

Taylor, Ken. *Rock Generation.* Melbourne, Australia: Sun Books, 1970.

Townsend, Charles R. *San Antonio Rose: The Life and Music of Bob Wills.* Urbana, Ill.: University of Illinois Press, 1976.

Index

General Index

Index to Song and Album Titles